LILITH'S CAVE

BY HOWARD SCHWARTZ

Poetry

Vessels
Gathering the Sparks

Fiction

A Blessing Over Ashes
Midrashim: Collected Jewish Parables
The Captive Soul of the Messiah: New Tales About Reb Nachman
Rooms of the Soul

Editor

Imperial Messages: One Hundred Modern Parables
Voices Within the Ark: The Modern Jewish Poets
Gates to the New City: A Treasury of Modern Jewish Tales
Elijah's Violin & Other Jewish Fairy Tales
Miriam's Tambourine: Jewish Folktales from Around the World
The Dream Assembly: Tales of Rabbi Zalman Schachter-Shalomi
Lilith's Cave: Jewish Tales of the Supernatural

LILITH'S CAVE

Jewish Tales
of the Supernatural

Selected and Retold
by
Howard Schwartz

Illustrated
by
Uri Shulevitz

1817

Harper & Row, Publishers, San Francisco

Cambridge, Hagerstown, New York, Philadelphia, Washington
London, Mexico City, São Paulo, Singapore, Sydney

Some of these tales have previously appeared in the following jour-
nals: *Agada, Fantasy & Terror, Four Worlds Journal, Midstream, The Mel-
ton Journal,* and *The St. Louis Jewish Light.* The Introduction first
appeared in *Judaism.*

FIRST EDITION

Designed by Donald Hatch

Library of Congress Cataloging-in-Publication Data

Schwartz, Howard, 1945–
   Lilith's cave.

   Bibliography: p.
   1. Jews—Folklore.   2. Jewish folk literature.
3. Tales.   I. Title.
GR98.S344   1987   398.2'089924   87-45196
ISBN 0-06-250779-6

88 89 90 91 92 HAL 10 9 8 7 6 5 4 3 2 1

For Tsila

H. S.

To the spirit of Gustave Doré

U. S.

CONTENTS

If you want to discover demons, take sifted ashes and sprinkle them around your bed, and in the morning you will see something like the footprints of a cock. If you want to see them, take the after-birth of a black she-cat, the firstborn of a firstborn, roast it in fire and grind it to powder, and then put some in your eye and you will see them.

The Talmud
Berachot 6a

ACKNOWLEDGMENTS

The editor would like to acknowledge those who have assisted in various ways during the research and editing of this book. In particular, thanks are due to Clayton Carlson of Harper & Row for his consistent and enthusiastic support; Ellen Levine of the Ellen Levine Literary Agency for her confidence in this project; Arielle North Olson for her friendship and for her valuable comments and insights on the text; Dov Noy and Edna Cheichel of the Israel Folktale Archives for opening the treasures of the archives to me; Evelyn Abel for research assistance in editing this book; and my wife, Tsila, whose help has been beneficial in every way. I also wish to thank the following people, who graciously offered their assistance at various stages in this project: Dina Abramovitch of YIVO, Rabbi Tsvi Blanchard, Marc Bregman, Matthew Chanoff, Elizabeth Cunningham, Marcia Dalbey, Joseph Dan, Rabbi Bruce Diamond, Steve Dietz, Brian Erwin, Diana Finch, Laya Firestone-Seghi, Nissim Binyamin Gamlieli, Jeremy Garber, Alfred Goessl, Robin Goldberg, Dorian Gossy, Sandy Greenberg, Yitzhak Greenfield, Zippora Greenfield, Jan Johnson, Kathy Kaiser, Yvonne Keller, William Hamlin, Holly Harem, Donald Hatch, the Khanem family, Joan Lorson, Sibylla Lotter, Rabbi Zvi Magence, Rabbi Abraham Ezra Millgram, Gedalya Nigal, William Novak, Clarence Olson, Jean Osborne, Cynthia Ozick, Mary Rapert, Robert Reis, Janet Reed, Sarah Robinson, Amy Rood, Steven Rowan, Barbara Rush, Yona Sabar, Rabbi Zalman Schachter-Shalomi, Charles Schwartz, Henry Shapiro, Peninnah Schram, Dan Sharon, Aliza Shenhar, Byron Sherwin, Ted Solotaroff, Zelda Sparks, David Stern, Michael Stone, Shlomo Vinner, Yehuda Yaari, Eli Yassif, and Ben Zion Yehousha.

LILITH'S CAVE

INTRODUCTION

One day a boy playing hide-and-seek sees a finger in the hollow trunk of a tree. Assuming he has found his friend, he puts a ring on the finger and pronounces the marriage vows, all in jest, but subsequently finds himself wed to a demoness. She, in turn, kills each of his human wives, until one of them finds a way to appease her—sharing her husband with the demoness for one hour every day.

This nightmare marriage is recounted in a sixteenth-century Yiddish folktale, "The Demon in the Tree."[1] Like most Jewish tales of the supernatural, it addresses one of the most crucial turning points in a person's life. Times of stress, such as birth, marriage, and death, inevitably become the focus of rituals, superstitions, and folklore, and the Jewish tradition is no exception. Indeed, the vast majority of legends and folktales that draw upon the supernatural take place at one of these turning points, or on such critical occasions as Bar Mitzvah, Yom Kippur, or other days of observance, including the Sabbath.

It was the supernatural that provided an explanation for all kinds of events, especially misfortunes. Surrounded by a myriad of dangers, opposed by both human and demonic enemies, the Jews turned to faith and superstition for an understanding of the world. Thus a stillbirth could be interpreted as the destructive powers of the demoness Lilith, or a sudden death as the punishment of vengeful spirits. These explanations, in turn, eventually became embodied as tales that were often retold in both the written and oral traditions. These include tales about wandering spirits, marriage with demons, possession by *dybbuks*, ghostly visitations, vampires, werewolves, speaking heads, corpses brought to life with the power of the Name of God, and every kind of supernatural adversary. These fantasies and nightmares, where danger is often overcome in a supernatural fashion, helped the oppressed Jews to find an outlet for their fears. For it is well known that hearing or reading even the most frightening tales can bring about a catharsis and release from fear. These folk explanations no longer have a primary place in our vision of the world, of course, but they still invoke and explore the dark side of the human psyche that is as evident today as it was in the time of our ancestors.

The role of the supernatural in Jewish life and lore is one of fascinating contradictions. On the one hand, there is the clear biblical injunction against supernatural practices: *There shall not be found among you any one that maketh his son or daughter to pass through the fire, one that useth divination, a soothsayer, or an enchanter, or a sorcerer, or a charmer, or one that consulteth a ghost or a familiar spirit, or a necromancer. For whosoever doeth these things is an abomination unto the Lord* (Deut. 18:10–12). On the other hand, even in the biblical account of King Saul and the witch of Endor (1 Sam. 28), this injunction is ignored, as Saul has the witch invoke the spirit of the prophet Samuel. Likewise, sorcery is resorted to on a great many occasions in the rabbinic literature, sorcery not only by wizards and witches, but even by some of the most respected rabbis. On one occasion Rabbi Joshua ben Hanania performs a magical invocation. He scatters flax seeds on a table, waters them so that they instantly take root and grow, then reaches into them to pull out the head of a witch who has cast a damaging spell.[2] In another tale from the Talmud, Rabbi Jannai diverts a witch who attempts to turn him into an ass, and transforms her into this beast instead.[3] These and many other examples clearly reveal the rabbinic ambivalence about the injunction against sorcery, and lead to hairsplitting attempts to define what kind of sorcery is acceptable and what kind forbidden. The conclusion the rabbis reach distinguishes between sorcerers who work through demons and those who work by pure enchantment. Thus, according to the talmudic sage Abaye, "If one actually performs magic, he is stoned; if he merely creates an illusion, he is exempt."[4] Although this distinction itself may seem to be an illusion, in many cases it accurately defines the difference between the sorcery of the rabbis and that performed by those who invoked the forces of darkness.

In practice, as well, the differences between sacred magic and sorcery are apparent. Although the black magic of the wizards is destructive in intent, that of the rabbis is protective—drawing magic circles that guard against any evil onslaught; using the power of the Tetragrammaton, the ineffable Name of God, to bring the dead to life; or exorcising *dybbuks*, spirits of the dead who take possession of the living. But on occasion, when sufficiently provoked, the wrath of the rabbis is terrible to behold: in his anger at witches who have kidnapped and mutilated the body of a Jew, Rabbi Hayim Vital turns them into black dogs in "The House of Witches"; Rabbi Shalem Shabazi causes three stories of a building to sink into the ground at his command in "Rabbi Shabazi and the Cruel Governor"; and in "The Cause of the Plague," Rabbi Judah Loew discovers that an evil sorcerer is responsible for a plague among the Jews, and turns the sorcerer's own destructive spell against him, causing him to burst into flames.

Such great power holds the danger of being abused, and this theme is found in several striking tales, especially that of Rabbi Joseph della Reina, who first tries to force the coming of the Messiah by capturing Asmodeus, King of Demons, and his queen, Lilith, in "Helen of Troy." Joseph della Reina succeeds in capturing them, but falls prey to their deception, is defeated, and afterward becomes a mad wizard, tutored by Lilith in the ways of black magic. Another tale, "The Homunculus of Maimonides," portrays the great philosopher and theologian as a sorcerer intent on creating an immortal being of unlimited powers. This has all the earmarks of a folk expression of the attitudes toward Maimonides found in the anti-Maimonidian controversy, in which the opponents of Maimonides portrayed him in the most negative terms. Both tales contain implicit warnings against messianic aspirations, and both emerge from periods dominated by such longings, with attendant false messiahs, especially Shabbatai Sevi in the seventeenth century.[5]

But most tales show a great reluctance on the part of the rabbis to invoke these supernatural powers, and it is only impending disaster that forces them to do so. The young Baal Shem Tov is forced to confront a werewolf to protect young children in "The Werewolf," and other rabbis are brought into magical combat with various demons—to save a kidnapped bride-to-be, for example, as in "The Bride of Demons," or to compel demons who have taken possession of a house to appear before a rabbinic court, as in "The Cellar." Thus these tales, which flourished in the Middle Ages, are an outgrowth in every respect of the biblical, rabbinic, and folk traditions that preceded them. Jewish tales with supernatural themes are derived from such biblical motifs as the speaking serpent in Eden, or Saul and the witch of Endor—and from virtually every phase of postbiblical Jewish literature, sacred and secular, written and oral. The written sources for these tales include the Apocrypha, the Pseudepigrapha, the Talmud, the Midrash, medieval Jewish folklore, and Hasidic texts. Some variants and additional tales can be found among those collected orally from various Jewish ethnic sources, including those published in this century in Yiddish by Y. L. Cahan and Immanuel Olsvanger, as well as the tales collected, primarily in Hebrew, by the Israel Folktale Archives.[6] Nor does the tradition end there, for these same legends have been selected by some of the most important modern Jewish authors, such as I. L. Peretz, S. Y. Agnon, Isaac Bashevis Singer, Bernard Malamud, and Cynthia Ozick, who have used traditional tales as the basis of short stories, novels, dramas, and poetry.

As might be expected, the imprint of the biblical sources can be recognized in many of these supernatural tales. For example, the binding of Isaac by Abraham at Mount Moriah is echoed in "The Devil's Fire," where a rabbi struggles to persuade the people in a Persian city that the practice of human sacrifices is wrong. The rabbi witnesses the abhorrent practice himself, and later learns that the reason the people are so willing to leap in the flames is because they believe they will soon return. This appears to be true, but when the rabbi investigates he discovers that the Devil has disguised himself as the one who comes back, perpetuating the illusion that the fire is harmless. With great difficulty, the rabbi finally manages to enlighten the people.

It is generally recognized that one primary purpose of the story of the binding of Isaac was to announce in clear terms that all human sacrifice for Jews had come to an end, and was to be replaced by animal sacrifice. And animal sacrifice came to an end after the destruction of the Temple. The rabbi in this tale, then, can be seen as attempting to blot out the practice of human sacrifice among pagans. At the same time the story is cast in the form of a tale of terror.

Another biblical theme, that of Joseph cast into the pit, is echoed in the tale "The Chronicle of Ephraim." Here an evil wizard causes a Jewish family to be cast into a pit to die. The mother gives birth there, and when the wizard learns this he offers to free them in exchange for the child, and with no other choice the family relinquishes their son to him. He raises the boy as his own, attempting to hide the boy's Jewish heritage from him. This theme is also echoed in midrashic literature, in the tale of Moses being cast in a pit, where he survives for ten years, secretly assisted by Zippora, whom he eventually marries.[7] In each of these cases the one cast into the pit has an extraordinary nature—Joseph, most beloved of his father and mother; Moses, the Redeemer; and the boy Ephraim, who is born casting an aura of light, as was said of Noah. Thus does the biblical episode of Joseph in the pit become an archetype for a stage in the experience of those destined for greatness—the dark pit symbolizing danger in which they miraculously survive.

In some cases it is possible to trace the evolution of a single legend from its biblical inception to its recounting in the Talmud, and from there to the version found in the Midrash and then retold in the Middle Ages in medieval folklore and echoed as well in some Hasidic tales. The Jewish literary tradition is unique in this, for in no other culture is it possible to trace the evolution of legends in written form throughout the ages.

Among the legends with biblical origins and rabbinic and folk elaborations, none had a greater influence than that of Lilith. It is not an exaggeration to say that much of the demonic realm in Jewish folklore grew out of this multifaceted legend, which came into being as a commentary on one passage of the Bible, *Male and Female He created them* (Gen. 1:27). This passage was interpreted by the rabbis to mean that the creation of man and woman was simultaneous, whereas the later accounts of the creations of Adam and Eve appear to be sequential. Working on the assumption that every word in the Bible was literally true, the rabbis interpreted this contradiction to mean that the first passage referred to the creation of Adam's first wife, whom they named Lilith, and the other referred to the creation of Eve.

This initiates the long legend of Lilith, whose name actually appears in the Bible only once, in a passage from Isaiah, *Yea, Lilith shall repose there* (Isa. 34:14), referring, probably, to a Babylonian night demon. Of the post-biblical texts, a few references to Lilith are found in the Talmud, where she is described as a demoness with long black hair,[8] and a demoness with identical characteristics is found in the apocryphal text *The Testament of Solomon*. But the earliest version of the legend that portrays all of the essential aspects of Lilith is *The Alphabet of Ben Sira*, of Persian or Arabic origin, in the eleventh century.[9]

The legend tells how God created a companion for Adam and named her Lilith. But Lilith and Adam bickered endlessly over matters large and small, with Lilith refusing to let Adam dominate her in any way. Instead she insisted that they were equal. Eventually Lilith pronounced the Ineffable Name of God and flew out of the Garden of Eden to the shore of the Red Sea. There she made her home in a cave, taking for lovers all the demons who lived there, and giving birth to a great multitude. This explains the proliferation of demons in the world.[10]

Adam complained to God, who sent three angels, Senoy, Sansenoy, and Semangeloff to command her to return to Adam. But Lilith refused. Not even the angels threatening to kill one hundred of her demon offspring a day moved her. Instead she proclaimed that she had been created to snatch the souls of infants, and she vowed that only if confronted with an amulet bearing the names of the three angels would she do no harm.

So widely known was this legend that such amulets became a familiar feature of Jewish life, and are used even today in some Orthodox Jewish circles.

Since Lilith's flight from Eden she has sought her revenge by slipping beneath the sheets of men who sleep alone and trying to seduce them. So too does she attempt to strangle infants in their cradles. But if she finds the amulet with the names of the three angels on it, along with the words *Out Lilith!*, she turns away and does not approach that child.[11]

Once a character was brought into being, the rabbis sought to discern or, in many cases, invent his or her entire history. So it is with Lilith, who is to Eve as a siren is to a mermaid: the negative side, from the rabbinic perspective, of woman. Lilith is assertive, seductive, and ultimately destructive; Eve is passive, faithful, and supportive. Thus were the opposite poles depicted in the rabbinic sources, and this negative characterization of Lilith served as the basis of a substantial body of demonic tales in medieval Jewish folklore and later Hasidic sources. These tales are not as restrained by the specific intentions of rabbinic commentary, and consequently have more imaginative freedom. This process of embellishment has a pronounced tendency to bring together as many previous themes and motifs as possible, yet at the same time the new tale takes on a life of its own.

In this fashion the archetype of Lilith became imprinted on Jewish folklore, and she reappears with a thousand names, among them Obizuth, Agrat bat Mahalath, and the Queen of Sheba, in early apocryphal, talmudic, and midrashic sources, as well as in medieval folklore and the later Hasidic tales. So too does Lilith play an important role in Kabbalistic texts, one that is essentially mythic in nature.[12] The talmudic and midrashic texts, of course, had the seal of rabbinic authority, while the apocryphal texts did not. Nevertheless, the latter had a strong influence on the development of Jewish lore.

Of the apocryphal texts, there are two, *The Book of Tobit* in the Apocrypha and *The Testament of Solomon* in the Pseudepigrapha, that greatly influenced the subsequent direction of demonology in Jewish folklore.[13] *The Book of Tobit*, dating from around 2 B.C.E., recounts the tale of Sarah, whose husbands all mysteriously die on their wedding nights. Finally Tobias is able to expel the evil demon Asmodeus whom, it turns out, had killed each and every husband. This key legend prefigures both the subsequent career of Asmodeus as the King of Demons and the pattern of a multitude of *dybbuk* tales, in which the evil spirit must be exorcised. *The*

Testament of Solomon, surviving in a Greek text, which is estimated to have been written between the first century and the fourth century, has the earliest version of what became the Lilith legend. It also serves as the earliest compendium of demons, who appear to King Solomon in succession at his invocation, and is the earliest text to cast King Solomon in the role of sorcerer, which became the primary model for him in subsequent Jewish lore. Among the demons compelled to appear is one who has all the witchlike characteristics of Lilith.

After using his magic powers to invoke the demons, King Solomon commands them to identify themselves. Among them is Obizuth, who describes herself in terms virtually identical to those later associated with Lilith: "At night I sleep not, but go my rounds over all the world and visit women in childbirth. Divining the hour I take my stand, and if I am lucky I strangle the child. . . . I am a fierce spirit of myriad names and many shapes."[14] Solomon demands to know by which angel she can be defeated (as every demon has an opposing angel that is its nemesis), and Obizuth replies: "By the angel of God called Afarol, also known as Raphael. If any man knows his name and writes it on an amulet for a woman in childbirth, then I shall not be able to enter her." This is the earliest textual reference to the amuletic tradition of warding off this demoness, which became so central a part of the Lilith legend.

Solomon's description of this demoness is also of interest: "When I, Solomon, heard this, I marvelled at her appearance, for I beheld all her body to be in darkness. But her glance was altogether bright and cheery, and her hair was tossed wildly like a dragon's, and the whole of her limbs was invisible, and her voice was very clear as it came to me."[15] This description links Obizuth even closer to Lilith, because the name Lilith has long been associated with *lilah*, the Hebrew word for "night," and Lilith's hair is said to be black. The fact that her body is invisible indicates the ability to transform herself into whatever shape she wishes, and she states as much herself. All of this indicates that the legend of a Lilith figure was a very old one indeed, going back to at least the first century, and probably earlier than that.

Sometime during the early Middle Ages the legend of Lilith, the dominant female demon, merged with the legend of Asmodeus, the King of Demons, and she became identified as his queen. Asmodeus was already a famous folk character because of the striking legends about him in the Talmud. One recounts his capture by King Solomon during the time the Temple was being built, and another describes how Asmodeus overpowered Solomon and threw him a great distance, turning him into a beggar king, and usurped his throne.[16] In retrospect the merging of the legends of Lilith and Asmodeus was inevitable, given their prominence.

The folk process invariably embellishes folktales that capture the folk imagination. Thus the fecund legend of Lilith, which grew out of a single line of Genesis, gave birth to a myriad of legends postulating the existence of another world, by some accounts existing side by side with this one, as close as the other side of the mirror; by others, in its own place, the *Yenne Velt*, Yiddish for "the Other World." In either case the demons were believed to reproduce and proliferate endlessly, creating difficulties at every turn: causing wine to turn into vinegar, fire to go out, man to be impotent, woman to be unable to give birth. And of course it was Lilith who was blamed every time an infant's life was lost. Thus the presence of Lilith and her cohorts was very real, and she served as a symbol of all that was enticing and destructive.

Thus there are two primary aspects of the Lilith legend: as the incarnation of lust, Lilith leads unsuspecting men into sin; in her incarnation as a child-destroying witch, she strangles helpless infants. It is interesting to note that these two aspects of this legend seem to have evolved separately, in that there is hardly a tale to be found in which Lilith plays both roles.[17] But the attachment of the witchlike role to the legend of Lilith broadens the Lilith archetype to include the most destructive kind of witchcraft as well. And such tales about witches are commonly found in Jewish folklore, as they are in the folklore of all peoples.

This, then, reveals a great deal about the workings of the folk process. One very old legend splits off into several sublegends, gives birth to a multitude of variants, and is embellished and retold for many centuries in new versions that are themselves embellished and retold until they bear little resemblance to the original. For it is clear that despite their age and familiarity, these supernatural themes retained great power for those who told them. And much of this power came from the fact that these stories embody universal fears and fantasies: Lilith is a projection of the negative fears and desires of the rabbis who created her.[18] If Lilith served no other purpose than to resolve the contradiction in the biblical text, such an extensive legend, with so many ramifications, would never have come into being.

As can be seen, the legend of Lilith gave birth to an elaborate Jewish demonology. One theme in particular, that of marriage with demons, evolved out of the legend of Lilith the seductress.[19] In these tales the demoness is not usually identified as Lilith, but nonetheless demonstrates all of her characteristics. One brief tale from *Midrash Tanhuma*, dating from around the eighth or ninth century, sets the pattern for many later tales, and also sets an important precedent in asserting that intercourse with demons does not constitute prostitution or adultery:

> On Yom Kippur, the Day of Atonement, a demon in the shape of a woman came to a pious man and seduced him and made love to him. Afterward the man was very sorry, until Elijah the Prophet came to him and asked him why he was so upset. And he told him all the things that had happened to him. And Elijah said: "You are free from sin, for this was a demon." After that the man reported this to his rabbi, who said: "Surely this judgment is true, for Elijah would never have come to a guilty man."[20]

The first and most important variant of this brief tale is *Maaseh Yerushalmi* ("The Tale of a Jerusalemite"), dating from the twelfth century.[21] Here a man is forced to marry the daughter of Asmodeus, the King of Demons, in order to save his own life. He is eventually permitted to return to his human family for one year, but when he refuses to return to his demon wife she comes to his city and challenges him before a *Beit Din*, a rabbinic court. Here the rabbis take her side, commanding him either to return with her or to pay the immense sum called for in their wedding contract, and when he still refuses she gives him one last kiss—the kiss of death. A late variant of this tale, "The Kiss of Death," is included here.

Maaseh Yerushalmi contains most of the essential elements of the later variants: the forced or accidental marriage of a man to a demon; an attempt to be freed from the unwanted vows; and a decision reached by a rabbinic court. This decision, however, contradicts the precedent established by Elijah in the tale from *Midrash Tanhuma*, which generally rules that such marriages are not valid and binding.

This theme was most popular in the sixteenth century, both in eastern Europe and Palestine. In *Maaseh Nissim*,[22] an important Yiddish collection of stories set in the city of Worms, there is the tale of "The Queen of Sheba." In this story a demoness by this name appears in a poor innkeeper's storeroom and seduces him both with her charms and with bags of silver coins. Another variant of this theme, the tale about the demon in the tree, has been mentioned, and there is a third variant from Palestine in the same century, from *Shivhei ha-Ari*, the tales about Rabbi Isaac Luria of Safed. In this tale, "The Finger," three young men out for a walk one evening find something that looks like a finger sticking out of the earth. One of them jokingly slips his ring onto it and pronounces the marriage vows. At that instant, without realizing it, he weds himself to a corpse, one who had not known her "hour of joy" while alive, and is not about to let it go now. The existence of such close variants from places so distant seems to confirm a substantial exchange of lore between Europe and the Holy Land in that period, for the versions seem too close to be a coincidence.[23]

Still another variant of this motif is found in the famous eighteenth-century ethical text *Kav HaYashar:* "The Cellar." Here a man's life is threatened by a demon, and he is spared only when he agrees to marry the demon's daughter. He does, and they produce demon offspring. Before his death, the man bestows on the demons the right to live in his cellar. When the house is sold to another family they unlock the cellar, and the demons fight them tooth and nail, tormenting them in many ways. At last the matter is brought to a rabbinic court for settlement, and the demons are expelled.[24]

One of the latest versions of this tale, "The Other Side," dates from nineteenth-century eastern Europe. Here an unsuspecting man is lured to the kingdom of the demons, not far from his own city, and step by step falls under the power of the demons, who finally wed him to one of their own, then dissolve the illusion, leaving him broken and mute. And it is only after the rabbinic court commands the demons to appear and rules against them that the man is freed from their curse.

All of the previous tales on the theme of marriage with demons concern a man married to a demoness. There are, however, a few tales in which a woman is wed to a demon, usually by deceit or by force. In one such story, "The Bride of Demons," from eighteenth-century Germany, Lilith lures a young girl into coming home with her, imprisoning her in order to force her to wed one of her demon sons.

Perhaps the most interesting of these variants is one from nineteenth-century Prague, in which a young woman, Haminah, follows her lover into the sea, prepared to end her life, only to discover that he is the demon ruler of the river, who makes her his bride in "The Underwater Palace." This tale combines two basic tale types into one. One of these is that of marriage with demons, and the other concerns a midwife who is brought to the kingdom of the demons.[25] Here the midwife motif is found in the subplot about the aunt of the girl, whose name is Shifra, and who, as a midwife, is brought to the underwater palace to deliver the child of the girl and her demon husband. (Note that the aunt's name is the same as that of the midwife in Exodus 1:15.) Such tales, involving a midwife needed to deliver a child or a *mohel* required to perform the circumcision, are found in both European and Middle Eastern sources. These stories emphasize the parallels between the lives of humans and those of demons, for the *Yenne Velt* is a distorted mirror image of this world. The older, written versions of this tale almost all concern a *mohel* who is led to Gehenna, and the more recent oral versions are almost all about a midwife who is taken to the land of the demons.[26] The fact that two such separate tale types have been combined here demonstrates how the folk process constantly remakes old themes in new ways, and thus keeps the tale alive in the retelling.

In one tale of considerable importance in which this theme of marriage with demons is found, it is possible to glimpse the historical kernel underlying it. In this tale, "The Demon of the Waters," collected in the 1930s from a Ukranian immigrant in Israel, the stairway to a *mikveh*, a ritual bath, collapses, throwing a woman into the river, where she is carried away, while her demonic double emerges from the waters, takes her place, and proceeds to behave in a violent and abusive manner.[27] It is not difficult to read between the lines of this tale to discern the human tragedy of madness. And the specific naming of the characters, the place, and the customs makes it clear that an actual incident lies behind it, not merely a fantasy.

Demons are not the only supernatural beings found in Jewish lore. There are angels, spirits, and other kinds of imaginary creatures, such as vampires, werewolves, goblins, and ghosts. Sometimes the spirit of one who is dead takes possession of a living being. This spirit is called a *dybbuk*, and from the sixteenth century on, accounts of possessions by *dybbuks* multiplied with alarming frequency. These are not folktales in the usual sense, because almost all of the literally hundreds of accounts of such possessions insist that the event actually occurred, and give all kinds of specific details about those involved. The pattern in these tales is almost always the same: the *dybbuk*, the spirit of one dead, takes possession of its victim. Eventually the matter is brought to the attention of a rabbi, who interrogates the *dybbuk* and eventually casts it out, usually through the little finger or toe of the victim.

This pattern is found in "The Dybbuk," a tale about how a widow of Safed was possessed, and how Rabbi Hayim Vital, disciple of Rabbi Isaac

Luria, succeeded in exorcising the *dybbuk*. This tale emerged in the six-teenth century, at around the same time as the major compendium of Yid-dish folktales, *The Maaseh Book*, appeared in eastern Europe, in which one of the earliest *dybbuk* tales can also be found.[28] It is these tales in *Shivhei ha-Ari* and *The Maaseh Book* that set the pattern for virtually all subsequent *dybbuk* tales.[29]

Sometimes the *dybbuk* finds a surreptitious way of entering the per-son, such as in the tale in *Shivhei ha-Ari* about a *dybbuk* who enters a fish, and when this fish is caught and eaten, the *dybbuk* is able to enter the body of the woman who eats it. In other cases the demon is able to approach a person because he or she said, "Go to the Devil," as in "The Bride of Demons." The first tale told by Rabbi Nachman of Bratslav, the great Hasidic storyteller, "The Lost Princess," begins with just such a curse, causing the princess to be taken over into the realms of evil, requiring an epic quest in order to set her free.[30]

Most often the spirit is able to enter its victim because of a lack of faith, such as not believing in the parting of the Red Sea, or because the text of the *mezzuzah* on the doors of the house is flawed or missing. Once the *dybbuk* finds a foothold, through one weakness or another, it inevita-bly takes possession. And only a ritual exorcism, such as that portrayed in the last act of S. Y. Ansky's drama *The Dybbuk*,[31] can succeed in expel-ling it. These tales served as a warning, of course, against permitting the forces of evil to gain such a foothold, and the fact that they are presented as accounts rather than tales shows how deeply such cases of possession were believed to be authentic.

A Persian tale, "The Soul of Avyatar," from an unpublished manu-script of sixteenth-century origin, describes how the soul of the sinner Avyatar entered into a horse and transformed it into a beast with great powers. This in itself is not uncommon, for *dybbuks* are often said to take possession of an animal, especially a dog or a cow. What is more unusual is that the soul of Avyatar remains trapped there, giving the horse great destructive powers, while other animals are shortly driven to madness. Possession usually involves a wandering spirit, that is, a *dybbuk*, although there are exceptions in which demons or other evil beings take posses-sion instead.[32] One such unusual account is "The Exorcism of Witches from a Boy's Body," from nineteenth-century eastern Europe, in which four witches take possession of a young boy at the same time. But as in the other cases of *dybbuks*, it is the power of God's Name that compels the witches to depart, just as the various *dybbuks* are unable to oppose it.

Underlying many of these tales is the Jewish concept of sin and its punishment. The punishments of *Gehenna* are recounted in "The Door to Gehenna," where a wife disregards a warning not to open a door. The moment she does she is pulled into *Gehenna*, where she is later found by her husband's steward. While many others are being openly tortured, her torture is more subtle and terrible: she is surrounded with gold and luxury on all sides, but everything is burning hot. This tale, as well as "The Devil's Fire," was recounted not only to convey the narrative, but also as a warning of what awaited sinners deserving of *Gehenna*.

In fact, the only sinners denied the punishment and expiation that *Gehenna* offers are those wandering spirits refused entrance there in the first place because their crimes are too terrible to forgive, and these poor figures are said to be chased for ages by vengeful angels bearing fiery whips. Because the punished soul cannot bear its suffering, it seeks refuge in the body of a living person or animal, thus becoming a *dybbuk*.

In addition to the uniquely Jewish tale types, such as those about *dybbuks* and Jewish demons, virtually all of the traditional types of supernatural tales are found in Jewish lore. This includes not only the expected tales about witches and wizards, but also tales about werewolves, ghosts, vampires, and even dragons. Naturally much of this material was taken in from the surrounding cultures in which the Jews found themselves, and is strongly molded by its source, but in many cases the tales are recast in a Jewish context.

There is, for example, a well-known werewolf tale about the Baal Shem Tov, founder of Hasidism, when he was a boy. In this tale, "The Werewolf," the singing of the children that the young Baal Shem (then known as Israel ben Eliezer) leads to school is so pure that Satan is threatened by it. Satan then sends an evil soul to take possession of an already wicked woodcutter, making him into an evil sorcerer who later transforms himself into a werewolf and attacks the children. The boy Israel ultimately defeats the werewolf, the very incarnation of evil, in the process showing evidence of his own great powers, which he kept hidden until the age of thirty-six, after which he revealed himself and took up the mantle of leadership.

One of the most basic types of supernatural tales is, of course, the ghost story, describing encounters with spirits of the dead. In Jewish lore the role of the ghost, per se, is a little different, because spirits are most often encountered as *dybbuks* after they have taken possession of the body of a living person. There are, however, more conventional ghost stories. The most famous ghost of all is, of course, that of the prophet Samuel, called forth by the witch of Endor for King Saul. Many of the characteristics of the ghost of Samuel, such as his anger at being brought back to this world, became the model for subsequent ghost tales.[33]

Of the supernatural tales in the Talmud, the ghost story is one of the most common types to be found. Rarely, however, do these ghosts haunt those who encounter them; instead, they are only reluctantly drawn into the world of the living. One such tale reports the dialogue between two ghosts who are overheard whispering in the graveyard.[34] Still another describes how the corpse of Rabbi Eliezer ben Simeon remains perfectly preserved for ten years after his death, and how his voice comes forth from the attic to reply to the questions asked of him.[35] This suggests in an allegorical manner how subsequent Jewish generations turned to the ancient sages for guidance, and even though they were dead, they still replied to the questions put to them. This, of course, was possible by consulting the ancient texts, especially the Talmud, where the opinions of the sages are still very much alive.

Ghosts also populate the oppressive world portrayed in *Sefer Hasidim*,[36] attributed to Rabbi Judah the Pious, from Germany in the late twelfth or early thirteenth century. One such tale reports a vision of a man who fell asleep in the synagogue. He awoke at midnight and saw many spirits wearing prayer shawls, including two men who were still alive. Those two died a few days afterward, and that was why he saw their spirits already among the dead.[37]

One of the finest examples of a ghost folktale is "The Dead Fiancée," where the ghost of a man's former fiancée appears to him and seems in every way to be alive. The man had wronged her many years before by marrying another when he was betrothed to her. This sin in turn caused the man to be without children, and the only way to could annul the curse was to seek the forgiveness of the woman—but she was dead. The man, however, does not know this, seeks to find her, and succeeds. Only after meeting with her does he learn from her brother that she has been dead for the past ten years, and thus realizes that he has met with her ghost. Her return is characteristic of many ghost tales in which a spirit returns to resolve an unfinished matter of great importance.

Far less frequent, but still to be found, are tales of vampires, which, while hardly a dominant theme in Jewish lore, appear in one of the oldest texts, *The Testament of Solomon*. Here a vampire sucks the blood of the child of the chief builder of the Temple until King Solomon finds a way to stop him. As to why the vampire motif is not more commonly found in Jewish lore, it seems likely that it has been replaced by the evil doings of Lilith and her daughters, who strangle their victims rather than drain the life out of them. In fact, it can be speculated that the Lilith legend may have given birth to the vampire myth. Lilith, after all, has several characteristics in common with the vampire: she can transform herself into an animal, usually a cat, and she makes diabolical attempts to do harm, often first deceiving her victims into believing she is either harmless or irresistible. In "The Other Side," for example, a demoness first appears to a man as a modest and lovely young lady, and in "The Kiss of Death," the daughter of Asmodeus snatches the breath of the man who has betrayed her, in a way strongly reminiscent of the fatal kiss of the vampire.[38]

Just as the ghost of Samuel serves as the earliest archetype of the ghost in Jewish literature, so does the witch of Endor serve as the archetype of the witch. Several tales about witches are found in the Talmud, including that of the eighty witches defeated by Rabbi Shimon ben Sheetah of Ashkelon.[39] Another talmudic tale is "The Rabbi and the Witch," included here. In this and other talmudic tales the witch conceals her true identity, but the observant rabbi sees through her. This also occurs in a talmudic tale where a rabbi recognizes that another rabbi's daughters are witches when he sees them stirring the broth with their hands.[40] And witches continue to populate Jewish folklore, especially in medieval texts such as *Sefer Hasidim*, where a witch casts a spell that puts a knife in a demon's heart in one tale and turns herself into a black cat in order to give the Evil Eye to a Jew in another.[41] Tales about witches are even found in Hasidic lore. Just as the young Baal Shem Tov defeats a werewolf, so too does he defeat a powerful witch in one tale and a wizard in another.[42]

Tales of the rabbi-sorcerer are, perhaps, the most commonly found among all these tale types. Moses serves as a magician in several biblical episodes, including the contest with the Egyptian magicians in Pharoah's court. This may indeed be the true model for the subsequent tales of such contests and magical combats. But it is King Solomon, not Moses, who is the primary model for the Jewish sorcerer. Solomon's exploits are a genre in themselves in Jewish lore, and only Elijah the Prophet is the hero of more tales. Solomon's mastery of over the forces of the supernatural was complete. He drew on the power of his magic ring, on which God's Name was engraved, and ultimately on the power of God. Solomon, however, was a king, and a model was needed for the rabbi-sorcerer. Several rabbis demonstrate supernatural powers in the Talmud, among them rabbis Simeon bar Yohai, Joshua ben Hanania, Jannai, and Eliezer ben Hyranos. But none of these could be described as a sorcerer.

Most medieval tales involving a Jewish sorcerer include a confrontation between the Jewish sorcerer and an evil sorcerer who often serves as a viceroy to an emperor or king, and whose primary purpose is to bring harm to the Jews. Among the medieval models for rabbi-sorcerer are Rabbi Samuel the Pious of Regensburg and his son, Rabbi Judah the Pious, whose miracles are recounted in *The Maaseh Book*.[43] There is also the legendary Rabbi Adam, who has vast kabbalistic powers at his command. He is the subject of several tales in which he draws upon supernatural objects, such as a magic lamp or mirror in order to protect Jews from impending disaster.[44]

In addition to Rabbi Adam, one other medieval rabbi in particular is portrayed in Jewish legend as having possessed great supernatural powers. This is Rabbi Judah Loew of Prague, who used his supernatural knowledge to protect the Jews from dangers arising out of the blood libel accusation, when Jews were accused of killing gentiles in order to use their blood in preparing *matzoh* for Passover—an accusation that occurred frequently and unfairly in the Middle Ages, often leading to terrible pogroms. Rabbi Loew himself is famous for the creation of the creature known as the Golem, a manmade man, created out of clay and brought to life with various magical incantations. This creature, according to the legend, protected the Jews of Prague from various dangers, especially that of the blood libel, with its disastrous consequences.[45]

Although the Golem cycle is the most famous of the legends of Rabbi Loew, there are many other tales in which Rabbi Loew exhibits his magical prowess, such as "Summoning the Patriarchs," wherein Rabbi Loew invokes the spirits of the biblical patriarchs at the bidding of the emperor, who wishes to be initiated into the secrets of the Kabbalah. So similar are the characterizations of Rabbi Adam and Rabbi Loew, that one of the tales about Rabbi Loew is identical to one that is told about Rabbi Adam: how he created a palace out of magic, and invited the king to a banquet there. The source about Rabbi Adam is the older of the two, and is a vivid illustration of how Rabbi Adam became the model for subsequent Jewish sorcerers.[46]

Hasidic legend, as recounted in *Shivhei ha-Besht*, the first collection of tales about the Baal Shem Tov, has Rabbi Adam identify the Baal Shem as his successor while the Baal Shem was still a boy.[47] Many of the tales of the Baal Shem cast him in the role of sorcerer. But although he, like Rabbi Adam, is heir to a tradition of kabbalistic magic, the power of the Baal Shem seems to derive more from his faith and less from kabbalistic formulas and invocations. In virtually all of these tales, even if a rabbi does not serve as the hero, the evil of the wizard is eventually uncovered, and a way is found to stop him.[48] Sometimes the one who defeats him is his own pupil, following the pattern of the tale of the sorcerer's apprentice, which itself is found in many variants. One of these, "The Wizard's Apprentice," based on an oral version collected by Y. L. Cahan in eastern Europe, is included here.

One indication of a tale's popularity is the number of variants in which it is found, and "The Wizard's Apprentice" is found in at least a half dozen variants. In the tale recounted in this collection, an evil wizard offers a son to a childless couple if they will leave the child with the wizard for one year. The desperate father makes the bargain, but fails to deliver the child when promised. The wizard then kidnaps the boy and raises him as his apprentice. When the time has passed, the father comes to take the boy back, but the wizard turns the boy into a bird and forces the father to agree to a test: if the father wins, the boy will be returned; if not, the boy will remain with the wizard for good. With the aid of the boy the father succeeds in freeing him, but the furious wizard pursues the boy in the form of various animals. Yet each time he tries to kill him, the boy, who has learned his lessons well, transforms himself into something that escapes the wizard's clutches. A theme such as this reworks a motif famous in world folklore, that of the sorcerer's apprentice, which was especially prominent in eastern Europe.

In the realm of folklore there are, of course, no boundaries. The Jews drew upon the folklores of the surrounding peoples, and the folklore of the Jews made its way into the traditions of other peoples. But even the Jewish tales with universal themes, such as those about demons, vampires, werewolves, or ghosts, almost always take on a Jewish coloration, even if the tales do not have a Jewish context. In these tales, then, the people found an expression for their fantasies as well as their primal fears, and the act of telling them was in itself an affirmation of faith and of the Jewish folk tradition. Above and beyond this, the inherent power of the tale is left to speak for itself.

Howard Schwartz
St. Louis

NOTES

1. Source information on the tales referred to in the Introduction is found at the back of the book, in the Sources and Commentary section.
2. Y. Sanh. 7:13. See "Rabbi Joshua and the Witch," p. 35 in *Miriam's Tambourine: Jewish Folktales from Around the World,* selected and retold by Howard Schwartz. (Abbreviated after this as *MT*).
3. See "The Rabbi and the Witch," included here, and the accompanying note.
4. B. Sanh. 67b. The passage in full reads as follows:

   > Abaye said: "The laws of sorcerers are like those of the Sabbath: certain actions are punished by stoning, others are exempt from punishment, yet forbidden, while others are entirely permitted. Thus if one actually performs magic, he is stoned; if he merely creates an illusion, he is exempt, yet it is forbidden; while what is entirely permitted? Such as was performed by Rabbi Hanina and Rabbi Oshaia, who spent every Sabbath eve studying the Laws of Creation, by means of which they created a third-grown calf and ate it."

   Note that this creation of a calf is parallel to the later creation of the Golem, a man of clay, by Rabbi Judah Loew.
5. See *Shabbatai Sevi: The Mystical Messiah* by Gershom Scholem. Refer to the Bibliography for additional information concerning this and other books available in English that are referred to in these notes.
6. To date the Israel Folktale Archives (IFA), under the directorship of Professors Dov Noy of Hebrew University and Aliza Shenhar of Haifa University, has collected more than sixteen thousand tales from every Jewish ethnic group in Israel and has published more than sixty volumes of these tales.
7. *Sefer ha-Ziokhronot* (Hebrew) by Jerahmeel ben Solomon, compiled by Eleazar ben Asher ha-Levi. Translated by Moses Gaster as *The Chronicles of Jerahmeel*. (London: 1899), 46:9–10.
8. B. Erub. 100b.
9. *The Testament of Solomon* (Greek), chapter 13, edition of F. F. Fleck, *Wissenschaftliche Reise durch das sudliche Deutschland, Italien, Sicilien und Frankreich*, vol. 2, (Leipz: 1837), 113–140. An English translation by D. C. Dulling can be found in *The Old Testament Pseudepigrapha* (vol. 1, 960–987) edited by James H. Charlesworth. *Alpha Betha de-Ben Sira*, edited by M. Steinschneider (Berlin: 1868), reprinted in *Otzar Midrashim*, edited by J. D. Eisenstein (New York: 1915).
10. The origin of demons is explained as follows: "The Holy One, blessed be He, created the souls of demons, but when He came to create their bodies, the sanctity of the Sabbath commenced and He could not create them" (Genesis Rabbah 7:5). This explains why demons have spirit bodies but not physical ones. Demons are described in the Talmud (B. Hag. 16a) in this way: "Six things are said respecting demons. In three ways they are like angels, and in three they resemble men. They have wings like angels, and like angels they fly from one end of the world to the other, and they know the future, as angels do. In three ways they resemble men. They eat and drink like men, they beget and increase like men, and like men they die." An additional characteristic of demons is derived from the talmudic account of the capture of Asmodeus, King of Demons, by King Solomon (B. Git. 68b): they have the feet of cocks.
11. The traditional use of such an amulet was widespread, and visitors to the ultra-Orthodox Mea Shaarim section of Jerusalem will even today find protective amulets against Lilith available for purchase. The text of a typical amulet against Lilith, drawn from the medieval Hebrew text *Sefer Raziel* (Amsterdam: 1674), reads as follows:

OUT LILITH! I adjure you, Lilith, in the Name of the Holy One, blessed be He, and in the names of the three angels sent after you, Senoy, Sansenoy and Semangelof, to remember the vow you made that whenever you find their names you will cause no harm, neither you nor your cohorts; and in their names and in the names of the seals set down here, I adjure you, Queen of Demons, and all your multitudes, to cause no harm to a woman while she carries a child nor when she gives birth, nor to the children born to her, neither during the day nor during the night, neither through their food nor through their drink, neither in their heads nor in their hearts. By the strength of these names and seals I so adjure you, Lilith, and all your offspring, to obey this command.

12. According to a startling legend found in the Zohar (III: 69a) after the destruction of the Temple and the Exile of the Shekhinah, the Bride of God, Lilith offered herself to God in place of his bride. And so fallen was the state of existence that God did accept Lilith as his consort.

13. For *The Testament of Solomon*, see note 9. For *The Book of Tobit*, see volume 1 of *The Apocrypha and Pseudepigrapha of the Old Testament*, edited by R. H. Charles.

14. *The Testament of Solomon* 13:3.

15. *The Testament of Solomon* 13:5.

16. B. Git. 68b.

17. David Meltzer's brief tale, "From the Rabbi's Dreambook," brings together the separate strands of the Lilith legend and weaves them into one. Here the daughters of Lilith both attempt to strangle an infant and seduce its father at the same time. The story can be found in *Gates to the New City: A Treasury of Modern Jewish Tales*, edited by Howard Schwartz, p. 516. See also "The Queen of Sheba," included here.

18. Lilith and Eve are really polar reflections of the rabbis' attitudes toward women, with Lilith representing the negative pole and Eve (despite her failings) the positive. Eve was, after all, a devoted wife and a good mother, and Lilith is portrayed as lacking any maternal feelings. A parallel myth in Western culture is that of the sirens and mermaids. Both are associated with the sea, but the sirens are seen as destructive feminine forces, luring sailors to their deaths, while the mermaids are described as helpful, guiding sailors through dangerous channels.

19. Although the majority of tales portray the marriage of humans and demons, a few variants describe marriages between humans and ghosts (such a tale is recounted by Zippora Greenfield of Yemen) or even humans and the dead (see "The Finger").

20. *Midrash Tanhuma* (Hebrew) 1:20, edited by Solomon Buber (Vilna: 1891).

21. *Maaseh Yerushalmi* (Hebrew), edited by Yehuda L. Zlotnik (Jerusalem: 1946). See "The Demon Princess" in Howard Schwartz, *Elijah's Violin & Other Jewish Fairy Tales* (hereafter *EV*) for a retelling of this tale.

22. *Maaseh Nissim* (Yiddish), compiled by Jeptha Yozpa ben Naftali (Amsterdam: 1696).

23. *Shivhei ha-Ari* by Shlomo Meinsterl. (Jerusalem: 1905).

24. *Kav ha-Yashar* (Hebrew) by Tsvi Hirsh Kaidanover. (Frankfurt: 1903). In almost all variants of this tale the *Beit Din* rules against the demons, but there are rare occasions when the ruling is in their favor.

25. For an extended discussion of the midwife tale type, see "Is There a Jewish Folk Religion" by Dov Noy in *Studies in Jewish Folklore*, edited by Frank Talmage, pp. 273–286.

26. Why is it that older written versions of the story all concern a man, and the prevelent oral versions all concern a woman? One possible reason is that the version about the midwife serves as an ideal story to be told by women to other women, especially girls, as a means of teaching a strong feminine role model. It seems likely that the medieval written version reentered the oral tradition and was transformed in the process into a woman's tale.

27. Even though this tale strongly appears to have been shaped by actual events, the pattern it follows is familiar in world folklore and is identified in *The Types of the Folktale* by Antti Aarne and Stith Thompson as type 926A, where a demon takes on the appearance of a man or woman. Interestingly, it is most often a shepherd in these tales that

recognizes the demon for what it is, just as happens in this story. The most likely explanation is that the mystifying events surrounding the wife's madness were best explained within the existing framework of this tale type.

28. *Maaseh Buch* (Yiddish) #152, compiled by Jacob ben Abraham of Mezhirech (Basel: 1601).

29. Both of these texts emerged in the sixteenth century, showing that accounts of *dybbuks* were told in both Palestine and eastern Europe at around the same time, probably due to travelers who brought such tales back and forth. Indeed, travelers from the Holy Land who sought funds in Europe were particularly welcomed because of their ability to regale their hosts with tales.

30. "The Lost Princess" in *Sippure Maaysiot*, (Hebrew) by Rabbi Nachman of Bratslav, edited by Rabbi Nathan Sternhartz of Nimirov (Ostrog: 1816). For a retelling of this tale, see "The Lost Princess" in *EV*.

31. Ansky's *The Dybbuk* was first produced in Yiddish by the Vilna troupe in 1920.

32. The earliest accounts of such possessions by demons rather than *dybbuks* appear much earlier, however, and are recorded both in the history of Josephus and in the Talmud. The account of Josephus, in the *Antiquities* (8:2.5), is probably the earliest Jewish report of possession and exorcism to be found, and the method of exorcism is attributed to none other than King Solomon himself: "He put to the nose of the possessed man a ring which had under its seal one of the roots prescribed by Solomon, and then, as the man smelled it, drew out the demons through his nostrils, and, when the man at once fell down, adjured the demon never to come back to him, speaking Solomon's name and reciting the incantations which he had composed." In the Talmud (B. Meilah 17b) we find the legend of Ben Temalion, a demon who agrees to assist Rabbi Simeon bar Yohai by entering the body of the emperor's daughter in a ploy to save the Jews.

33. 1 Samuel 28:15. For a modern variant of this tale, see "Partnership with Asmodeus" in *EV*, pp. 102–106.

34. B. Ber 18a. A variant legend found in *Sefer Hasidim* (#266) tells of the spirit of a man reluctant to join the other spirits because he had been buried in a shroud with a torn sleeve. See note 36 for a full citation.

35. B. Bab. Mez. 83b–85a.

36. *Sefer Hasidim* (attributed to Rabbi Judah the Pious), Parma edition, Hebrew manuscript De Rossi 33, published by Yehuda Wistynezki. (Berlin: 1891).

37. *Sefer Hasidim* #711.

38. Another one of the rare Jewish vampire tales is found in *Sefer Hasidim* #1465. Here the vampire is Astryiah, an old woman who uses her hair to suck the blood from her victims. Another brief tale in *Sefer Hasidim* describes how to be certain that a witch does not come back from the dead to haunt her enemies. This is reminiscent of the method of killing vampires with a stake in the heart:

> Even after a witch dies, she is dangerous. Once a witch was captured and when they were about to put her to death she said: "Even after my death you will not be safe from me." And they said to her: "Tell us, how can we be safe from you after you die?" She said "Take a stick and push it through my cheek so that it enters the earth, and then I will not be able to do any more damage."

Why the witch revealed this secret is not reported, but these tales are clear evidence of the fear of vampires and witches among the people, and of the countermeasures they were prepared to take. Another example of witch lore found in the *Sefer Hasidim* (#1465–1467) holds that the mouth of a witch must be stopped up with dirt when she is buried; otherwise she will resume her destructive activities.

39. Y. San. 6.9 and Y. Hag. 2.2. See "The Witches of Ashkelon" in *EV*, pp. 25–28.

40. B. Git. 45a.

41. For the tale about the knife, see "The Knife," p. 88. The tale of the black cat is found in *Sefer Hasidim* #1466.

42. The tale about the witch is found in *Shevhei ha-Besht* (Hebrew) #98, edited by Samuel A. Horodezky (Berlin: 1922). See "The Boy Israel and the Witch" in *EV*, pp. 203–209.

The tale about the wizard is included here: see "A Combat in Magic" p. 181, and the accompanying note. Jewish lore about witches has survived even into the present. One famous example is the witch of the Israeli city of Dovev, who has been sighted frequently and described as having "evil eyes and talon-like fingernails." (*The Jerusalem Post*, April 26, 1986).

43. *Maaseh Buch* #158–183.
44. See "The Magic Mirror of Rabbi Adam" in *EV*, pp. 187–195, and "The Magic Lamp of Rabbi Adam" in *MT*, pp. 230–237.
45. *Niflaot Maharal* (Hebrew) by Yudel Rosenberg, first published in 1909.
46. See "The Tales About Rabbi Adam Baal Shem and Their Different Versions as Formulated in Shivhei ha-Besht" (Hebrew) in *Zion* 28, 1963. For the version of this tale about Rabbi Adam, see "The Enchanted Palace" in *MT*, pp. 245–249.
47. *Shivhei ha-Besht* #7.
48. This motif is parallel to that in a tale about Rabbi Samuel the Pious found in *The Maaseh Book* #174. See the note to "Rabbi Joseph and the Sorcerer," p. 228.

The Queen of Sheba

n the city of Worms there was an innkeeper who was very poor. His inn, known as the Devil's Head, was on the outskirts of the town. Few travelers stayed there, and those who did could barely pay for lodging. Wealthy travelers stayed at the other inn, The House with the Sign of the Sun. The poor innkeeper was very jealous of it and wished that his inn would flourish instead.

One day the poor innkeeper was in his storeroom, bemoaning his fate, when a lovely voice said, "Your riches are but an arm's reach away." Startled, the man looked around and saw a beautiful woman standing there, with hair of gold—the most beautiful woman he had ever seen. Her dress clung to her body, revealing a ripeness that astonished the man. And her demeanor was worthy of a queen.

"Who are you?" the man stammered. "I am the Queen of Sheba," she replied. "I have been sent to fulfill your dreams. If you will come to me at this time every day and give yourself to me, I will make you a wealthy man." The man could hardly believe what he heard. His head began to spin. His blood became hot and he was filled with desire for the woman who stood there, the very incarnation of lust. He did not consider how she had gotten there or how she could be the Queen of Sheba. And before he knew it, he found himself in her embrace. Afterward, the Queen of Sheba handed him a bag filled with silver coins, and when he saw what it contained, the innkeeper was overjoyed, for now he would be able to pay all his debts and live as a wealthy man at last.

The next day at the same time, the man came back to his storeroom, to which he alone held the key. There he found the Queen of Sheba bathing in a golden basin. When he entered she stepped out of the bath, naked, and he was once again overwhelmed by her beauty. As soon as she was dry she lay down on a bed. The man did not ask himself where the basin and bed had come from, but gave himself up to the delights she offered, and it was midafternoon before he emerged, bearing another bag of silver coins.

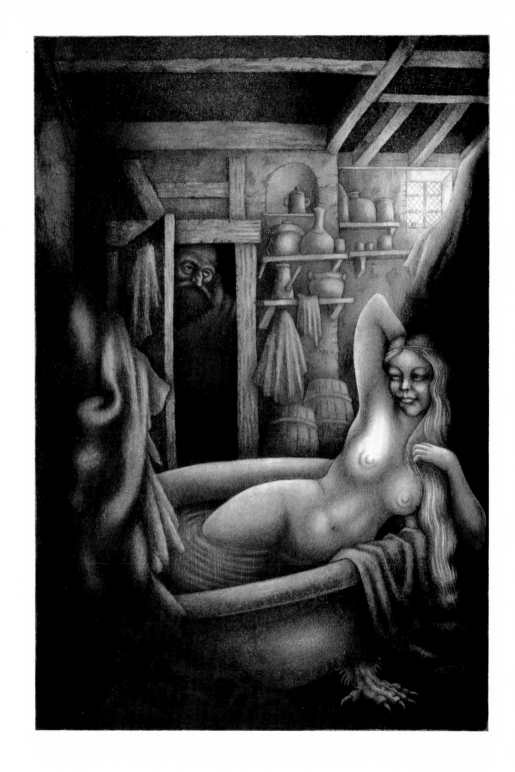

That day the man hurried off to purchase a beautiful dress and a golden ring for his wife to wear on the Sabbath. His wife was astonished by these gifts, but she did not ask to know where their wealth had come from. Instead she celebrated with her husband, relieved that a little good fortune had come their way at last.

All that night the innkeeper dreamed he was back in the arms of the Queen of Sheba, and his body trembled with sensual delight. In the morning he could barely wait for the time to go into the storeroom. At last he did, and there he found his mistress waiting for him as before. They embraced as lovers, and afterward, as the man lay back exhausted, the Queen of Sheba said, "By now you know how much abundance I have to offer you. Stay with me and you will be a wealthy man. But if you speak about me to anyone at all, it will be on penalty of death."

The man was startled to learn this, but he insisted he would never tell anyone, for his wife would surely demand a divorce, his children would never forgive him, and no one would frequent his inn. So she said no more about it, and gave him another bag of silver coins, from a store that he guessed must be inexhaustible.

In the days that followed, the way of life of the innkeeper and his wife was completely transformed, as was the inn itself, which he had remodeled until it became far more luxurious than The House with the Sign of the Sun. The wife of the innkeeper purchased an entirely new wardrobe, and it became her custom to wear beautiful dresses not only on the Sabbath and holidays, but on every day of the week. They acquired many servants to maintain the inn, and the innkeeper found that all of his tasks were taken care of by someone else. The only problem was that his wife began to wonder where the riches came from, but the innkeeper refused to discuss it, much to her frustration. And in the days of luxury that followed, she had very little to do but to muse about this matter and harp on it every chance she got.

Meanwhile, the man returned to the storeroom every day to do the bidding of the Queen of Sheba. And she, in turn, saw to it that his riches continued to grow. By this time the man had become a slave to the desires of the Queen of Sheba. He served her in any way that she saw fit, for by then his dependence on her was complete.

Because the innkeeper refused to divulge the secret of their wealth, his wife began to spy on him to see what she could discover by herself. Before long she noticed that he disappeared late in the morning and was not seen again until the middle of the afternoon. Soon she found out that he was in the storeroom during that time, and she wondered what he was doing in there. One day she casually asked him about it, and he replied that he had gotten into the habit of napping on sacks of grain.

This reply did not satisfy the wife, however, and early one morning she took the storeroom key and had a copy of it made for herself. Then she returned her husband's key, undetected. One afternoon, when her curiosity could not be restrained any longer, she quietly opened the door to the storeroom while he was in it. So it was that she saw her husband asleep in the arms of the Queen of Sheba. Overcome by the sight, she quietly shut the door, so that no one would know that she had been there. But the Queen of Sheba observed all that had taken place. And she woke the man and said, "You must have told your wife our secret, and now you must die!" The man pleaded with her, saying that he had never told anyone, especially not his wife, but the Queen of Sheba said that his wife had just opened the door and seen them together. The man was terrified to learn this and saw that his luck had run out. But he so begged for his life that at last she agreed to spare him. "But you will never see me again," she said, "for I will never come back to you. So too will your wealth disappear. I am taking back everything. And I intend to strangle the two children that I have had with you—you did not even know about them, did you? I will wring their necks. In three days' time, go to the bridge over the Rhine River, and there you will see a coffin floating on the water, and inside will lie the children you fathered with me." And then, all at once, the Queen of Sheba disappeared, and the golden basin in which she bathed disappeared as well, as did the bed they had been sleeping on, and the bag of coins she had brought to give him. It was then that he realized that she must have been a demoness, maybe even Lilith herself.

The innkeeper staggered out of the storeroom and ran to the place where he had hidden all of the silver coins he had received from her. He found the bags there, but when he reached inside, he found that the coins had all dissolved into foul water, which soiled his hands. From there he rushed to his wife's closet, where he found that all her new dresses had vanished, along with everything else they had bought with those coins. So too all of the repairs done on the inn had vanished, for they had been an illusion to start with, and the servants, merely cohorts of the Queen of Sheba. And the man and his wife were just as poor as they had been before he had met the Queen of Sheba, but it was much more terrible this time.

Germany: Sixteenth Century

The Bride of Demons

n the city of Frankfurt a girl was about to be married, and on the eve of the Sabbath before the marriage she and her mother had a dispute over what she was going to wear. The girl refused to wear the wedding dress of her mother; she wanted one of her own. In particular, there was a dress she had seen in the market that she could not get out of her mind. She wanted to buy it, even though it would take all of her savings. But her mother wanted her to save the money. At last her mother became so angry with her that she said, "Go to the Devil!" And she walked out of the girl's room and slammed the door.

Shortly after that the girl left the house. She walked into town and went directly to the merchant who had the wedding dress of which she dreamed. For she was prepared to purchase it, even over the objections of her mother. Just as she arrived she saw a splendidly dressed woman of great beauty shopping there with a servant. This woman had selected many dresses for herself, and among them was the very dress the girl longed to have for her own.

Trembling, the girl went up to the woman and said, "Please, madam, do not be angry with me, but I was hoping to purchase that one dress for my wedding." The girl pointed to the dress in the pile, and the woman pulled it out and put it on top. She said, "What a beautiful girl you are. I am certain that you would indeed look magnificent in the dress. Perhaps I can give it to you as a wedding present." Now the girl was quite surprised to hear this, but at the same time she saw that the woman possessed great wealth, and might even regard the gift as only a small act of charity. Still, she said, "No, I would not ask for that. Only that you permit me to purchase the dress myself." "No, my dear," said the woman, "I would love to make this dress a wedding present for you, and I will do so. I only ask that you come with me to my house, so that I may see how fine you look in it."

Now the girl was overjoyed, for she longed to have that dress. And she thought to herself how happy her mother would be when she learned that no savings had been spent to get it. So she thanked the woman for her kind offer and said that she would be happy to go with her to her home.

After that the woman completed the purchase, buying all of the dresses, including the one that the girl so wanted. Then she led her to her waiting carriage, and they set out together. All this time the girl was in a daze, and she could not wait to try on that dress.

In a very short time they arrived at a great mansion, which to the girl looked more like a palace. The girl had not even dreamed that such wealth could exist in the world. She walked into the house, staring at everything, and not believing her eyes. Once inside, the woman quickly took out the dress and handed it to the girl, directing her to a room where she might try it on. The girl entered that room and saw that it was filled with many mirrors, in which she could see herself from every angle. She closed the door and quickly took off her old dress and put on the new one.

The dress was truly magnificent, woven with gold and silver threads, with many ornaments forming a beautiful pattern. And when the girl put it on she recognized for the first time just how beautiful she was, and at that moment she made a wish: that she could always be like she was at that moment, dressed as a bride in that room of mirrors, in which her image was reflected everywhere. Then the happy girl went to the door to show the woman how well the dress fit her. But the door was locked.

The girl did not return home that afternoon, nor did she come back in time for dinner. After dinner her parents went out to look for her, but they could not find her, and the next day was the Sabbath. So they hurried to Rabbi Naphtali Cohen, who told them to observe the Sabbath as usual, as if she were there, and continue all the preparations for the wedding. And this is what they did.

That night, before going to sleep, the rabbi asked a dream question, in which he sought to learn why the girl had disappeared and what had happened to her. And in a dream he learned the truth.

Now when the family of the bridegroom arrived and saw that the bride was not there, the rabbi asked the bridegroom if he were willing to risk his soul for her. And when the bridegroom said yes, the rabbi ordered his carriage to be made ready, and he and the bridegroom set out together and rode until they were out of the city.

At last they arrived at a field, and the rabbi took the young man to the center of the field and told him to stay there. After that the rabbi made a great circle with his staff around the bridegroom, and he said to him,

"Know that your bride has been kidnapped by Lilith, Queen of Demons. She has taken her away to be a bride for her son, who is also the son of Asmodeus, King of Demons. You are your intended's only hope, for only one who would be willing to risk his soul for her could save her in this hour of danger.

"Now I must leave. Soon you will see around you a great many groups of demons. All of them will curse and humiliate you and attempt to harm you. But do not be afraid of them, nor reply to them in any way. After that many carriages will arrive, which will ignore you, and you should also ignore them. Then a golden carriage will arrive, whose driver will be blind in one eye. And next to him will sit another, who is the King of Demons. And you must look him in the eyes and say, 'Why did you take my bride?' And you must not turn away from his gaze, no matter what."

And so it happened, exactly as Rabbi Naphtali had said. Crowds of demons arrived from nowhere and stood outside the circle and taunted him in every possible way and threatened his life, but the bridegroom ignored them and said nothing. After this, many carriages arrived, and the last was a golden carriage, driven by a man with one eye. And next to the driver sat a most imposing man, whom the bridegroom knew at once must be the King of Demons.

The trembling bridegroom refused to succumb to his terror, and he looked into the eyes of the King of Demons and said, "Why have you taken my bride?" And Asmodeus stared back at the bridegroom and replied, "Because her mother gave her as a present to me, and because she herself made a wish to remain in my palace forever." The bridegroom answered, "Her mother cannot do that, because she was already betrothed to me, nor do I believe that my bride truly intended to remain a prisoner in your kingdom." Just then the bridegroom heard a cry, followed by weeping and sobbing. And he knew that it must be his bride, held prisoner in that very place. And he longed to look at her, for he had never in his life met her, but he remembered the words of the rabbi and did not turn his gaze away from that of the King of Demons. If he had, he would have seen his bride buried in the earth up to her neck, for she was almost lost to the Devil. But just the knowledge that she was there gave the young man renewed strength. A great anger came over him and he stared into the eyes of Asmodeus and said, "She is mine, not yours. She will come with me." And while the two continued to stare at each other, neither turning aside, the rabbi and his people suddenly arrived, and they dug her out of the earth while the other demons looked on but did not harm them. She was still wearing the dress that Lilith had given her, but it was no longer beautiful, for it was covered with worms and maggots. They took her away and tore off the wormy shroud, replacing it with a clean garment. And at that moment the demons disappeared, including Asmodeus.

When the rabbi was certain that the demons were gone, he led the bridegroom out of the charmed circle to his carriage, where his bride wept great tears of relief. And as they rode back to town the rabbi said to him, "You have done well indeed, for had you turned your eyes away from those of Asmodeus for even an instant, the girl would have been lost for good. But because you did not, she was set free."

When they returned to Frankfurt they celebrated the wedding with great joy. The girl wore the wedding dress that had belonged to her mother, and everyone said that they had never seen a more beautiful bride.

Germany: Eighteenth Century

The Homunculus
of Maimonides

oses ben Maimon, known as Maimonides, was a student of the prophet Elijah, who not only revealed to him all the mysteries of the Torah and the sciences, but also gave him two secret books—*The Book of Creation* and *The Book of Healing*. With the aid of these two wondrous texts Maimonides was able to understand the greatest secrets of nature and to heal all diseases. His fame spread over all of Europe, and in the most distant lands people spoke of the great wisdom of the famous Jewish doctor in Cordova.

Now it happened that the only son of a rich businessman in London, whose lust for learning could not be satisfied by the teachers in his own country, secretly left his parents' home and traveled to Cordova. It would not be enough, this young man thought, to be the student of this doctor; he wanted to observe the greatly esteemed man in his own home and enter into the secrets and mysteries that the teacher reserved for himself alone. Therefore the young man employed a cunning device to achieve his goal. He appeared before the rabbi, dressed in a poor and humble manner, and presented himself as completely dumb. By means of piteous expressions and beseeching gestures, he made the rabbi understand that he wanted to serve him.

Maimonides was moved by the fate of the young man and accepted him as his servant. And by virtue of his attentiveness and punctuality, the speechless servant so earned the favor of his master that his help was soon requested at each experiment. During this time the student increased his theoretical knowledge as well. For in his master's absence he studied his master's books and writings with great industry, so that after only a few years he was almost his equal.

Now it so happened that a distinguished man of the court fell ill of a strange disease. Although there was no sign of injury on any portion of his body, from time to time he would fall into a kind of frenzy and twirl about, as if driven by unseen forces, until he fell to the ground exhausted.

All the Spanish doctors tested their skill in vain; the disease grew worse and worse, and the courtier's life was in great danger. As a last resort they sent for the Jewish doctor Maimonides. He immediately recognized the problem. "The sick man has a worm in his brain. There is only one way to save him: bore through the skull and remove the worm." For a long time the courtier could not persuade himself to undergo the operation. But as the disease got increasingly worse, he finally agreed.

Maimonides and his speechless servant came into the sick man's house with all the necessary instruments and found that a large number of doctors had assembled there to observe the procedure. With a sure and skilled hand Maimonides performed the dangerous operation. A portion of the skull was removed, and they could see the worm lying motionless on the delicate brain. Everyone present was astonished at the wisdom and skill of the Jewish doctor. Now Maimonides reached for some small pincers to remove the worm. Just then a strange voice from behind him cried out, "Stop, master! You'll kill the man!" Startled, Maimonides dropped the pincers and turned in amazement to the speaker. It was his servant. "What is this? Have you deceived me?" asked Maimonides in anger. "Forgive me, master. I will explain the reason for my deception later. But now let us save the sick man. Look, the worm has been suck-ing powerfully on the brain, and if you pull it away with force, you will injure the organ and the man's life will be lost." "What can we do to remove the worm?" asked Maimonides. "Sir," replied the student, "you explained it yourself in your writings. Lay a plant on the place and the worm will willingly leave its position to bore into it." So Maimonides sent for a plant, the courtier was cured, and Maimonides became the king's offi-cial physician.

After this operation Maimonides forgave his pupil for his deception and treated him as an equal. In time the two became inseparable. Their researches were pursued largely in common, and when one of them was at a loss, the other came to his assistance. Thus together they studied almost all branches of knowledge.

One day as they were sitting together in the study, the master said, "I see that you have almost surpassed me in learning. For you have at once absorbed what took me years of struggle to understand. And your power-ful free spirit can go much further than mine, for it is more in tune with earthly matters than my own. Let us therefore follow a path together that past generations have never pursued. We want to observe the secrets of creation and destruction in nature, and then solve the great riddle of creation." "My lord and master," answered the young man, "I am young, and I am not certain how to distinguish what is true from v̵ ̵ ̵ is false. I do not yet understand how far it is permitted for the human spirit to enter into the secrets of nature, but such daring seems to me sinful for a son of man and can only incite the wrath of the Creator." "All of this," the master replied with a sweep of his arm, "belongs to the human spirit, which can observe and employ it as it wishes. The human spirit can search until it finds the truth, until it can even create a world." "Sir, your words frighten me. I am, however, ready to follow you wherever this may lead. By your side I cannot stumble."

"Now I recognize once more my worthy pupil," said Maimonides, as he turned to the bookshelf and removed a large folio of *The Book of Creation* from a hidden drawer.

"Have you read any of this book?" he asked. "Often have I read with amazement, and not without terror, the wonders it contains," the pupil replied. "What do you think of the secrets found here?" Maimonides asked. "I doubt that they are true," said the pupil. "But it seems that your powerful spirit wishes to be convinced."

"We shall make experiments," Maimonides said. He opened the folio and pointed to a particular passage. "Here it says, 'Kill a healthy man, cut his body into pieces, and place the pieces in an airless glass container. Sprinkle upon them an essence gathered from the sap of the Tree of Life and the balsam of Immortality, and after nine months the pieces of this body will be living again. It will be unharmable and immortal.'"

"Master, whom shall we get for this dangerous experiment?" the young man asked anxiously. "You or me," responded Maimonides, "the lot shall decide. But first let us swear, in the Name of the Eternal One, that the living one will permit the dead pieces to ripen, and will not, for whatever reason, hypocritically destroy the apparatus prematurely, in order to destroy the embryo life." Both men laid their hands on the Holy Scroll and swore to the Almighty. The lot was cast and fell to the pupil. Maimonides conjured up the Angel of Death, and the young man fell lifeless to the ground. Maimonides cut the body into pieces, placed it in a glass container, sprinkled it with the wondrous essence, and left the room, which he carefully locked and did not enter for four months.

Finally, tortured by doubt and curiosity, he looked at the mass of dead flesh. And behold, there were no longer severed pieces but structured limbs, as if crystallized in the glass container. Happy about the restoration of his student, he left the room and waited a month. In the fifth month the form of the human body could already be recognized. In the sixth the arteries and nerves were visible, and in the seventh movement and life in the organs could be perceived. The researcher, however, became worried. Maimonides was now convinced of the veracity of *The Book of Creation*. And he was terrified about the future. "What horror threatens the human race if I let this come to fruition? If this immortal man, with all his power, wanders among his brothers, will not people deify him and pray to him, and will not that holy revelation, the Laws of Moses, be denied and finally entirely forgotten?" Thus thought Maimonides as he left the room. At the end of the eighth month, uncertain and deeply troubled, he approached the growing being and was staggered as the almost completely developed face smiled at him. Unable to bear the demonic grin, he ran out of the room. "Oh, Lord, what have I done! It is true that man should not investigate too deeply; what is beyond this sphere leads to Hell."

A few days later Maimonides appeared before the Great Council and explained the case. After lengthy reflection the learned rabbis agreed: to protect against a horror for mankind, and to preserve God's honor, that vow might be broken and such a man killed. This decision they based on a verse in Psalms: *Disregard the law; the time has come to act for God.**

At the beginning of the ninth month, Maimonides stepped into the room, intending to destroy his creation. He brought a dog and a cat with him, and he released them and let them fly at each other. In the midst of this fighting, the glass container crashed to the floor and broke into a thousand pieces. The dead man lay at Maimonides's feet. After he recovered himself, Maimonides buried the body and took the pernicious volume and threw it into the flames of the fireplace. But nothing was the same again. Maimonides was attacked by the learned men of the court, accused of magical practices, and escaped judgment only by a timely flight to Egypt. But even there he was pursued and treated as an enemy both by his fellow Jews and by unbelievers, and from then on his life was filled with sorrow.

Eastern Europe: Nineteenth Century

*Psalms 119:126

The Wizard's Apprentice

here once was a pious Jew and his wife who had tried for years to have a child. They had sought every known remedy, but none had succeeded in bringing them the blessing of a child. Now one day, while the wife was shopping in the market, she overheard a conversation about a powerful wizard, who was said to live in those parts. She questioned the speakers about this wizard and learned from them that his magic could accomplish virtually anything. She asked them if this included a cure for barrenness, and they told her that such a cure was indeed possible.

When the woman returned home that day, she told her husband what she had heard. But even though his longing for a child was as great as hers, he did not want to ask a wizard for help. Anyone with such great power might also be dangerous. The desperate woman was willing to take the risk, however, and nagged her husband day and night, until he could no longer resist her pleas.

Now the wizard lived deep in the woods, and the man made his way there with a heavy heart, for he feared the Dark Arts. Yet he also put his trust in God and prayed that the Holy One, blessed be He, might protect him from any danger.

When he finally arrived at the wizard's hut, the man was very surprised, for it was a small, modest hut, such as might be owned by any peasant. This simple home reassured the man, for it was evident that the wizard was not seeking material gain. So the man went up to the door and knocked. When the door opened, however, he had a very great shock. For he found himself standing not in a humble shack, but in the doorway of a great palace. And before him stood the wizard, dressed in a silken robe, who invited him inside. The man could not comprehend how that palace could fit inside a simple hut, and when he entered, his amazement only deepened, for it was the most immense palace he had ever seen, even larger than that of the king. How was such a thing possible?

But before the man could ask, the wizard explained, "It is not difficult for a wizard to contain the world in a nutshell. Therefore, imagine how easy it was for me to contain a palace within a hut! Nor is it difficult for a wizard to see into the future. Therefore, I knew that you would be coming, and what you would want. You want a child of your own; neither you nor your wife will ever be happy until you have received this child. Is that not correct?"

The man was deeply shocked that the wizard knew everything in advance, and he stood in awe of his amazing powers. He acknowledged that everything the wizard had said was true and pleaded for help. Then the wizard's eyes turned hard, and he asked the man what it was he might offer him in return. The man, who was of modest means, did not know what to say, for it was obvious that he had nothing of value with which to repay the wizard. After a long silence the wizard said, "Listen, then. If you will do as I say, I will see to it that you have a child of your own, a son. Go home, and nine months from now your child will be born. Raise him well, and when he is ten years old you must bring him to me and leave him here for one year. Then you may come to take him back."

On the one hand, the man was very happy to learn that a son would be born to him, but on the other hand, he wondered greatly at the condition the wizard had set. Yet he also recognized that the wizard would not help him without this condition, so he agreed to do whatever was requested. The wizard nodded and then told the man before he departed, "Just remember, you must bring him to me when he is ten. If you do not, I will come and get him. Then he will not be as easy for you to take back!" The man assured the wizard that he would bring the boy to him, and he took his leave. And all the way home he delighted in the thought that he would soon be a father, and he gave little heed to the wizard's condition, for it seemed so far off.

Naturally the man's wife was filled with joy when she heard of the wizard's prophecy. And she too gave little thought to the wizard's demand. For all she could think about was the child that was soon to be her own.

Just as the wizard had said, the wife gave birth to a fine and handsome son exactly nine months later and, needless to say, his parents were delighted. They raised him in the ways of a pious Jew, and he was the joy of their lives. The years passed swiftly, and before long it was almost time for the boy's tenth birthday. At that time, the man recalled the condition of the wizard and spoke of it to his wife. She was alarmed to hear of it, for long ago she had put it out of her mind. And she argued hard with her husband that they must not take the boy to the wizard, for she could not bear to be separated from him for a year. The man found himself in a dilemma and could not decide what to do. In the end he did nothing. The birthday of the boy came, and no decision had been made, nor had the father told his son of the wizard's demands.

Meanwhile, the evil wizard knew from looking into his magic mirror on the boy's birthday that the father had not set out to bring the boy to him, and his anger grew greater as the day passed. Just before sunset, when they had not arrived, the wizard pronounced a powerful spell. And far away, in the home of the boy whose birthday it was, he and his family had just sat down to dinner when a terrible thing happened: the boy suddenly vanished, and in his place was a bird, which flew around the room and then out the window. In terror the father and mother witnessed this, and when they had recovered from the first shock, they realized that the wizard must have cast a spell over the boy, turning him into a bird. And they grieved deeply over the loss of their son.

As for the boy, he suddenly found himself a bird, flying relentlessly into the woods, drawn there by an unseen force. Soon enough he flew into an open window in a small hut, and the bird became a boy who found himself standing inside an immense palace. This had all happened so quickly that the boy could only believe that he had somehow fallen asleep at the table and was dreaming. And yet he had the eerie feeling that he was not dreaming at all, that, in fact, all these things were happening while he was awake.

All at once the wizard appeared out of thin air. He called the boy by his name and told him of the bargain his parents had made so that he might be born and that he had to spend the next year in that palace. The boy was heartbroken at the thought of being separated from his beloved parents for so long, but when the wizard told him he would be free at the end of that time, the boy overcame his fears and agreed to cooperate. For he saw at once that the wizard's power was very great and that he had no other choice.

Naturally, the boy was very curious to know what the wizard intended to do with him. He asked about this, and the wizard told him that he was going to teach him how to be a great wizard like himself. For he wished to share the vast knowledge he had gathered over the years, and therefore he was going to make the boy his apprentice. What he didn't tell him was that he intended to make him his slave for life. Now the boy had no desire to study the Black Arts, for he preferred to spend his days in the study of the Torah. But he was well aware that he must not antagonize the wizard, so he agreed to become his apprentice.

So it was that the wizard began to reveal, little by little, the mysteries at his command. And because the boy paid close attention, he was able to master the Black Arts much sooner than even the wizard had expected, and in the span of that year he came to know almost as much as his master.

Now that year passed ever so slowly for the boy's poor parents, but at last the time came when it was once again the boy's birthday. Then the father returned to the forest and went to the hut of the wizard. The wizard opened the door and when he saw who it was, he looked at him with disdain and said, "I see you have arrived here on time. But that was not the case a year ago. And therefore it is far from certain that you may take your son back with you." All at once he pronounced a spell, and the boy, who was in another room, was suddenly transformed into a bird again, one with black feathers and a white crown. But at the same time, two frogs that lived in the pond behind the house were also transformed into birds, which flew in the open window. So it was that there were three birds flying around inside the palace. Then the wizard laughed and said to the man, "One of these three birds is your son. Tell me which one and I will reverse the spell. And if you choose correctly, you will know it soon enough. And if not, you will find yourself in possession of a frog, and your son will be compelled to remain with me for the rest of his life!"

The poor father was terrified at these words, for the fate of his son was in his hands. Yet he had no way of knowing which of the three birds to select. Now the boy, who had become a bird, had overheard the wizard's demand and realized that his fate hung in the balance. For he had long suspected that the wizard had no intention of letting him return home. At first the boy-turned-bird tried to pronounce the spell to change himself back into a boy, but he found that he could not—the wizard was somehow preventing him from doing this. Yet his poor father was going to have to make a decision at any moment, and the boy was desperate to give him a sign. So the boy-turned-bird pronounced a spell, and all at once the colors of his feathers changed so that they were no longer black, but black and white like the stripes of a *tallis*. Further, the crown of his head became all black, so that it resembled a *yarmulke*. And when the father took one last look at the birds and recognized the resemblance to the *tallis* and the *yarmulke*, he realized that his son was trying to assist him, and he selected that bird.

Then the face of the wizard grew very red, and he angrily pronounced the spell that changed the bird back into the boy. He could not understand how the man had made the right choice, for he had not noticed the changes in the bird's appearance, nor would he have known what they represented. So he thought the father had made a lucky guess. Then he spoke bitterly, saying, "You guessed correctly, so the boy is free to go with you. But heed my warning—because he is not remaining here, he is not to make use of the magic skills I have taught him. If he does, you can be sure I will make him my apprentice once again. And the next time there will be no way for you to get him back!"

Now when the father and son had departed from the den of that wizard, they embraced and shed tears of joy. The father could not believe the evil wizard had let the boy go, but the boy explained that all conditions of a spell must be fulfilled. The wizard could not go back on his word once the right bird had been identified. And they both gave thanks to the Holy One, blessed be He, for having set the boy free from that wizard, who had been so reluctant to let him go.

Now there was a grand celebration when the boy arrived home with his father. And before long they were back to their lives of old, in which the boy and his father studied the Torah together every day. And the boy was careful not to use any of the magic skills he had learned during his year in the wizard's palace, for he had not forgotten the wizard's warning.

So it was that things went well for several months, but the time came when the fortunes of the father began to wane, and he soon found himself penniless. Things reached the point that the family was about to lose its home, when the son went to his father and said, "So far I have not used the magic I learned in that long year, Father, but perhaps the time has come. Let me pronounce a spell that will turn me into a horse of great value, and you can take me to the fair and sell me there. And when you sell me, you should remove my reins, so that I will be able to turn back into a boy within a few hours and return home. But do not forget to remove the reins, or I will be compelled to remain a horse for the rest of my life!"

Now at first the father rejected this plan, for it defied the wizard's warning. But when it became clear that there was nothing else they could do to save their home, he reluctantly agreed, after the boy promised to pay back his victim as soon as he could. Then he and his son prayed to God to forgive them for acting thus in their great need, and soon afterward the boy pronounced a spell and was instantly transformed into a black horse of immense value. The father then put reins on the horse and led it to the fair, where he received a price of one hundred rubles for the horse from a wealthy nobleman. Then the father took off the reins, explaining that they were not included in the sale, and the nobleman led it away.

That night the nobleman locked the horse in his stable, but when he went to admire it the next morning, it was gone! He searched for it everywhere, but there was not a single sign to be found. He did not know that the horse had turned into a boy and that the boy had climbed out of the stable window and had run back to his home. Thus the family saved their house and brought themselves a period of peace. And when the wizard did not appear, they thought he did not know the boy had used magic. But, in truth, the evil wizard was well aware of what had happened. He was simply waiting to strike when he was ready.

As time passed, however, they became even poorer, until things grew desperate enough that the boy again proposed to his father that he transform himself into a horse. As before, his father was very reluctant, but he recognized their desperate plight, and at last he agreed that they would do as before. Once again the son reminded his father to take off the horse's reins before handing him over to whoever purchased him. For if he forgot to do this, the boy would never be free to come home again.

This time the boy changed himself into a magnificent white horse, worth at least two hundred rubles. And no sooner had they reached the fair than an old nobleman walked toward them and immediately agreed to pay this price. But the old man talked so much that he confused the father, and the nobleman ended up taking the horse and the reins as well. Then, before the father could stop him, he mounted the horse and in a flash had ridden off into the woods. The father ran after them, but they were nowhere to be seen, and he returned home filled with grief at his terrible error.

Meanwhile, the nobleman dismounted the horse deep in the woods and tied it to a tree. Then he revealed himself to the boy-turned-horse, saying in a cruel voice, "Did you forget my warning not to use the magic you learned? Now your punishment is to begin!" And the evil wizard took a whip and began hitting the horse. He hit him so hard and so long that eventually the reins fell off, and as soon as the reins were gone the boy changed himself into a wolf and ran off as fast as he could. When the wizard saw this, he quickly pronounced a spell so that he too became a wolf and chased after the other.

With the second wolf howling behind him, the boy-turned-wolf ran as fast as he could until he reached the river. By then the howling of the second wolf had brought together a pack of wolves, all of which chased after him. Therefore the boy changed himself into a fish as soon as he reached the water and swam off as fast as he could. And when the wizard saw this, he too turned himself into a fish, a much larger one, which swam after the other, determined to swallow it.

The boy-turned-fish saw that the big fish would soon catch up with him, so he swam for the other side of the river. And just as he reached it, he saw that a princess, with her royal servants, was bathing there. At that instant the boy changed himself into a gold ring, which the princess found in the water at her feet. She was astonished at the ring's beauty and put it on her finger and showed it to all her servants, who gasped in awe. And the wizard, in the form of the fish, saw all that happened and realized that the boy had escaped him for then. But he was determined that he would still capture him and punish him in a terrible way.

So the wizard changed himself back into a man and went to the king and told him that he had lost a gold ring at the edge of the river that day, which he believed the princess might have found. The king told him that if this was the case, the ring would be returned, and he called the princess into his presence. When she arrived the king asked her about the ring, and she acknowledged that she had found a ring exactly as the wizard had described. The king then asked her to give it to him, and just as the princess went to take it off, the ring fell off her finger. As it struck the floor it turned into a huge serpent, which lunged at the wizard and bit him, causing him to die on the spot. And an instant later the serpent changed back into the boy, who told the astonished court the whole story.

Now when the king heard this remarkable tale, he was filled with sympathy as well as awe, for the boy had truly learned all that the wizard had to teach him. And when the princess saw what a handsome and clever lad he was, she lost her heart to him. So it came to pass that the boy and the princess were wed. He came to inherit half of that kingdom and repaid the noble whose horse had vanished. Then he invited his mother and father to stay in the palace, and they all lived happily ever after.

Eastern Europe: Oral Tradition

Helen of Troy

ne day in a small town in the south of France, a disheveled man arrived and purchased an old house. This man's body was hunched over, as if with defeat, his eyes focused on the ground. But when he lifted his head, it was seen that his eyes had a ferocious look, like that of one obsessed. This man's name was Joseph della Reina, but that is all he revealed about himself. He refused to say where he had come from, or in what kind of work he had been engaged. Rarely was he seen to depart from the house, not even to go to the market, and his absence made him the subject of rumors among the people of that town. Some said that he was a sorcerer, others that he was the Devil himself. He had sometimes been heard speaking to someone in his house, although he lived alone and no one was ever seen entering or leaving there. His presence in that town was unsettling.

Now, if the truth be known, this old man was indeed a wizard. Once, long ago, he had been a sage and had even been regarded as a holy man. But fate had dragged him to the other side, and now he was wedded to Lilith, the Queen of Demons. For it was none other than Lilith herself to whom he spoke, for she instructed him in the ways of Black Magic. It was through the use of this magic that he sustained himself by transporting exotic fruits from around the world: carobs from the Holy Land, olives from Greece, mountain apples from the lands of the south. In his youth he had spent many a day fasting for some holy purpose. Now he loved to savor succulent fruits and partake of delicious dishes, and with the help of Lilith he was able to indulge himself as much as he wished.

But he was driven by other desires besides that for food. Most of all he wished to possess the most desirable woman in the world. Nor was Lilith jealous of this; on the contrary, she encouraged him to fulfill his every lust. Now in all of Europe it was known that Queen Dolphina of France was the most beautiful woman alive. And Joseph della Reina was determined that she would be his, on his own terms, in his own house. And with the help of Lilith, he was able to snatch her for himself.

First, using the spells that he had learned, many of them involving holy names that he had once used for holy purposes, Joseph della Reina created the illusion that the modest house in which he lived was a palace. From outside it seemed exactly as it had been, old and dilapidated, but on the inside it appeared vast and without end, with many floors, each with an infinity of rooms. For with the help of Lilith, he had cast a spell that had transported the palace of Asmodeus, King of Demons, inside his very house. And because that palace was itself an illusion, it was no problem to make it fit in such a small place. In fact, this was a much larger home than was usual for the palace, which normally was hidden in a secret cavern of a remote cave in the Mountains of Darkness.

Once he had created the impression of vast wealth, Joseph della Reina pronounced the names that enabled him to snatch Queen Dolphina just as she fell asleep, so that her body vanished from the royal bed and suddenly appeared on the elaborate bed of Joseph della Reina. The queen was awakened from her sleep by the touch of hands undressing her, and when she opened her eyes and saw the terrifying visage of Joseph della Reina hovering above her, she almost fainted. To comfort herself she kept repeating that it must be a dream. But it was not.

In fact, the horror was only beginning, for the look in Joseph della Reina's eyes was so terrible that the queen sorely feared for her life. Thus she did not resist when he plucked the flower of her beauty, for she saw that it would be futile.

Afterward Joseph della Reina spoke for the first time. "You were wise, Your Majesty, not to try to withhold your favors from me. For know that you are fully within my power, and your very life rests in my hands. Know too that you will return to the palace of the king in the morning, but that you must remain here with me all night. Indeed, the night belongs to us, and we will meet on many occasions, as you shall see." And the queen trembled when she heard these words, knowing that she had fallen into the hands of a mad wizard. She looked around the room and saw that it was decorated with more precious objects than was her own palace, and she knew that such wealth, combined with the power that had transported her there, was a formidable menace indeed.

The thought that she must remain all night with a madman terrified the queen, and in desperation she sought to establish a conversation with him, that she might be spared his renewed lust. She said, "I did not know that such a master made his home in our kingdom. If you had come to the palace and revealed your great powers, surely you would have been made my husband's viceroy. Even now it is not too late. Return me to my chamber, and I shall put all that has happened out of my mind and see to it that you receive an audience with my husband, the king."

Joseph della Reina laughed hideously when he heard this. "Why should I serve the king, who is but a king among men? My King rules all the forces of the Other Side, all the legions of demons, all the gates of Hell!" And poor Queen Dolphina realized that she was the victim of one who had made himself a slave to the powers of evil, and she could barely conceive that such a thing could be happening to her. Still, she tried to remain calm. "Who, then, are you?" she asked. "And how did you come to be here?"

Now when Queen Dolphina asked this question to Joseph della Reina, a terrible pang of remorse passed through him, and for a moment he recalled the promise that he had thrown away when Redemption had been almost at hand. Since that day, so many years ago, he had not spoken to another human being. His only companion had been Lilith, who had infected him with her evil ways, so that not a spark of holiness remained within him. No man alive knew what had happened to him. For those disciples that had embarked on his folly with him had all lost their lives at that same disastrous moment. And a great longing to reveal his history came over him, and, as if in a trance, Joseph della Reina began to speak.

"My name is Joseph della Reina. I dare to disclose my name because there is no mortal power greater than my own. When you return try, if you wish, to seek me out. Send the palace guard, send an entire legion of your army; it will do you no good. No one can find me. So safe am I from any revenge on the part of your paramour that I will reveal to you all that you have asked, even more: I will tell you my history, as terrible as it is, and you will know to whom you have given yourself. Know that in the world there are only a handful of sages to whom the prophet Elijah comes to reveal the hidden truths of the Torah, and long ago I was one of these. Elijah was my constant companion; from his lips I drew down the fire of Sinai as if for the first time. From him I heard the very same truths that were revealed to Moses on high, and whose echo has been lost in this world from that time. And from all the secrets and mysteries that became transparent to me, I came to realize that my greatest desire was not an impossible wish, but one that could be accomplished. What was this, you wonder? I longed, more than anything else, to bring to this world the Age of Redemption; I longed to hasten the coming of the only one who can bring the End of Days any closer; I sought to beckon the Messiah himself from the palace known as the Bird's Nest, where he makes his home on high.

"These thoughts haunted me for many days, until I could not restrain myself any longer, and one day I begged Elijah to reveal to me the secret behind this mystery. At that, Elijah grew silent and departed. Nor did he return. When I realized that he had abandoned me, I fell into a great sorrow. I recalled how Adam had stood in the river Gihon after his sin, until his skin began to sag, and I too stood in the river and wept and prayed and fasted for many days. And at last Elijah sought me out and asked why I had prayed so insistently for his return. I told him that my only desire was to restore the *Shekhinah*, the Bride of God, to her rightful abode and to bring her exile to an end. Elijah told me that what I sought to do was very dangerous, and that the likelihood of success was very small, and he asked me to abandon the quest. But when he saw that I would not and that I was willing to give up my life to accomplish this deed, he imparted many secrets and revealed many mysteries. And I listened to those words so intently that as soon as each one was spoken, it was engraved in my memory for all time. For Elijah told me all that I would have to do in order to bring an end to the reign of evil. And this was to capture none other than the rulers of the Dark Kingdom, Asmodeus, the king, and Lilith, the queen. The same Lilith who now is my wife!" The searing memory of his great fall suddenly struck Joseph della Reina anew, and for a long time he was silent. And Queen Dolphina began to recognize for the first time a kernel of humanity in him that was still capable of regret.

Now Joseph della Reina's silent brooding lasted for a very long time, and finally the sky began to grow light. When he realized that dawn was imminent he jumped up, turned his back on the queen, and whispered in reverse the holy names that had made it possible for him to snatch her in the first place. An instant later the queen found herself back in her own royal chamber, next to her husband, the king, who was sound asleep. The queen was greatly relieved when she realized that she had escaped from the clutches of that madman, but she was still haunted by the horror of that night. Worst of all was the memory of his promise to snatch her away again. Did he mean the very next night? She could not even bear to consider the thought. And even though she remembered well his warning that they could not find him, she did not intend to be his victim without a struggle. And without any further hesitation, she woke the king and told him her terrible tale.

Now, as might be expected, the king had a hard time believing the story of the queen. After all, guards had been posted at the door all night, the windows had been locked, and he himself had been sleeping beside her. He thought that it must have been a terrible and very vivid dream that had afflicted her. Still, even such a dream would be a bad sign, and that day he called upon his soothsayers to reveal its meaning. But when the soothsayers, who were far more familiar with the ways of black magic, heard all that the queen had to say, they quickly confirmed her account to the king, who finally came to accept it as true. And then a great fury possessed him, a veritable darkness and lust for revenge. For his wife had been ravished and his honor had been sullied in the most terrible way. Nor had the danger passed, for the queen remained in very grave jeopardy indeed.

That evening the king saw to it that guards were posted not only outside their chamber, but also within. He himself remained awake, for he intended to see with his own eyes if the queen did, in fact, disappear, for he still hoped against hope that it was only a dream. The soothsayers had warned them that the most dangerous time was at midnight, and as it approached the king became even more vigilant, holding his wife tightly in his arms. Then, just at the stroke of twelve, the queen suddenly vanished. No one had entered, but she was snatched from his arms before their eyes. And when the king saw this, his terror was so great that he fainted.

Far away, in the south, the queen suddenly found herself once more in the palace of illusion of Joseph della Reina. As before, his intention was to possess her at once, and she felt even more helpless than before, for all the efforts of the king to save her had failed. Afterward, without being asked, Joseph della Reina continued his story, and that is when the queen realized how eager he was to tell it. He said:

"From the prophet Elijah I had learned that the secret of how to capture Asmodeus and Lilith, the very rulers of the Forces of Darkness, could be imparted only by Metatron, Prince of the Angels. And in order to invoke Metatron and call down his fiery chariot, it was required that my disciples and I subsist on as little as possible for twenty-one days, until our bodies were purified. Furthermore, we were to immerse ourselves twenty-one times every day. We were to strengthen ourselves as necessary only by smelling spices, especially pure frankincense. And after the twenty-one days, we were to fast three days and nights, and on the third day, at the time of the afternoon prayers, we were to put on our *tefillin* and cover our faces with our prayer shawls, and then, and only then, we were to pronounce a series of holy names that Elijah revealed.

"We did exactly as Elijah had directed, until, by the end of the third day of complete fasting, it felt as if our souls were about to take flight. We each put on our *tallis* and *tefillin*, and at last I spoke the holy names that Elijah had revealed. Thunder and lightning roared over us, and the sky split open, and we fell on our faces in terror. The whole Earth shook as if it were about to split asunder. A great whirlwind swirled around us, and out of the whirlwind spoke a terrible voice: 'Speak, you who are flesh and blood, dust and worms! Why have you called me here? Is this how you honor your Maker?' I replied, 'I am like a lifeless stone in your presence. Without your help I have not even the strength to speak.'

"Then the angel Metatron—for that is who it was—touched me, and a shock passed through my body, as if I had been struck with lightning. I found that my strength had not only been restored, but was much increased. I revealed my intention to the Prince of the Angels, and when he saw that I sought to restore the world to its prelapsarian state, at last he revealed the great mystery that I so longed to learn: how the capture of the evil rulers might be accomplished. And Metatron warned us to be very careful not to forget any detail of what he had told us. Then the angel departed in his fiery chariot, leaving us in a state of shock and awe, for all that we had sought was now within our grasp."

Here again, as Joseph della Reina recalled how close he had come to completing his quest, he fell into a morose silence, while Queen Dolphina continued to pray for the night to end. And yet, if the truth be known, she also found herself curious to know how this madman had sought to capture the Rulers of Darkness and how he had failed. And she wondered if this tale might contain a hint of how she might be set free from his grasp.

At the first light of dawn Joseph della Reina arose as before, spoke the spell with his back turned, and an instant later the queen found herself back in her bedroom, where the king and his guards had spent a miserable night. The king was so happy to see his wife that he shed tears and embraced her, and he vowed that he would find a way to save her from the monster who had snatched her out of his arms. That day the king called in all of his soothsayers and told them that their lives would be in danger if they did not protect the queen from this terrible magic. The soothsayers tried to explain that the level of sorcery was far greater than they had ever encountered, but the king refused to listen. At last one of the soothsayers came forward and said, "I have read, Your Majesty, that the only way to gain power over such a sorcerer is to obtain an object that belongs to him. It does not seem likely that we can prevent him from taking her again tonight, if that is indeed his wish, but perhaps the queen can find a way to bring back one of his possessions. Then we can make use of our own magic." And when the queen was informed of this, she promised to bring back something, whatever was possible, for she, more than anyone else, wanted that nightmare to end.

That night at midnight, it happened again—the queen vanished in sight of all of those attempting to guard her. Again she found herself in the arms of a madman, who ravished her without hesitation. As he did, the queen tried to turn her thoughts away from him and concentrated on finding something that she might take back with her that night, something that might serve to reveal to the wizards the precise location of that palace. It was then that her eyes lit upon a golden wine goblet next to the bed. She reached for it unseen by Joseph della Reina and slipped it beneath the pillow. And this single act helped her to endure the long hours that remained before dawn.

As before, Joseph della Reina had barely satisfied his lust when he began to speak, continuing to tell the tale as if in a trance. "No sooner had Metatron departed in the fiery chariot than we set out to complete the quest. As he had directed us, we traveled to Mount Seir and ascended it. And there we performed many matters of holiness and we ate little and immersed ourselves in the prayers of unification. The angel had assured us that everything we did below would also be performed on high, and thus the sacred power would be able to surround that evil, making possible its capture and defeat.

"After that we began to search everywhere on the mountain, for the angel had made it known that in a certain ruin the wicked Asmodeus and his wife, Lilith, would be found in the form of two black dogs, male and female. Before long we did indeed discover that ruin, and by peering through the holes in the wall we saw the two terrible dogs, just as the angel had described them. So too did the dogs see us, and they began to growl, low at first and then louder and louder, until they were howling. That terrible noise raised the hair on the back of my neck and caused me great pain, but we did not turn back. No, we entered the ruin, in our hands two chains, the links of which were engraved with God's Name. We held these chains out before us and went forward toward the dogs, who did not attempt to flee, but seemed frozen in place. At last we threw the chains around their necks, and all at once the dogs vanished, and in their place stood the two demons, on whose faces were inscribed the agony of defeat.

"Then a great thrill passed through all of us, for we had accomplished what none other had even dared to attempt, and the Rulers of Evil were our own prisoners, to do with as we wished. Now the angel had warned us to take care not to give them any kind of sustenance. And soon enough the two of them began to beg to eat and drink, but we gave them nothing at all. Instead we led them down the mountain, for that is what the angel had directed us to do. All along the way the two pleaded with us for at least a drop of water, for they claimed that their throats were parched. These requests moved me, but I still managed to deny them, for I reminded myself of the angel's warning.

"Just as we were about to reach the base of the mountain—that mountain on which the power of the demons was most abundant—Lilith and Asmodeus made the most heartrending pleas, claiming that they could not go on, for they were without strength. They begged that at least they should be permitted to sniff some incense, to regain enough strength to complete the descent. And here I found it hard to refuse, for I could not imagine that such a minor gesture could be dangerous. Therefore I did permit them one such sniff of our incense, and that is all it took for both of them to cast off their chains. A moment later I saw Asmodeus grab the first of my disciples and cast him such a great distance that he soon vanished from our sight. One after another, each of my disciples was cast from the mountain in that way, and all of them, I am certain, met their death.

"In less than a minute I was the only one left alive. Asmodeus looked at me fiercely and my heart almost stopped beating. Then he picked me up and cast me as he had the others, so that I found myself flying through the air as if I had wings. That flight seemed to last so long that I felt that I must have passed over half the Earth. Suddenly I found myself crashing downward, into a green area, and then, all at once, I found myself landing in arms that broke my fall and embraced me. And when I realized that I was not dead, because those arms had blunted my fall, I looked up and saw that it was none other than Lilith herself who had caught me. Of course I was much amazed, and when she saw this, she said, 'You may wonder why I have saved your life, when it was your intention to destroy me. The answer is that I have recognized in you an ember of evil, and now that you are mine I shall fan that ember until it bursts into flame!' "

With these words Joseph della Reina stopped speaking and glared at

Queen Dolphina. The look in his eyes was so terrifying that she was afraid that he might kill her then and there. But that moment of hatred passed, followed by one of great grief, and as before he fell into a morose state and was silent. Queen Dolphina remained completely still, barely breathing, for she was so afraid of what he might do next. But at the same time she marveled at the tale he had told her, and she understood at last how he had become so evil. For she knew that he was completely in the power of the demoness Lilith, who had enabled him to transport her, the queen, to his chamber, to do with as he wished.

It seemed years before dawn at last arrived. And as it did, Joseph della Reina pulled himself up and mumbled the words that released the queen from his spell. But just as he turned his back, she reached under the pillow and clutched the golden goblet, and when, an instant later, she found herself back in the royal chamber, the goblet was still in her hand! The king was the first to see it. He grabbed it and gave it to the soothsayers and demanded that they discover from whence it came. Then the soothsayers hurried off to do their magic, hoping that the secret might be revealed. And lo and behold, before even an hour had passed they returned smiling, for their spells had worked, and now they knew the very town in which the evil sorcerer resided; even more, they knew the very house in which he could be found. Upon learning this the king did not hesitate, but ordered that all of his palace guards set out at once, in order to reach that town before midnight. And within minutes the guards were urging their stallions to gallop in that direction.

Now it was normally a two-day journey to that town from the capital, but this time the soldiers did not stop to eat or drink or rest, even for a moment. They pushed themselves and their horses relentlessly, so that they might arrive before midnight and thus spare the queen another night of torture. And at the very stroke of twelve they arrived at the door of the house where they knew the sorcerer was to be found. True, it did not resemble the palace the queen had described, but the soothsayers had warned them that that might be the case. And without a moment's hesitation they broke down the door, just as Joseph della Reina was about to pronounce the spell to transport the queen to his bed. He could not believe he had been found. For a terrible moment they stared at one another, then he pronounced a spell—not the spell to snatch the queen, but one to make himself invisible—and suddenly he vanished from before their eyes.

The soldiers could not believe they had lost him so suddenly, and they searched the palace from top to bottom, but not a sign of the sorcerer was to be found. For he had walked among them, invisible, and slipped out the door.

Now the spell of invisibility lasted for only a few hours, and then it could not be renewed until a full day had passed. Joseph della Reina knew that he had to find a safe place to hide by the time the spell wore off. For the soldiers had seen him, and now there would be guards searching everywhere. Joseph della Reina remembered that there was a cave near the sea, on the side of a cliff. Lilith had first taken him there when he had been cast from the Holy Land to France by Asmodeus. And beneath the light of the full moon he set out for the sea. He reached it shortly before the spell wore off and quickly hid himself inside the dark cave, where he could not be seen even when he was visible. And only when he was finally safe did he realize how frightened he had been. How had they found him in the first place? He could not imagine, unless the queen had taken some object of his back to her palace. Now he would have to give the queen up. He could not dare risk trying to capture her again.

For the first few days after this near catastrophe, Joseph della Reina slept in the dark of the cave. Each time that he awoke and recalled his humiliation, he forced himself to fall back to sleep. At last his hunger kept him awake, and he knew that he would have to sustain himself. Once again he invoked the spells that Lilith had taught him, transporting the palace of Asmodeus, with all of its furnishings, into that very cave. So too did he make use of the spells that provided him with whatever he wanted to eat. And in that place he slowly recovered from his shock. For it was not the first great shock of his life, yet somehow it was almost as hard for him to bear. To have failed as a holy man was one thing, but to have failed as a wizard was another. Thoughts of revenge often obsessed him, but he realized that the king had his own sorcerers waiting to combat his magic and that it was too dangerous to challenge them again.

At last Joseph della Reina's lust was restored to him. And one day a thought occurred to him that gave him something for which to live. Perhaps it was true that Queen Dolphina was the most beautiful woman in the world, but that was true only of that time. In the past there had been many others far more beautiful, and above them all was one whose beauty had provoked the Trojan War—Helen of Troy. The thought of possessing such a legendary beauty for himself slowly took possession of Joseph della Reina, blotting out the memory of Queen Dolphina and the humiliation he had known at her hands. And before long he became consumed with the thought that he must make Helen of Troy his own.

Now between the secrets that the angels had revealed to Joseph della Reina and those that Lilith had supplied, his powers were very great, and at last he found a way not only to transport a human being across a great space, but across the centuries as well. The first time he cast the spell he shivered in anticipation. For a moment the illusory palace in which he lived seemed to flicker, as if the illusion were about to end, then all at once the cries of an infant shocked Joseph della Reina, and he found, to his amazement, an infant loudly crying on his bed. The shock soon passed, though, when he realized that he had succeeded in his basic attempt, but that he had called Helen from out of the past too young for his purposes.

Quickly, impatiently, Joseph della Reina pronounced a spell that sent the infant back, and then he spoke again, to summon an older Helen. His lust for her was so great that it was palpable, and he was certain that it was about to be sated. Again the palace flickered, this time more than before, then a figure suddenly appeared on the bed, that of Helen of Troy. But it was not Helen as Joseph della Reina had expected to find her. No, this Helen wore a worm-eaten shroud and consisted solely of bones. But what was far more horrible was that the skeleton was alive—in invoking it from the past Joseph della Reina had brought it back to life. And as he watched in horror, the arms of the skeleton opened and reached out to embrace him.

A wave of pure horror washed over Joseph della Reina, and he dashed from that room, but there too the bones of the once-lovely Helen awaited him, seeking an embrace, and the terrified sorcerer ran from the house. In his terror he forgot that the palace was but an illusion, and that his true home was in a cave on the side of a cliff overlooking the sea. No sooner did he step out of the door than he found himself falling. And a second before his body shattered on the rocks below, he saw the bones of Helen awaiting him, her arms open.

Palestine: Sixteenth Century

The Finger

ne night long ago, in the city of Safed, three young men went out for a walk. Reuven, the eldest, was to be married the next day to a beautiful and wealthy maiden, and his companions laughed and joked and teased their friend. The moon was full that night, and the young men decided to leave the beaten path and walk in the thick forest that surrounded the city.

The moonlight illumined even the darkest parts of the forest, and they passed through it fearlessly. At last they reached the riverbank and rested on large rocks near the shore, while they watched the river below. Here they continued to make merry, for they felt as if they were intoxicated.

It was during this time that one of them noticed something strange nearby. It was an object the size of a finger that stuck out of the earth. They got up to examine it, assuming it was a root. But when they came closer, they saw to their amazement that is was indeed a finger that emerged there.

Now on a different night the young men might have felt pity for one buried so near the surface. But filled with high spirits, they jested about it instead. One of them said, "Who among us will put a wedding ring on this finger?" And Reuven, the groom-to-be, quickly replied that it must be he, because he was to be the first one to marry. Then, as his friends looked on in amusement, Reuven took off his ring and slipped it on that finger, pronouncing as he did the words *Harai at mi'kudeshet li*—"You are betrothed to me"—three times, as the Law requires. But no sooner did he finish speaking than the finger began to twitch, much to the horror of the young men, who jumped back at the sight.

Suddenly the whole hand reached out from the earth, twitching and grasping. And as they stared at it in horror, frozen in place, the ground began to rumble, as if the earth were about to open. Suddenly the body of a woman, wearing a tattered shroud, rose out of the earth, her dead eyes staring directly into those of Reuven, her arms open as she cried out, "My husband!" in a terrible and terrifying voice. Hearing this, the three friends screamed in horror and took to their heels, running through the forest as fast they could go. But this time the way was dark, for the moon had slipped behind a cloud, and as they ran they tore their clothes on thorns and branches, but never did they stop running or even dare to look back until they had reached their homes in the city. For all the time they ran they heard the unearthly wail of the dead woman close behind. Only when they were safely in their own homes, with the doors locked and the windows barred, did they dare breathe a sigh of relief and tend to the many cuts they had acquired in their wild dash through the forest.

The next morning the three friends met together, still pale and shaken. And they agreed to keep the horrible events of the night a secret, for they were deeply ashamed of their jest and its terrible consequences. Then Reuven went to the ritual bath to prepare for the wedding and left his friends alone with their confused thoughts.

Now a great many people had gathered, for Reuven and his bride belonged to two of the most distinguished families in Safed. But just as the ceremony was about to begin, a bloodcurdling shriek came from the back of the crowd, followed by many others' screams, provoking a panic. For there stood the corpse of a woman wearing only a worm-eaten shroud. Most of the crowd—including the bride and the families of the bride and groom—ran away when they saw her, until none were left there except for Reuven and the rabbi, who had been about to pronounce the wedding vows.

The rabbi, alone among all of those present, retained his composure. He addressed himself to the corpse and said, "Why is it, woman, that you have left your final resting place and returned to the living?" And the corpse replied, in her unearthly voice, "What blemish does the bridegroom find in me, that he should want to wed another? For cannot all the world see that he is wed to me?" And she held up her hand, on which the ring of the bridegroom could be seen, with his initials engraved on it. Then the rabbi turned to the bridegroom, who was crouched in terror behind him, and asked if what the woman said was true. In a trembling voice the young man told of his walk through the forest with his friends and of the jest they had played when they had found the finger sticking out of the earth. And the rabbi asked, "Did you pronounce the sacred vow three times?" The young man meekly nodded. And the rabbi asked, "Was it done in the presence of two witnesses?" Again Reuven nodded. Then the rabbi looked very grave and said that the rabbinic court would have to be convened to discuss the matter, for in the eyes of the Law it appeared that the young man had indeed bound himself to that corpse in matrimony. When the bridegroom heard these terrible words, he fainted dead away and had to be carried off to his home.

In the days that followed, the city of Safed was in an uproar, for who had ever heard of a living man marrying a corpse? And the parents of Reuven begged the rabbi to find a way to free their son from the terrible curse. As for the rabbi, he immersed himself in meditation and in the study of *responsa*, searching for a precedent. But there was none; instead one would have to be set. On the day the court was convened, the rabbi called upon the corpse to appear, and she did so, still wearing the worm-eaten shroud in which she had been buried. Under oath she told what young Reuven had done in the forest. Then the rabbi called upon the two friends, who reluctantly confirmed what she said. At last the rabbi called upon the bridegroom, who also confessed that the vow had been made, but pleaded with the court to annul the marriage, for he had never intended for it to happen.

Then the court addressed the dead woman and asked her if she would relinquish her claim, but the corpse was adamant that the marriage must be consummated. For while she had lived she had never married and had thus been denied her hour of joy. And she was determined to receive after death what she had been denied in life.

Then the rabbi called upon the parents of the bridegroom, who testified that the betrothal of their son to the daughter of the wealthy man had been made even before the birth of the children. The two couples had vowed that if one had a boy child and one a girl, then they were to be wed. And the parents of the bride confirmed this vow.

Finally, when all the testimony had been taken, the court gathered together to discuss the case, while young Reuven trembled, his eyes avoiding the terrible corpse that also stood waiting among them. At last the court reached a decision, which the rabbi announced. He said, "It is true that Reuven did, in the presence of two witnesses, unwittingly make a vow of marriage that appears to be valid." Here the rabbi paused, and the young man and his parents were filled with terror. Then the rabbi continued, "There are, however, other factors that must be considered. First, the wedding vow would deny the betrothal, and it is widely known that one vow may not be permitted to negate an earlier one. Second, the vows of the bridegroom were not made with intention. Finally, there is no precedent for a claim on the living by the dead. Therefore the vows cannot be accepted as valid, because the bride is not from among the living. The marriage is thus declared null and void!"

Now when the rabbi uttered these words, young Reuven fainted again, this time from relief. But the corpse, having lost her chance to wed either in life or in death, let forth an ear-shattering shriek, which pierced the souls of all those assembled there and filled their hearts with horror. Then she collapsed upon the ground and became again as one of the dead.

When those assembled had at last calmed down, the rabbi gave orders to have the corpse reburied, with proper ritual and at a greater depth, so that a tragedy like the one that had just occurred would never happen again. And after her burial the rabbi called upon the parents of the true bride to fulfill the vow they had made before their daughter had been born and to complete the wedding ceremony, which had been so terribly interrupted. This was done and at last the wedding of Reuven and his true bride took place.

Palestine: Sixteenth Century

The Punishment

ong ago, in the city of Safed, a rich man sought out Rabbi Isaac Luria, known as the Ari, and said, "You are known as a seer; but can you envision even the darkest secrets hidden in a man's past? If such a thing is possible, then I am prepared to repent; if not, then I see no reason to have faith in God." The Ari turned to the man, peered into his eyes, and told him everything about himself, from the time he had been born, including every one of his sins. The rich man was startled at what he heard, and he confessed to everything, except that he denied having sinned with his maidservant, who had since died.

So the Ari motioned with his hand and drew her forth from the *Sitra Ahra*, the Other Side. When the man saw her, he stiffened, grew pale, and fell at the Ari's feet, confessing his sin with her. Then he begged the Ari to send her away, for the soul that he had called forth clung to his own, and he could not bear it. But the Ari refused to remove her from his presence, saying, "Our masters taught that whoever joins himself to a woman in sin shall be bound up with her for all time, in this world and the next. For in both worlds she will cling to him and refuse to depart. Only one thing can wrench her free." "What is it?" screamed the man. "Tell me, for I cannot bear the pain in my soul!" And the Ari said, "In your case the only penance can be death by fire."

The man cried out, in great pain, "Even such a death would be better than to lose my soul like this!" "Know then," said the Ari, "that the Law requires that hot lead be used." The man flinched at this, but said, in a strangled voice, "I am ready to die." The Ari commanded that lead be brought and heated over the flames. He ordered the man to once again make a full confession of his sins, and he did. Then he told the man to throw himself to the ground, stretch out his hands, close his eyes, and open his mouth. The man did all this and awaited a terrible death, his soul coiled in terror. At that moment the Ari poured honey into his mouth and said, "Your sin has been lifted and your soul freed. Nor shall you die." And when the man tasted the honey and heard these words, he fainted.

But when he opened his eyes he was like a new man, for the great weight of the sin had been lifted, and along with it had vanished the soul that had clung so tightly to his own. And he lived all the rest of his days in righteousness, his repentance complete.

Palestine: Sixteenth Century

The House of Witches

n Damascus there was a house of witches not far from the Jewish cemetery. Those witches used their powers in strange and unspeakable ways. Their evil struck like an arrow, without warning. They were the pestilence that walked in the darkness and the destruction that laid waste at noon. Even the dead were not spared their ghastly intentions—for the witches had begun to steal the bodies of pious Jews from their coffins and to do evil things to pollute their souls, which were still in the process of parting from the shells they had inhabited so long.

At last the Ari sent Rabbi Hayim Vital to exterminate that nest of evil. And when he arrived he told the Jews of the community to inform him at once if any one of them died. When the first such death was reported to him, Hayim Vital attended the funeral and followed the coffin as it was carried to the grave. But those carrying the coffin felt that it was too light, and when they opened it they found, to their horror, that it was indeed empty. Then they knew that the witches had snatched the body of that man. Hayim Vital told the four coffin bearers to wait in the cemetery, for he would be back within an hour. And before he left he gave them special holy names to pronounce should they find themselves in danger. The men repeated those names over and over to themselves, so that they would not forget them.

After that Hayim Vital went directly to the house of the witches. He crept up to the window of the house and peered inside. There he saw the witches laughing together, and from their comments he understood that they had done something terrible to the body of the man in order to force his spirit to become a wandering soul that would never find any rest. Then Hayim Vital grew very angry and pronounced a holy name that made him invisible. After that he went to the door of the witches and knocked. When they asked who it was, he said, "It is the soul of he that you have condemned to wander. I have returned to seek my revenge!"

Now when the witches heard this, they became frightened. For although witches are unafraid of living men, they are terrified of spirits, especially angry ones. The witches all sought to hide, but before they could, Hayim Vital pronounced the series of holy names that the Ari had given him. And at that moment every witch in the house turned into a black dog and went dashing out the door toward the cemetery.

All at once the coffin bearers saw the dogs rushing toward them, barking horribly. At first the men were frozen with fear, but then they recalled the names Hayim Vital had given them. And as soon as they began to pronounce them they found themselves strengthened, until they felt as brave as he was. The dogs ignored them completely, however, and ran right by, as if they did not see them at all. And they split up and ran to the four corners of the cemetery. When the men saw this, they followed after them, and that is how they found the parts of the body of the man who had died, for the witches had cut his body into four parts and carried them to the corners of the cemetery. And now they were rushing to recover the body and bring it back together in order to free themselves from the spirit's terrible revenge.

It was then that Hayim Vital reached the cemetery and saw how the witches had scattered the poor man's body. His anger grew so great that he pronounced another spell, and all of the witches turned into worms and other vermin, and that is what they remained.

Then the coffin bearers gathered the parts of the man's body and placed them together in the coffin. The rabbi closed it and pronounced a series of holy names. When they reopened it, they found that the body of the man was intact, as if the witches had never touched it at all. And they knew that his soul, as well, had been saved. Then Rabbi Hayim Vital and the others buried the man and said *Kaddish* for him, the prayer for the dead. And never again did the witches cause harm to the Jews of that city.

Syria: Oral Tradition

The Beast

here once was a wealthy man and wife who longed, more than anything else, to have a child of their own. Over the years the wife had tried every known remedy in order to conceive, including potions of every kind, but still the couple was without children. Now the man, who was a merchant, heard from others that there was a wise old man among the Jews, whose name was Elijah, who could help them have a child. And when they had exhausted every other means, the merchant and his wife went to the Jewish Quarter of Cairo and sought out the old man.

They found that Elijah lived in an almost empty hut in the poorest part of the quarter. He possessed nothing except for the robe he wore and a prayer book. The merchant and his wife wondered to themselves how such a poor man could be of help to them. Still, they were desperate, so they told the old man how much they wanted to have a child, and they offered to pay him whatever he asked if he could help them. Elijah said, "What do you want, a son or a daughter?" The merchant replied, "To have a son of my own is what I want more than anything else in the world." Then Elijah told them to bring him pen and paper, and when they did, he wrote out an amulet, using holy names. He told them to place that amulet in a cup of wine and for both of them to drink from that cup, and in nine months' time they would have a son of their own.

Somehow the quiet confidence of Elijah soothed the pair and gave them hope. Then the merchant said, "We will always be grateful if what you have said comes true. Tell me, how can I repay you?" Elijah replied, "Do nothing for now. But when the child is born, make a donation in the charity box of the synagogue on the corner of this street, which serves the poorest Jews. That will suffice." Then the merchant and his wife thanked him many times, and turned to go. But before they left, the old man said, "Wait. There is one more thing that I must tell you." The merchant and his wife turned back, wondering what it was. And Elijah said, "The son that will be born to you is not destined to be wed. He must remain unmarried all his life. For it is written that on the night he weds, he will be devoured by a beast!"

As they heard this prophecy, the high hopes of the couple were suddenly shaken. They stood silent, but at last the merchant said, "Is there nothing we can do to spare our child this terrible fate?" And the old man answered, "No, I am sorry to say. All that you can do is avoid making any match for him, and when he is old enough to understand, explain that it is his destiny to remain unwed." And the merchant and his wife assured Elijah that they would heed his warning, and that if indeed they were blessed with a son, they would see to it that he was never betrothed. Then they took their leave, but this time they were much more solemn.

When they returned home the merchant placed the amulet that Elijah had written into a silver goblet and filled it with his finest wine, a bottle that had been saved since he had been born. The merchant and his wife drank from the goblet, one sip at a time, until it was empty. It was then they discovered that the amulet had dissolved into the wine; not a trace of it was to be found. And when the couple saw this, they sensed that the prophecy of the old man would indeed come true, and they would become parents. But they did not think about his admonition.

To their mutual delight the merchant's wife soon found that she was with child, and all during the pregnancy she took great care so that the child should not be lost. And at the end of nine months she gave birth to a beautiful son, and the merchant and his wife felt that they had been greatly blessed. The merchant did not forget his promise to Elijah to give money to the synagogue for the poor. He gave them a great donation, enough to sustain them for a full year. But he did not dwell on the warning of the old man, for the time his son would think of marriage was far off.

In the years that followed, the man and his wife raised their son with loving care, for he was more precious to them than anything in the world. From time to time a marriage was proposed for him, for such early betrothals were the custom. The boy's parents always turned down these offers, giving one excuse or another, but never, of course, the true reason. The day came, however, when the young man himself informed his parents that he wished to be wed. The parents argued long into the night about whether to tell the boy the prophecy of the old man. In the end they decided not to, and instead made up their minds to see to it that the boy was indeed wed, but under circumstances that would protect him from every danger.

Now in his travels the merchant had once come into possession of a small island in a distant sea. That island was uninhabited by man or beast, and the merchant thought it would be the perfect place to have the wedding. Therefore, once the match had been made, the merchant saw to it that a fine mansion was built on that island, surrounded with a large stone wall that would protect his son from every kind of danger. So too did he have guards posted to guard the mansion day and night.

One year later, when the time for the wedding had arrived, the merchant was informed that the mansion was ready. Then the merchant had his finest sailing ship outfitted and brought both families on board, along with the bride and groom and many guests. (Of course the bride and groom were never permitted to glimpse each other, as was the custom.) The voyage was a time of great rejoicing, and the merchant and his wife never dwelled at all on the prophecy of the old man. For they felt that they had done everything possible to protect their son from danger.

When the ship at last docked on that lovely island, all expressed wonder and delight. The sand of the beaches was pure white, and there were fruit trees of every kind, as well as wild grapes and berries. So too were all the guests astonished at the extravagant mansion. It was constructed of marble, like a palace, and the chamber of the bride and groom was set at the top of a spiral tower. There, the merchant felt sure, his son would be safe.

The wedding festivities continued for three days and nights before the vows were finally said. It was then that the merchant's son saw his bride for the first time. She was astonishingly beautiful, with raven hair that reached to her waist, and the young man felt himself to be the most fortunate groom in the world. At last he and his bride climbed the stairs to the tower together and stood on the threshold of the bridal chamber. The young man led his bride inside and closed the door. As he gazed at her he was filled with awe at her beauty. He admired especially her hands, with their fine, slender fingers and long nails. He smiled shyly at her, but she seemed afraid to lift her eyes from the floor. When at last she did, the young man was astonished to see a look of wild desire in them unlike anything he had ever seen. When he stepped forward to embrace her, he suddenly heard a low growl. The young man looked around in confusion, wondering where it could have come from. He turned back just in time to see the fangs of the beast as it leaped at him from the very place his bride had been.

Egypt: Oral Tradition

The Rabbi and the Witch

ong, long ago, strange things began to happen. Jews disappeared for no reason and were never heard from again. They left the city but never reached their destinations. Or they started back but never reached home. At first the people thought it must be the work of thieves, but it seemed strange that the only victims were Jews. As more and more disappeared, most of them merchants, the people became alarmed, and they turned to Rabbi Jannai for help.

Rabbi Jannai learned that everyone who had vanished had passed along the same road. Disguised as a merchant, he set out on that very road in a wagon filled with wine barrels, certainly a tempting target. Some of the other rabbis had warned him that such a journey might be filled with danger, but he had assured them that no harm would befall him, for he was undertaking the mission in the name of God.

Rabbi Jannai rode all morning and afternoon, and nothing unusual happened. As evening approached he came to an inn and decided to spend the night there. Now an old woman ran that inn, and she recognized at once that Rabbi Jannai was a Jew, for it was clear for all the world to see. She smiled to herself and invited him to make himself at home.

After that long journey Rabbi Jannai was thirsty, and he asked the old woman for a drink of water. He noticed that she turned her back to him as she poured it, and he became suspicious. So too did he see how her lips were moving as she brought it to him, and he wondered if she might be casting a spell. When she turned away to tend the fire he spilled a little of that water on the floor, and he didn't blink an eye when he saw the puddle turn to snakes and slither away. Then he spoke to the woman and said, "My thanks, good woman, for the water. I'll drink it later. Now perhaps I could interest you in purchasing some of my wines."

The old woman was delighted to learn that the Jew was a wine merchant, for she knew that all his possessions would soon be her own. But she concealed these thoughts and said, "Well, perhaps, but I must taste any wine before I will buy it." And Rabbit Jannai said, "Of course. That is only to be expected. Wait here and I will bring you some."

Then the rabbi left the inn and returned to his wagon, taking the glass of enchanted water with him. He poured some of it into a wineskin that he finished filling from the spout of a barrel. Then he returned to the inn and handed the wineskin to the old woman, encouraging her to taste his wares. She emptied it in a single gulp. And no sooner had she done this than she turned into an ass. The beast began to run wildly about the inn, causing great damage.

At last Rabbi Jannai dragged the ass outside and tied it to his wagon. Then he took it, braying and kicking, back to the city. There he mounted the ass and rode it into the marketplace, intending to reveal the cause of the mysterious disappearances.

Now there was a witch living in the city who was a sister of the old witch who ran the inn. And when she saw Rabbi Jannai riding that donkey, she not only knew that it had been enchanted, but she recognized her sister as well. She quickly mumbled the spell to turn the ass back into a human being. And as soon as the spell was spoken, the ass became the old woman, crawling on her hands and knees, with Rabbi Jannai riding upon her.

So it was that Rabbi Jannai was seen in public riding upon a woman. The wags and gossips still laugh when they tell the tale, but they speak of the rabbi with pride, for he outfoxed the witch. And so greatly did she fear his powers that she confessed turning the missing merchants into donkeys and vowed to reverse the spells if the rabbi would let her go. He agreed, and within moments the hoofbeats in the field around her inn turned into footsteps, and all the missing merchants hurried home.

As for the witch, she and her sister dined together at an inn that night and drank many glasses of wine to celebrate her escape from the Jew. But no one seems to have seen them after that, and no trace of them was ever found—except for the two ornery asses they were said to have left behind.

Babylon: c. Fifth Century

The Door to Gehenna

here once was an older man who married a young bride. His wealth was very great, as was his desire for his young wife. But she cared only for his fortune. For the man himself, she felt nothing. Perhaps because she was young and he was old, this man was very possessive of his wife, and he never let her out of his sight. And she began to feel that she had been trapped in a golden cage.

Now the wealthy man had one servant whom he trusted completely. This steward had served him for many years and had never betrayed him. It happened that urgent business called the man away from home, and he entrusted his wife to his loyal servant. He told her that she could pass the time exploring the great mansion, but he warned her in the strictest terms that under no circumstances was she to open one particular door in the courtyard. And he warned the servant as well. Any other rooms, however, were available to them. Then the man kissed his wife good-bye and set out on his journey.

Now this young woman had grown lonely in that vast house, never seeing anyone but her husband and his servant. And because she did not care for her husband, she had begun to have fantasies about the handsome steward. So it happened that no sooner had her husband's carriage set out than she felt flushed with desire for the servant and decided to seduce him.

At first the steward did not recognize her intentions. But her behavior became increasingly brazen. On the first night she let her hair down in his presence; on the second she appeared to him wearing a robe; on the third she saw to it that the robe slipped open; on the fourth she wore nothing beneath it. By the fourth night the poor steward was fully in the power of his lust. So when the robe slipped open on that night and he saw her naked, he gave in to her without thinking and possessed her, as Adam had Eve.

Only afterward did the full meaning of his sin become clear to him. He turned his face to the wall and sobbed. But the woman felt no grief at all. And now that she had conquered the steward, she began to wonder about the door her husband had forbidden her to open. This thought took root in her mind with the persistence of an obsession. While the servant mourned his unfaithfulness to his master, the woman slipped out of the room. She lit a torch and began to explore the mansion, moving toward the courtyard and the forbidden door. And the steward was so lost in his emotions that he was unaware of her absence.

So it was that the forbidden door drew her to it, like a moth to a flame.

When the steward finally came to his senses, he discovered that his master's wife was no longer there. He sighted her in the courtyard, and he suddenly realized that she had already reached the forbidden door, where she stood, like Eve before the Tree of Knowledge. This sight left him petrified. He watched in a daze as she reached beneath the vines that had grown over the door and found the handle. She turned it. The vines restrained her at first, but she pushed with all her might and tore them loose. The door swung open: a hand reached out, grabbed her, and pulled her inside. The door slammed shut. At that instant the frozen man came back to life. He rushed to the door and tried to open it. But it was locked.

When the master finally returned home, he found neither his wife nor his steward and began to search through the house. He heard a moaning sound and found the poor steward, sobbing to himself. At that moment the master knew that his wife must have opened the door. He shook the steward, demanding to know if this had happened. And when the steward nodded to confirm it, the husband fell into a terrible rage and beat him mercilessly.

When the livid husband had vented his wrath, he demanded to know exactly what happened. Since the steward could not bear to reveal their sin, he told his master that his wife had secretly left her room at night and gone to the courtyard. He said that when he had discovered that she was missing, he had hurried after her but arrived too late. And he told his master of the hand that had reached out the instant the door had opened.

Then the husband pulled the steward up, stared into his eyes, and told him that the door his wife had opened was none other than the door to Gehenna, where the souls of the wicked are tortured; the very gate to Hell. The servant realized that his master had known this all along and had been afraid to say anything, lest curiosity overcome them. And the servant's grief over his betrayal was even greater.

Later that night the master became calm again. He told the steward that he was prepared to forgive him, although he could never redeem himself in his eyes because of what had happened. To the steward this was the mildest of punishments, and he knew that his bitterness at his own failure would always be even greater. Then the master told the steward how it had come to pass that such a door was to be found there. And this is the tale that he told:

"By birth I was a common man, and when I was younger I was a hunter. Once, when hunting in the forest, I found a young man lying half-frozen in the snow. I did everything I could to warm him, and in this way I saved his life. When the young man was restored to his senses, he told me where he lived. I helped him to his home and found that it was more like a palace.

"That is when I learned that the young man's father was none other than Asmodeus, King of Demons. When he learned how I had saved his son's life, he told me that from that day on I would be a wealthy man and live like a lord. And he gave me this mansion. But he also warned me that one door in the courtyard was never to be opened, for if it were, disaster would surely occur. I asked him why, and he finally revealed the reason, so that I might be spared from finding out myself. He told me that it was the door to Gehenna, the very gate of Hell, and whoever entered there was doomed. And he explained that there were two entrances to Hell in this world, one there, in that courtyard, and another one, far off in the forest."

The steward listened to this tale with amazement, and at the end he asked only one question: why had his master accepted a house with such a door in it. And the master replied, "Only in this way could I receive the great wealth I had always lusted after, nor did I fear the door, because I knew what was behind it. Nor was my wife in danger, as long as I was with her. But when I had to leave, I thought it best to warn her of the door's dangers. That was my mistake. If I had said nothing, surely nothing would have happened. That is why I did not kill you. For I know deep down that I am to blame."

That night the steward had difficulty sleeping. Half the night he tossed and turned. Just before dawn he finally fell asleep, and as soon as he did, he had a vivid dream. In the dream the steward was ordered to go to Gehenna to find his master's wife. He packed at once and left, leaving his master a note saying that he would come back only if he succeeded in finding her. And he set out on a long journey. In the dream he found a clue that led him onward. It was a turtle shell, and he suddenly realized that it formed a map. So he followed that map, and it led him to a remote forest. At first he was reluctant to enter there, but he knew that his life was worth nothing unless he redeemed himself.

So he walked into the forest, dark and dense. And before long he was completely lost. This time when he looked at the symbols inscribed on the shell, the lines were blurred in his vision. And it seemed that no matter where he went, he was only going in circles. He could not find even a hint of a path. Finally, in frustration, he cast the shell against the ground. At that very instant a head and legs emerged from what had been a hollow shell, and a turtle scurried away. This miracle left the man dumbfounded and made him realize how precious that shell was. He raced after the turtle, but it disappeared in the forest. He had let the magic turtle go! All at once the world seemed to grow dark. The sun had set, and he had not even seen it go down. And it was then that he really became afraid, for it seemed as if there were no way out of that dark place.

Fear and exhaustion led the man to seek out a place to sleep. He saw a large and prominent tree and sat down against its trunk. The steward was starting to feel drowsy when something cold and wet fell on his eyes. He jumped up, but it was too late. He was blind. In terror the man wiped his eyes and smelled the substance that had fallen on them—it was blood.

Now blind and lost in that desolate place, the steward realized that he was being punished for his sins, and he felt that his death was near. Still, he found the strength to stagger away from that bleeding tree, but then he tripped and fell into a pit. The bottom was covered with leaves, which softened the fall. He pulled himself up and tried to crawl out, but he could not. He was trapped. So he lay down in a stupor. Finally, a ringing sound aroused him. It sounded like a woodcutter in the distance. At first he was filled with hope that someone might find him there in that pit. But then the ringing sound grew louder and louder, until it was like thunder. The man became confused and wondered if he were dead or alive. He knew that in any case he could not escape. So he lay there, awaiting his fate.

Just then the chopping sound ceased, and the man heard the earth-shaking crash of a giant tree being felled. A chill of terror passed through his body, for he realized that whoever the woodcutter was, his size was far greater than that of any mortal man. He trembled and shook in the bottom of that pit, like a calf waiting to be slaughtered. All at once he heard the sound of branches breaking and heard the sound of trees snapping under the weight of giant steps, coming closer and closer to the edge of the pit. The servant said his prayers and prepared himself to die. Just then a thunderous voice bellowed, "Who are you and what are you doing there?" "I am a man, blinded by a bleeding tree," the poor steward replied. "I am lost in the forest. Help me, please, to find the way out." "Ah, the bleeding tree!" the giant roared. "Every day there is another victim. But fear not, for I myself was once blinded by it, when I tried to cut it down. A man such as yourself saved me then by bringing me the herb that can cure blindness. When I recovered my sight, he showed me where this herb grows, and I always carry it with me." These words, even though they echoed like thunder, sounded like a mother's lullaby to the terrified man. He reached out for the herb, and the giant gave it to him. And when he rubbed it into his eyes, it was as if a dark veil had been lifted. And he looked up and saw that the giant was indeed as tall as the great trees of that forest, but kindly, and he thanked him with all his heart for saving his life.

"Where do you want to go?" roared the giant, and the tone was not bellicose, but even if he whispered the sound would terrify any man. "I must find the way to Gehenna, for my master has sent me there," the man replied. "But those who go to Gehenna are not lost," said the giant, "neither are they of the living. Are you a living man or not?" "I am alive," the man shouted, with all his strength. "I am on a mission to find my master's wife, who is in Gehenna. Can you tell me how to get there?" "If I were you, I would turn back and go the other way," bellowed the giant. "But if that is where you want to go, here, come with me." And with that, the giant bent down and lifted him out of the pit with one hand. At first the man closed his eyes in terror, but when he opened them he saw that the giant was taking great strides, which seemed to span miles. All at once he found himself standing on the earth again, before a glowing gate. The giant roared, "That is the gate that you seek." And when the man turned to thank him, the giant was already gone, and only his thunderous footsteps could be heard.

In great confusion the steward approached the gate, touched it, and badly burned his hand. Had he come all that way at such great risk only to be turned back at the gate of Gehenna? At that moment he heard many voices sobbing, and looking up he saw a line of wraithlike beings coming out of the forest, whipped onward by an angel. The man could barely believe his eyes and ran to hide behind a tree. From there he saw the angel and his victims reach the gate, which the angel struck once with his fiery whip so that it swung open. Then the angel forced all the others inside, even though they tried to resist. But they were no match for his whip. And the steward knew that if he entered there on his own he might never escape and that the punishments awaiting those wraiths might be visited on him as well. But he dismissed these thoughts at once and rushed inside under the very arm of the avenging angel, slipping in just as the gate slammed shut.

No sooner had he stepped inside than he almost fell into an abyss, for he had arrived on the Bridge of Gehenna, which was no wider than a thread. The man saw how even the spirits of the dead had to struggle to cross that bridge, and now and then one tumbled over it, his diminishing scream the last they heard of him. How then was a living man to cross there? He clung with all his strength and somehow made his way to the other side.

Once across, he was greatly relieved, even though that place was Gehenna. But then the steward looked up and almost fainted. He saw bodies strung everywhere, hanging by their eyelids, their ears, their hands, or their tongues. Some women hung by their nipples. Their shrieks were beyond description. Even in his darkest fears the man had not expected punishment like that, and he sought refuge in that place of horror.

In the distance the man saw a palace. Although it was surrounded with flames, he ran to it, for there was nowhere else to hide. When he reached its entrance, he saw that it had been constructed of gold and was more precious than any palace on Earth. Flames of red and blue surrounded the walls, so that the whole palace seemed to be burning inside a great flame. The man burned his hand as he opened the door, and when he stood on the threshold he felt the heat of the floor rising up through the soles of his shoes. But what he saw made him forget his pain: inside that golden chamber, seated on a golden throne, was his master's wife. She was wearing garments of gold, and all the objects surrounding her were made of gold as well. Many servants attended her, some pouring wine into a golden goblet, others bringing food on a golden tray. The steward was completely dumbfounded. Is this how she, the greatest sinner he knew, was punished? Or was she herself the Queen of Demons?

Just then the woman looked up. She saw the steward and recognized him. And she beckoned for him to come to her. The man came forward in great fear, because he dreaded that he might fall under her power again. And she said, "How is it that you have come here?" He replied, "I vowed to find you, to redeem myself in the eyes of my master, whom I betrayed with you. But how is it that you are held in such high esteem here, while the others are tortured in such terrible ways?" She replied, "It is not as it appears. You believe that I am a queen here, surrounded by slaves. But the truth is that I am being tortured in this place. Everything, as you can see, is made of gold. But all the gold is molten, and every moment I am burned: when standing up, when lying down, when eating, when drinking. The wine is molten gold; the food is burning jewels. There is no sustenance here and no respite."

The steward realized that what she said was true, that her opulence was a false illusion, and that she was suffering as much as those hanging by their hair. Then the woman spoke again, and she said, "Go now, return to the world. Tell them what awaits them here. Take my ring with you, and they will know that it is true." With that she took off her ring and dropped it into her golden goblet. Then she put the goblet inside a marble vase and gave it to the man. He looked inside and saw the burning ring and heard it hiss. Then, trembling at the horror of that place, he took his leave and ran as fast as he could to the entrance of the palace. And the moment he stepped out of the doorway he awoke. He found himself lying in his own bed, in his master's home, which he had never left.

The man was staggered to learn that the long, exhausting journey had been a dream. But then he looked up and saw a strangely familiar marble vase on the table next to his bed. He jumped up and looked in the vase, and there, to his complete astonishment, was the golden goblet with the white-hot ring from Gehenna. The steward picked up that vase and hurried to show it to his master. And when his master saw that burning ring and heard the tale, he knew it was true, even though it had been a dream. And all who saw that ring knew that the warnings of the prophets were not idle talk and sought refuge in the ways of the righteous.

France: Thirteenth Century

The Devil's Fire

nce a ragged traveler made his way to Jerusalem. He found refuge for the night in the home of a pious Jew, and after they had shared a modest meal, the traveler offered to regale his host with tales about his travels. The Jew replied, "Yes, I would like nothing better than to hear your strangest tale, a tale of the most extraordinary thing that has occurred in your travels."

The wanderer grimaced when the Jew said this and looked him in the eyes. "My most unusual experience took place in a Persian city, where it is the custom to offer human sacrifices. Now in our day such things are not common. Yet the custom itself is not as disturbing as the fact that those who are sacrificed go gladly to this fate, and sometimes even offer themselves to be burned in the fire."

Now the Jew, whose name was Rabbi Zacharia, could not believe that such a thing was possible, for who would willingly abandon his own life? Yet the wanderer insisted it was true, saying, "This is the strangest part of all: the reason the people do not fear being sacrificed is because one month later, in every instance, the one who was consumed in flames comes back to the city, alive and well. Those returning always wear pure white robes and report that they have traveled to another kingdom, where they were well received and greatly rewarded. They seem so calm and peaceful that all who see them are convinced that the fire holds no danger. Instead, they believe it is the doorway to another world, one in which their lives will be abundant."

"But how do they survive the fire," the rabbi asked, "for such a thing cannot occur!" The stranger replied, "You are right. And yet I myself have seen one who was consumed in flames return one month to the day after his death. Otherwise I too would never have believed it possible." And when Rabbi Zacharia heard this, he was awestruck, for he saw that the traveler was a man of his word, and even something of a prophet.

This bleak tale filled the rabbi with sorrow, because he refused to believe for a moment that those who returned were the same as those who had been sacrificed. No, some kind of deception had taken place; perhaps an evil spell had been cast. And the tale continued to haunt the rabbi long after the wanderer had departed for still another land.

At last Rabbi Zacharia decided that he must somehow try to free those people from the terrible delusion that the flames offered them no danger. So he set out for that very city, in remote and distant Persia. In order to get there he joined a caravan going that way. The caravan, which consisted of three dozen camels and the same number of riders, crossed a vast desert that loomed in every direction like a great sea. It took them more than six months, but at last they reached their destination.

When Rabbi Zacharia made his way to the center of the city, he saw that a great crowd had formed there, but he could not see what was taking place. Then he noticed that one of those at the edge of the crowd was observing something in a small mirror, which he held above his head. The rabbi asked the man if he might also peer in the mirror, and the man handed it to him just in time for the rabbi to see a young man cast himself into a mighty bonfire, where he was quickly consumed, amid many terrible screams. This sight horrified the rabbi, who saw for himself that the young man had offered no resistance, but had gone willingly to his death.

Rabbi Zacharia returned the mirror to the man and told him that he was a stranger passing through that city. He asked him why that young man, with so much to look forward to, had willingly leaped into the flames. The man replied, "You can find out for yourself. Simply remain in this city, and one month from today go to the home of that young man. Then you will understand."

Rabbi Zacharia decided that he would indeed remain in that city for the allotted time, in hopes of resolving the mystery. So he stayed at an inn and passed the days strolling in the marketplace, trying to learn more about that strange custom of self-sacrifice. But he found that the people were reluctant to talk about it, and if they said anything at all, it was that he must find out for himself.

When a month had passed, Rabbi Zacharia went to the modest hut in which the young man had lived with his wife and family. Entering, he saw that many residents of the city had gathered there, including the man who had lent him the mirror. Rabbi Zacharia took a place next to this man and asked him to point out the young man's wife and children. When the man singled them out, Rabbi Zacharia saw that neither the wife nor the children were in mourning, even though the young man had departed from this life long before his time. Rabbi Zacharia could not understand this at all, and he asked the man's children why they did not weep. The children told him that their father had simply gone to another place, one in which there was always enough to eat and nothing to fear. So too were they certain that he would return from there to visit them that very night. And they invited the rabbi to remain among them as their guest to help celebrate their father's homecoming.

So it was that Rabbi Zacharia waited with them, and, at the stroke of midnight, they saw a man, dressed in a white robe, approaching the house. Even before he came inside the children all began to cheer, for they were certain it was their father coming back to them. And when the door opened Rabbi Zacharia saw to his complete amazement that the man who stood there was none other than the very one who had cast himself into the fire a month before. The robe he wore was woven from the finest silk, and upon his countenance was a look of great joy.

The man embraced and kissed his family and told them that all was well with him, far better than he had ever known. He encouraged them to join him by passing through the fiery gate. The rabbi was horrified to hear him say this, for even though the man appeared to be the one whose death he had witnessed, he still was not convinced it was the same man. And he vowed not to rest until he found out the truth.

When the man took his leave that evening, his family accompanied him along the road. Rabbi Zacharia followed them to the foot of the mountains, which was the place where those who had returned from the beyond always parted ways with their families. But even after the man's wife and children had turned back, promising to join him shortly, Rabbi Zacharia continued to follow him. He remained a safe distance behind as the man climbed up a path to a high ledge that could not be seen from below. There the man stood in a certain spot and said, "Open ye fiery gates, in the name of he who commands you." In an instant a great creaking was heard, and the stone wall of the mountain opened as if it were a door, and the man hurried inside. And as soon as he had entered, the stone door closed, and the mountain was restored to its original shape.

Rabbi Zacharia, who had witnessed this wonder, could barely believe his eyes. Yet at the same time the use of the spell confirmed what he had believed all along—that sorcery was somehow involved. He decided that in order to discover the truth, he would have to enter that passageway himself, even though it brought his life into danger. So Rabbi Zacharia climbed to the very same place he had seen the man stand and spoke the very same words. Then, just as swiftly, the stone door swung open, and Rabbi Zacharia hurried inside.

Inside the mountain it was pitch black and thick with the smoke and stench of brimstone. From where he stood, Rabbi Zacharia thought he heard distant screams and shrieks, and fear almost drove him to escape while he still could. But he restrained himself; he would not turn back until he had discovered the truth.

Then suddenly Rabbi Zacharia heard mocking laughter nearby. In terror he felt along the wall with his hands, searching for a place to hide. And just as the voices came closer, he discovered a crevice that was barely wide enough for him to enter. He tried to breathe quietly and wished he could still the loud beating of his heart. From where he was he could see the man who had come back from the dead, accompanied by a legion of fearsome demons. A terrible fire burned in the demons' eyes, a fire filled with hate. And now Rabbi Zacharia saw how that very same fire had begun to glow in the eyes of the man who had claimed to have escaped unscathed. And as Rabbi Zacharia watched, the man's body was transformed into that of the most terrible demon of all—Satan, the Devil himself.

"It worked again!" the Devil said. "More victims will be coming soon." And when the demons heard this, they all laughed hideously. That is when Rabbi Zacharia finally understood the truth. In each case the Devil had disguised himself as the latest victim of the flames and had gone back to convince the others to destroy themselves as well. Rabbi Zacharia felt sickened by the terrible deception, and he understood once and for all that there was nothing the evil ones would not stoop to do in order to dominate the world.

All this time Rabbi Zacharia had barely breathed, for fear of being discovered. But when the horde of demons finally passed he moved quickly, feeling his way along the wall again until he came to the place where he had come in. As soon as he reached the rock that had swung open, he whispered the magic words, still terrified that he might be overheard. But the rock did not budge. He decided that he had not spoken loudly enough and tried again. Still nothing happened. Rabbi Zacharia began to panic. Could it be that the words worked only from the outside, but not from within? He desperately repeated the magic words one more time, but without result. Then the cold truth sunk in: he was trapped in the underground cavern of the demons, who would, without doubt, find dozens of ways of torturing him should he fall into their hands.

In the distance the rabbi still heard the perverse laughter of the demons, and he decided that his only hope lay in following them, to learn what magic words worked from within. So he let their voices lead him down one passage to the next. And he kept wondering how they could see where they were going, for he was as good as blind in that dark cave.

As he walked, the screams and shrieks that Rabbi Zacharia had first heard grew louder and louder, until they pierced his ears. Somewhere nearby, multitudes were being tortured. The sound was so terrible that Rabbi Zacharia shivered with fright, yet he forced himself to go on. Little by little he found that he was becoming used to the dark. And he thought he could make out something faintly glowing in the distance that made it possible for the first time to see the dim passages before him. He wondered what it was that burned so darkly and shed so little light.

Suddenly the rabbi almost stepped into a great pit. He teetered on the edge for a terrifying moment, then found his balance and backed away. That is when he saw how the path had taken a very sharp turn, leading around the edge of that abyss. The shrieks from below were so terrible that Rabbi Zacharia could not bear the din. Looking around, he saw the young man who had leaped into the flames. He was in chains, and he was being dragged by a dozen demons. He screamed hysterically while the demons jested among themselves. While Rabbi Zacharia watched, the demons strung their victim upside down from a long pole. Then, as he pleaded for mercy, they dropped him into a bonfire of dark flames, where he screamed in even greater agony. They kept him there for an unbearably long time, while Rabbi Zacharia watched in horror. Then they pulled him out again, waited a brief moment, and then pitched him into the flames again, over and over, until they finally tired of their torture. At last they pulled him up and left him hanging upside down from the pole, and when they were gone Rabbi Zacharia crept up to him. Because he had gone to the young man's house, he knew his name. And when he was as close as he dared to come without being seen by the others, he called out to him.

Hearing his name the poor young man groaned, "Who is it?" And Rabbi Zacharia whispered that it was one of his own, a human being, one who had witnessed his plight. He asked the young man to tell all that had happened to him since he had leaped into the flames. Then the young man told this terrible tale: "At the moment I leaped into the flames my soul was lost, and I found myself falling a great distance, until I landed in a sea of boiling oil. That oil scalded me to the depth of my soul, and

I died a thousand deaths, but I could not die for good. For though my body had perished in the flame, my soul is imperishable, yet it is also subject to unimaginable pain. At last I was dragged out of that oil by burning pincers, and since then the other tortures have never ceased."

Rabbi Zacharia was horrified to hear this. Then he told the young man how the Devil had taken on his very image and tried to convince his family to follow in his footsteps. The poor man groaned with more pain than when he had been thrown into the flames. He said, "Please, I beg you, see to it that they do not, for their souls would be lost as well." And the rabbi replied, "I want to warn them and all of the others. But how can I get out of here? The spell that opened the boulder in the mountain does not work from within."

Then the unfortunate man replied, "The thought of escaping from this dreaded place consumes those who are tortured here. Yet it is said that no one has ever succeeded. For never are we free of our chains for a single second. I have heard, however, that there are three entrances. One is in the mountain, where you entered. Another is hidden in the desert, where Korah rebelled and was condemned. And the third is in Jerusalem. From what I have heard, the place where you entered does not open from within. When the demons want to get out to do their evil deeds, they leave by way of the desert." "But tell me quickly, how can I find that place?" the rabbi pleaded, for he knew the demons would soon return. "Seek out the rock from which the flames burst forth. That is the source of the fire of Gehenna—for know that you have reached the fires of Gehenna and nowhere else." And when Rabbi Zacharia heard this, even though he had known it must be so, he shook with fear. He whispered good-bye and was about to run off, when the man said frantically, "Here, take my ring so that my family will know you are telling the truth. But do not touch it with your fingers, for it will burn you to the very soul if you do." Then the man slipped the glowing ring off his finger, where it had been burning into him without cease. When it fell at Rabbi Zacharia's feet, he bent down and used a rock to push it into the leather pouch he wore and ran off as fast as he could. And a moment later he heard the chilling screams of the man, who was being thrown back into the flames.

He hid again, sickened by the acts of torture in the abyss, where worms crawled up and down their bodies as they hung helpless, slowing devouring them; scorpions walked over them at will, stinging them again and again with their terrible venom; burning embers poured down relentlessly on those who could not even lift their hands to protect themselves; and everywhere there was the thick smoke and acrid smell of brimstone that had overwhelmed him ever since he had entered that cursed cavern.

Not in his worse nightmare could Rabbi Zacharia have conceived that the tortures of Gehenna could be so cruel. And he knew that if he did not find a way out quickly, he might well lose his mind. It was then that his eyes fell upon a great rock that spewed forth the rain of fire that fell every-where. The demons, however, seemed oblivious to the flames; only the victims suffered its effects. And the rabbi knew that this must be the fountain of fire of which the poor young man had spoken.

Now this fiery rock was near the ceiling of the cavern, on the oppo-site side of the pit, and Rabbi Zacharia knew that he would be taking a great risk to go there. Yet he clung to the sides of the cavern like a shadow, hoping beyond hope that he would not be sighted. And he found that the demons were so preoccupied with the pleasures of torturing that he was able to reach the fountain without being seen.

Rabbi Zacharia climbed up as high as he could on the great rock from which the fire burst forth. It was so hot that his feet began to blister and burn. But through a crack in the ceiling of the cavern he could see faint stars through the thick smoke. If only he could climb through that crack! With his last strength he leaped up and clung to its edge with his finger-tips. Slowly he managed to raise himself, until at last he climbed out, and a fresh wind carried off the stench of smoke and brimstone that he had breathed for so long. The rabbi felt great relief, but he knew that he was still in peril. He quickly gazed at the world that stretched around him. It was a barren desert, a wilderness, although he could see dim lights in the distance. He dashed off as fast as he could and did not stop running until he was miles away. That night he slept in the open and was haunted by the most terrible nightmares he had ever known. But when he woke up he found that he was still a free man. And he gave thanks to God that he had not been trapped forever in that abyss.

Two days later Rabbi Zacharia reached the city in which the sacrifices had taken place. And as he came into the town square he saw that a great crowd had gathered. He realized at once that another victim was about to leap into the fire. Rabbi Zacharia asked one of the bystanders who it was and learned, to his horror, that it was none other than the wife of the young man whose soul was being tortured at that very moment. The rabbi rushed to the platform and cried out for her to stop. She stepped back from the edge of the abyss on which she stood and regarded him strangely, for she recalled that he had been present when her husband had rejoined them. The crowd, however, was infuriated at this interruption of their sacred rites, and Rabbi Zacharia knew he must convince them that what he said was true, or he would lose his life.

Then, gathering all his strength, the rabbi stood before the angry crowd and began to speak. "Hear me, for what I tell you will cause your blood to curdle. You believe, wrongly, that the woman who stands before you, who is ready to throw herself on the pyre, will not die there, but will go on to another kingdom and a better life. Know now that this is the direst falsehood. Never will you see this woman again. The one who will return is none other than the Devil himself, disguised as his victim, come back to convince other willing victims to throw away their lives for eternal damnation—for that, not any other reward, is what awaits all those who curse their souls by leaping into these flames!"

On hearing this, many devout believers within the crowd began to grow angry and started to jeer Rabbi Zacharia, and it was then that he recalled the ring the tortured young man had given him. Quickly, before they attacked him, Rabbi Zacharia said, "If you do not believe me, let me prove to you that what I say is true. For I myself have just escaped that abyss, and there I saw the young man who was the most recent victim. He was hung upside down and cast into a terrible fire that tortures him without end. That is his fate. He gave me his ring to bring back to his family to prove that what I say is true."

From the crowd came shouts of "The ring! The ring!" mixed with more angry threats. And the woman, who had stepped back from the edge of the abyss, cried out, "Yes, let me see the ring. For there is none other like it." Then the rabbi opened the pouch and dropped the ring onto the platform, where it glowed like a live coal, still bearing the flame of Gehenna. Rabbi Zacharia warned them not to touch it, because it was white hot. But one man, who thought him lying, knocked the ring into a bucket of water brought there in case the fire got out of hand. The instant the ring hit the water it began to steam and sizzle, and this continued without abate until all the water was gone—and still the ring glowed. When the people saw this, word began to spread, first a low murmuring, then screams of horror, as they realized that what Rabbi Zacharia had said was true and that they had been victims of a hoax too terrible to imagine.

The wife of the young man, who had been about to throw away her soul, as well as her life, was convulsed with weeping, both for herself and for her beloved husband. And the grief of the people soon turned to anger and hatred, and they railed against the Devil for so deceiving them. Nor did any of them ever cast themselves into the flames again. And after that the Devil had to use all his wiles to get any new souls from that city. For everyone there had been tricked by him once, and after that they were on their guard for all time.

Eastern Europe: Nineteenth Century

Rabbi Joseph
and the Sorcerer

t happened one year in the city of Salzburg that three young and beautiful Jewish girls disappeared on Yom Kippur, the Day of Atonement, as they walked through the streets on the way to the synagogue. When this terrible news became known, the Jews of Salzburg all gathered together and poured out their hearts to the Holy One, blessed be He. But the girls were never heard from again.

The next year, on the same holy day, the very same disaster struck again. Three of the most beautiful young Jewish girls vanished somewhere between their homes and the synagogue. This time, when the news reached the members of the congregation, who had already sustained a year of mourning, they trembled to their very souls. And when the Day of Atonement ended, they set out in a methodical search through all of Salzburg and the surrounding area, but they found nothing, nothing at all.

Virtually all Jews and righteous Gentiles kept a close look out for those girls everywhere they went, but not a single sighting was reported. How could this be? The people began to fear that it was some kind of terrible punishment the Lord had brought down on them, because of their sins, and they prayed and repented and fasted from Sabbath to Sabbath. But still none of the lost girls was heard from again.

The third year, as the time drew near for Yom Kippur, the people began to tremble with dread, especially the parents of young and beautiful maidens. Many of these parents came to the rabbi of Salzburg and begged him to find a way to protect their daughters that year, for they all feared the worst. The rabbi, like all of the Jews of the city, had suffered greatly over the loss of those precious maidens, and he too feared future dangers. Yet every avenue had been searched, and still nothing had been found. What could he do?

That night the rabbi sent up a dream question, in which he begged the Holy One, blessed be He, to help them find a way out of their dilemma.

And in the dream that came to him, the rabbi found himself walking through the streets of a strange city as though he knew his way, and at last he reached the house that was his goal, although even in the dream he did not know what this was. He knocked on the door in great anticipation, but just then the dream ended and the rabbi awoke.

The rabbi vividly recalled this dream, and he realized at once that it was in some way a reply to his dream question. But what did it mean? For now that he was awake, the rabbi realized that he did not know the city in which he had been walking. Certainly it was not Salzburg. And even if he were able to find out the name of that city, how could he ever find his way to that same house, which he had come to in the dream? The rabbi tried to recall any detail of the house he could. And at last he recalled that the door had a bronze knocker in the shape of a dove, surely quite rare. It was only a tiny clue, but at least it was a start.

With three months remaining before Yom Kippur, the rabbi of Salzburg set out on what he feared would be a futile quest. He traveled to many German cities, looking for the one in his dream. But he could not find it. After two months of futile searching, he began to fear that he had failed and would have to turn back, for he had to be with his congregation on Yom Kippur. That year of all years he could not abandon them. Still, he continued his quest, urging his horse onward until so little time remained that he knew he could visit only one more city, and if that were not the right one, he would have to turn back in defeat.

It was late afternoon when the rabbi reached that city, but he thought nothing of his own needs and set out at once to ride through the streets. No sooner had he done so than he began to find them familiar, as if he had once lived there, but so long ago that he could not even recall when. And all at once, with a burst of joy, the rabbi realized that he had reached the city of his dream. Then, as if in a trance, he found himself following the same path he had taken that night so long ago, through streets that circled like a labyrinth, until at last he found himself standing before the door of a house. And the bronze knocker of that door was in the shape of a dove!

With trembling hand the rabbi raised the knocker, praying that this should not prove to be a dream as before, but salvation for his tormented city. He knocked three times. The door opened, and the rabbi found himself face to face with an old Jew of deeply pious appearance. The old Jew invited the rabbi to come inside and said that he had been expecting him. And the rabbi of Salzburg was so relieved by these words that he burst into tears. Then the old Jew comforted him, saying that he knew why the rabbi had come to him and assuring him that the time of trial would shortly come to an end. The old Jew introduced himself as Rabbi Joseph and told the rabbi of Salzburg to join him for a meal and then to rest. And in the presence of Rabbi Joseph, the rabbi of Salzburg felt himself grow calm, until he sat for the first time in months with a sense of peace. That evening, however, his sense of urgency returned, and he told Rabbi Joseph that they would have to set out the next day if they were to reach Salzburg in time for Yom Kippur. Then Rabbi Joseph told him, "Stay with me until the eve of the Day of Atonement." The rabbi of Salzburg, upon hearing this, began to sob again. Rabbi Joseph asked him, "What is bothering you? Why are you crying?" And the rabbi of Salzburg answered, "My city is a week's journey from here, and only eight days remain until Yom Kippur. If we do not leave by morning, we will not return in time to save three beautiful girls from being kidnapped." But Rabbi Joseph assured him that there was no danger of their not arriving in time, and the pious Jew reluctantly agreed, for he saw that he had no other choice.

So it was that they remained together in Rabbi Joseph's house, and as each day passed, the rabbi of Salzburg grew more and more anxious, for he could not imagine how he would ever return in time. But Rabbi Joseph had no such doubts. Then, on the day preceding the Day of Atonement, Rabbi Joseph brought the rabbi of Salzburg to a small, empty synagogue. The rabbi let himself be led, for he had finally come to the conclusion that the matter was in the hands of God. Rabbi Joseph walked up before the Ark of the Covenant where the Torahs were stored and opened it. Then he turned to the rabbi of Salzburg and said, "Follow me." A moment later Rabbi Joseph stepped into the Ark and disappeared. The rabbi of Salzburg almost fainted when he saw this, but overcoming all doubts and fears, he too stepped into the Ark, and the next thing he knew he found himself in his own synagogue in the city of Salzburg, standing before the Ark. Then the rabbi of Salzburg knew that his faith in Rabbi Joseph had not been misplaced. But before he could consider the miracle that had just happened, Rabbi Joseph turned to him and said, "Come with me." And the rabbi of Salzburg meekly followed, as if in a trance.

Rabbi Joseph walked through the streets of Salzburg as if he had made his home there all of his days, and as late afternoon approached and the time for *Kol Nidre* was near at hand, the two men arrived at a house on the outskirts of the city. Before they knocked on the door, Rabbi Joseph went around to the back, where they saw six asses tied up to a tree. When the asses saw them, they began to kick and bray with heart-rending cries, which were almost human. And suddenly the rabbi of Salzburg realized that Rabbi Joseph had revealed the terrible secret to him: the girls had been turned into asses by some kind of diabolical magic. He whispered to Rabbi Joseph, "Can the spell be broken?" But all that Rabbi Joseph said was, "Come with me."

They went back to the front of the house, and Rabbi Joseph knocked on the door. The door was opened by a wealthy man, who eyed the two rabbis with great suspicion and asked what they wanted. Rabbi Joseph said, "Can we come in? There is a matter we would like to discuss with you." The man replied with hatred in his voice, "No Jew can step foot into my house. If there is something you want to say, say it from where you stand." Rabbi Joseph remained completely calm, saying, "We have simply come here to make a purchase. Our people are in need of beasts of burden, and we noticed that you have six fine asses tied up in back of your house. We are prepared to pay a considerable price for them." Then Rabbi Joseph reached into his pocket and pulled out a bag of golden coins, and when the man saw them, he was overcome with greed. He said, "These asses are an exceptional breed. A bag of gold would purchase no more than one of them."

Rabbi Joseph replied, "One bag is all we have with us, so perhaps we shall purchase one of the asses now and bring the rest of the gold later." The evil man could not believe his good luck, for that much gold could purchase six hundred such animals. But he pretended as if the Jews were driving a hard bargain. He said, "I suppose that I can accept your offer. Tell me which of the asses you want." Rabbi Joseph replied, "Come with us and we will show you." But the evil man said, "I will not be seen in the company of Jews. You walk around to the back, and I will look on from a window." And Rabbi Joseph said only, "That is what we shall do."

Rabbi Joseph signaled the rabbi of Salzburg to remain silent and led him around to the back of the house. When they arrived there, they found that the man had already come to the window and opened it. He leaned out and called to the rabbis, "Hurry now, it's getting late; there is some-where I must go. Tell me, which one do you want?" Rabbi Joseph turned around to point at one of the animals, but as he did he pronounced a mystic name, and at that moment the window from which the man leaned out suddenly shut, trapping his head. The man cried out and tried to push the window open, but it was frozen in place. Then Rabbi Joseph approached him and spoke, with deep anger, "Know that your secret has been revealed to us. It is you who have kidnapped Jewish maidens on Yom Kippur and transformed them into these asses! Confess at once how the spell can be broken!"

Then the evil sorcerer, for that is what he was, realized that he had met his match. In terror he begged for his life and he confessed that he had cast the spell that had turned the girls into asses and led them to his home, where he broke the spell at night in order to possess them, then recast the spell in the morning. The two rabbis were heartsick to learn these details, and their anger grew even greater. And the sorcerer, knowing full well his peril, pronounced the spell. The asses turned back into girls, and they cried out to the rabbis to save them from their tormentor.

Then Rabbi Joseph turned to face the sorcerer and pronounced another name. And the window fell down all the way, cutting off the head of the sorcerer and ending his evil life. The two rabbis comforted the girls, who cried hysterically because they had finally been freed. After this the men led them back into the city, and they reached the synagogue, where all of the Jews of Salzburg had gathered, just before *Kol Nidre* was to begin. And when the two rabbis entered, followed by the six girls, the people broke into a joyous uproar. The families of the girls ran to embrace them, and there were tears in the eyes of everyone.

That was the happiest Yom Kippur in the history of Salzburg, for the people knew before it began that the Holy One had revealed His judgment, and that it was good. The rabbi of Salzburg led Rabbi Joseph to the Ark and asked him to blow the *shofar*, which he did, blowing blasts that ascended all the way to the Throne of Glory. None who heard him blow the *shofar* that day ever forgot it. Then the Ark of the Covenant was opened and the Torah taken out, and just as the appropriate portion was about to be read, Rabbi Joseph turned to the Ark and stepped inside. In front of all of those seated there, he vanished. And all of the Jews of Salzburg, without exception, knew that a great miracle had taken place.

Germany: Twelfth Century

The Haunted Violin

n Worms there was a carpenter who was called upon to make a coffin. When the coffin was finished, there was one board left. The carpenter decided to carve a violin out of it. That night, however, he had a dream in which the dead man for whom he had made the coffin came to him and warned him not to do so. The carpenter recalled this dream when he awoke, but dismissed it, as he did all dreams.

That day he started to carve the violin. He proceeded very slowly, perfecting it over a period of weeks. When he was finished he saw that the violin was very well made indeed, and he was proud of himself. He polished the wood and strung the violin and looked forward to the time that he might play it, once he had made a bow. That night the dead man came back to him in a dream and again warned him not to play the violin. But upon waking, the carpenter again dismissed the dream.

That day he carved the bow and polished its wood until it shone like that of the violin. It was late at night when the bow was finished, so he decided not to try it out until the next day. That night the dead man came back to him once again, and told him that he was warning him for the last time not to play the violin. But when the carpenter awoke, the first thing he did was to take down the violin and run the bow across its strings. A haunting melody rose up, as if on its own, and no sooner had he played but a single refrain than the room grew dark, as if the sun had been blotted out. The carpenter ran to the window, opened it in confusion, and peered outside, but the darkness was so deep that he could not see anything.

Suddenly a great force from behind, like invisible hands, shoved him out the window. Before he knew it, the carpenter found himself tumbling down, and an instant later he plunged into something soft and treacherous, like mud. With horror he realized it was quicksand, relentlessly sucking him under the earth. It had already reached his arms when he understood how imminent was his danger, and he thrashed about wildly, but it was too late. The quicksand dragged him under as he drew in his last breath.

The son of the carpenter found his father's body lying on the floor of his workshop, a violin in his hands. That night the same dead man who had warned his father came to the son in a dream and revealed all that had happened. The very next day the son burned the violin. And as it went up in flames he heard the voice of the carpenter crying out as if from a great distance. Then he knew that somewhere his soul was still being tortured.

Germany: Twelfth Century

The Sorcerer
and the Virgin

here was a fine, generous man, a wealthy scholar, who lived near the well in the city of Worms. He had an only daughter, who was pious in every respect. One day a student passing through the city glimpsed this girl as she went out to draw water from the well. He was smitten with her beauty and desired her for himself. Now this student was an apprentice in magic. He had studied for several years with a sorcerer and decided to use this knowledge to force himself upon her.

Brazenly, the student went up to her house and knocked on the door. When the girl answered, the student said, "Tonight I will come and possess you. You will not be able to escape." And with that he turned away and left. Now the terrified girl hurried to her father and let him know what the student had said. Her father became very frightened and brought ten rabbis to his house that evening to guard his daughter throughout the night. He seated her in a prominent place before them, and he himself remained with them for the vigil.

At midnight the ten rabbis and the girl's father suddenly became very drowsy. They tried to stay awake, but they could not. Soon all of them had rested their heads on their arms and were sound asleep. The girl ran from one to another, calling to them and shaking them, but nothing woke them up. At that moment the student entered the room, although the door had been locked and bolted. He stood before the maiden and said, "You have no choice. So give yourself to me."

Even though she was alone and faced with his great powers, the girl replied, "I would rather die." The student grabbed her, forced her down, and was about to rape her, when she snatched a knife from the table and stabbed him in the back. Then she ran outside screaming and woke the neighbors, who hurried in and found the young man lying dead on the floor, and the ten rabbis and her father still sound asleep.

The neighbors raised a great cry, and before long others came in to see the strange sight, among them some Gentiles who lived nearby. These neighbors passed on the news, and soon an old witch heard about it. She came to the house and said to the Jews, "Go inside quickly, and see if there are candles burning in the hearth." They looked and saw eleven candles burning there. And when they reported this to the witch, she said, "The young man was supposed to have put out the candles in order for those sleeping to wake up. But because he is dead there is no remedy, and they will have to sleep until they die."

Now when another rabbi heard of this tragedy, he came to the scene of the crime. He saw the body of the young man and, nearby, the sleeping rabbis and the girl's father. Everyone there was bemoaning the terrible enchantment—except for the visiting rabbi. He calmly took a piece of parchment and wrote out the Name, placing it in the mouth of the dead man. Then he whispered the secret pronunciation of the Name into his ear, and all at once the dead man stirred and came to life. He found himself confronted by the rabbi, who said, "Foolish man, you have been destroyed by those you sought to destroy. Now all that you have left to save is your soul. Hurry, blow out the candles in the hearth, for if you do not your soul will burn in Hell another century for each of those whose lives you snatched!" The young man, who had already tasted the scorching fire of Hell, said not a word, but walked over to the hearth, bent over, and blew out the flames. And at that moment he slumped over and died again, while at the very same moment each and every one of the sleeping men awoke. When they found out how close they had come to never waking from that endless sleep, they all gave thanks to the Holy One, blessed be He, whose power had saved them from a living death.

Germany: Sixteenth Century

The Knife

here was a man whose widowed mother died without leaving a will. This man knew very well that she had been wealthy, and he searched everywhere in the house but he could not find where her fortune was hidden. The matter became an obsession to him. He searched through everything again and again. He even looked between the pages of each and every book she owned. Nothing. Then he dug up the yard to a depth of three feet. Still nothing. After that he began to tear out the floors, in case the money was hidden there. It was not. At last he realized that he simply could not find it on his own. So he decided to go to a witch for help.

Now this witch was famous for the power of her spells, and she demanded one half of the fortune for herself if she succeeded in finding it. The desperate man agreed to this at once. Then the witch told him to leave her house, for none could be present when she worked her magic. And when he was gone she took out a knife and said a spell over it. Then she hid the knife beneath her pillow and went to sleep.

That night, a demon who had a knife in his heart came to the witch. It was the same knife over which the spell had been cast. The demon spoke to the witch and said, "Why did you do this to me?" And in the dream the witch replied, "So that you would bring me the woman who hid her son's inheritance. And until she reveals where she put the treasure, the knife will stay exactly where it is!" At that she woke up, and she felt beneath the pillow and found that the knife was gone. And she smiled to herself.

The next night when the witch went to sleep she dreamed that the same demon came back to her, the knife still in his heart. With him were his son and the woman who had died without leaving a will. "Now," said the demon, looking desperate, "take out the knife!" "No," the witch replied, "not until this woman reveals where she hid her fortune." "That I will never do," the woman said. "Why not?" asked the witch. "After all, you are dead; what good will it do you now?" And the woman replied, "If I had wanted him to know where the money was, I would have told him. I don't want him to know." With that the dream ended and the witch awoke. And the knife was still gone.

The third night the demon came back, in the same company, the knife still in his heart. He looked feeble and unable to speak. His son spoke for him and begged the witch to remove the knife, or the damage would be fatal. The witch told them that she would take it out as soon as the woman revealed the secret. Then the demon's son begged the woman to take heed of the suffering of his father and to speak, and at last she relented, saying, "To spare you any more pain I will reveal this much, and this much only: the money is hidden in a box." At that the dream ended.

When the witch awoke the first thing she did was to pronounce another spell. Then she put her hand beneath the pillow and found that the knife was there. So she knew that the demon no longer had the knife in his heart. Then she hurried off to the home of the man and told him the hint she had wrenched out of his mother's spirit. This clue astonished him, because he had looked in all the boxes first, and several times thereafter, and he had found nothing. That is what he told the witch, but the minute she went away he took each and every box apart, and in this way he found one with a false bottom, under which the fortune was hidden.

Now that the reluctant inheritance was his, the man decided to leave town at once, for he had no intention of sharing the money with the witch. This he did, and the witch soon discovered that he was gone. But she was not worried. That night she placed the knife under her pillow again.

Germany: Twelfth Century

The Charm in the Dress

n the city of Worms there was a beautiful woman, God-fearing and kindhearted, who devoted herself to good and charitable works. She was beloved by rich and poor alike, all of whom praised her and spoke well of her. One day her husband was shopping in the marketplace when he saw beautiful material for sale, and he thought that it would make a fine garment for his wife. So he purchased it and took it to a tailor to make a dress from it. This the tailor agreed to do, and the man left the material with him and departed.

Now the tailor soon cut and sewed that dress, and when it was almost finished a Gentile wizard happened to enter the tailor's shop. This man saw the lovely dress and said to himself, "The garment becomes the wearer, and the wearer is surely beautiful." And he craved her.

What did the wizard do? He went home and wrote out a magic charm on a slip of paper, came back, gave it to the tailor, and told him to sew it into the dress, and to hide it well so that it would be neither felt nor seen. The tailor was reluctant to do it, but the wizard offered him a considerable sum, and he let himself be bribed.

. The next day the woman's husband picked up the dress from the tailor and brought it home as a gift for his wife. She found it to be exceptionally beautiful and decided to save it to wear on the eve of Yom Kippur, which was soon approaching. And because this tailor had made many other dresses for her and knew her size very well, she did not even try it on, but put it away for that time.

On the eve of Yom Kippur, after the meal before the fast, the woman donned the dress for the first time to wear to the synagogue. But the moment she put it on an impure spirit took possession of her, and she was filled with desire for a man she had never met, but that she somehow knew how to find. When her husband asked her to accompany him to the synagogue, she replied that she was not feeling well and would follow a little later. So he went to the synagogue by himself, and after he had gone the woman stepped outside, but instead of following after him, her legs carried her toward the villain's house, as the charm commanded.

The dazed woman walked until she found herself before a strange door and knocked on it. And no sooner did the wizard open the door than this woman, who had never seen him before, fell into his arms and kissed and hugged him as if they had always been lovers. So too did she transgress by eating and drinking everything he offered her, without a thought that it was Yom Kippur and that the food, in any case, was unacceptable. And after the meal the wizard led her to his bedroom to lie down.

The woman followed after him unquestioningly, as if in a trance, and when he began to undress, she did as well. But as soon as she removed the dress, the unclean spirit immediately left her and she came to her senses, and her remorse was terrible to behold. She decided to leave at once and reached for her dress, but the instant she put it on her desire for him returned, twofold. She forgot her determination to go and was ready to give herself to him again.

Once again she undressed, in order to consummate their lust, but again, the moment the dress was off, waves of remorse washed over her. It was then she realized that the dress must be exerting some kind of power over her, and she decided then and there to leave without it, before she committed an even greater sin. Thus, dressed only in her chemise, she hurried out of the house and through the streets of the Jewish quarter, terrified that someone would see her. But, of course, everyone was in the synagogue for Yom Kippur, and so no one saw her before she reached home.

Once there she wept bitterly over what had occurred and also gave thanks to God that her sin had not been greater. She was terrified that her husband might find out what had happened and decided to keep it secret, lest he cast her out. So it was that when her husband returned from the synagogue and asked why she hadn't come, she told him that she had felt too ill to go and had decided to stay at home. And her husband, who trusted her completely, did not question her explanation at all.

A few days later the wizard decided to sell the dress in the marketplace, in hope of finding another beautiful victim for his lust. And it happened that the woman's husband was shopping there, and he saw the dress and recognized it at once, for there was none other like it. Naturally he was stunned by the sight and could not understand how it came to be there. Still, he did not reveal his feelings, but bartered for the dress and purchased it for a second time. And the wizard sold it to him, ignorant of the fact that he was the husband of his first victim, for the wizard was hoping another victim would soon be knocking at his door.

When the husband came home that day he said to his wife, "Where is the dress that you wore on Yom Kippur?" She pretended to go and look for it, and after a while she came back emptyhanded and said that she could not find it, and he saw that she was afraid. Then he took out the dress that he had purchased in the market and showed it to her and said, "How is it that this dress came into a stranger's hand in the marketplace, where I purchased it for the second time today?" And when the woman saw the dress, she fell down in a faint, and when she recovered she confessed to her husband all that had happened to her, fantastic as it was.

The man immediately took the dress to the rabbinic court and asked them to examine it. They ripped apart all of the seams and studied it thoroughly, and in this way they discovered the hidden charm. And when they read it, they understood why the woman had lost her will when she was wearing the dress. Then the rabbis accompanied the husband to the tailor who had sewed the dress and confronted him with the charm. And when he saw it, he grew very afraid and confessed how he had been bribed by the man to sew it into the dress.

After that the rabbis went to the authorities and accused the man of witchcraft and offered as evidence the dress, the charm, and the testimony of the tailor and the righteous woman who had been the victim of the spell.

So it was that a few days later the wizard heard a knock on his door, and assuming it was his next victim, he opened the door with a smile, only to find himself confronted with guards, who dragged him off to court, where he was shortly condemned to death. And within a week the sentence was carried out, and justice was done. As for the tailor, he was punished by being forbidden to practice his livelihood, because he could not be trusted, and was forced to become a water carrier, bearing the heavy yoke of the buckets all day long. And with every step he took, he repented his sin and gave thanks that it had not cost him his life.

Germany: Sixteenth Century

The Scribe

n the Sabbath the tortures of Gehenna cease for a day, and the spirits that are punished there and the demons that punish them are set free to roam the world until the Sabbath ends. But not all return to the place of punishment on time; some lag behind until dawn and seek ways to cause turmoil in the world once the sanctity of the Sabbath has been lifted.

In one town there was a scribe who was writing a Torah. This Torah was to be used the first time in a newly built synagogue. The scribe lived in fear of not completing the Torah in time for Simhat Torah, when the Torah reading begins anew with the first verses of Genesis. So it was that as soon as the Sabbath had ended and the *havdalah* prayers had been said, even though the rabbi had warned him to refrain from working, this scribe hurried to his desk. He was in such a hurry, in fact, that he failed to recite Psalm 91, which protects against the dangers of demons.

The scribe worked like a demon himself until midnight, but then his eyes grew bleary, and he knew that he must stop, for if he made a mistake he would have to write the Torah all over again. And as he reluctantly went to sleep, the scribe wished that someone would help him complete his work, so that the Torah would be ready on time.

Now every wish is overheard, either by an angel or a demon. And in this case it was a demon on its way back to Gehenna who overheard the scribe's wish and decided to fulfill it at once.

This demon tried to enter by slipping beneath the front door, but because the text of the *mezzuzah*, which the scribe had written himself, was flawless, it could not. Then the demon circled the house, searching for an open window, and at last it found one that was open just a crack. But that was enough for the demon, who quickly slipped inside and hastened to the scribe's desk, where the incomplete Torah lay open.

The demon picked up the scribe's pen, dipped it in the ink, and began to write. It copied the text at a great speed, for the demon knew it by heart, because demons are as familiar with the Law as are the angels. And before very long the demon had filled up that page of the parchment and had started in on the next. Soon that page was filled as well, and the demon, lost in the task, continued to write long into the night, until a great many folios of the parchment had been written, and only one page still remained.

The demon hunted for more parchment, but not a scrap was to be found. And the demon, in a frenzy to complete the task before being forced to return to Gehenna at dawn, hastened to the bed of the scribe and began to strip the skin off the man's back, despite his howls of pain, then continued to scribble away on it until the task was done.

Germany: Fifteenth Century

The Bleeding Tree

 woodcutter once entered a part of the forest that he had never explored. He approached one large and conspicuous tree and raised his ax to cut it down. But as he did, something fell upon his coat from above, and when he looked to see what it was, he found, to his horror, that it was blood. Terrified, he dropped his ax and ran away as fast as he could, and he didn't stop running until he reached his village.

There he told the rabbi what had happened and showed him his bloodstained coat. The rabbi looked very concerned and said, "You did well to run away at once. But tell me, you did not leave anything behind, did you?" When the woodcutter told him about the ax, the rabbi became very solemn. For a while he seemed lost in thought, then he said, "Although it involves great risk, I am afraid that you have no choice but to retrieve the ax, because if it falls into the hands of demons, it could come back to haunt you. For whatever object the demons obtain of a person, they hold the power of that object over him. And because the ax earns your keep, you would be risking your livelihood as well as your very life if you did not get it back. For surely that tree is infested with demons, and that blood, supernatural. Take the coat and burn it, as far from your house as you can. For if the evil were to be unleashed there, the demon might take possession of your house."

The woodcutter could not wait to get rid of the coat. He burned it at the edge of the forest, far from any habitation. And when it burned, a terrible stench rose up, searing his nostrils and filling him with fear, so that he ran off, and still the stench followed after him. Only when he passed the House of Prayer did it depart.

When the woodcutter got home and told his wife all that the rabbi had said, and of the terrible stench of the burning blood, she became very frightened. They talked over the matter in hushed tones, so that the children would not hear them. And they decided, with great reluctance, that the woodcutter must indeed try to get the ax back. Otherwise, the whole family was at risk, including their three children. That was too great a hazard to bear.

The woodcutter set out the next morning, determined to recover the ax no matter what. At first he was frightened, but before long his fright turned to anger, and he vowed not to let the demons destroy his life.

By early afternoon he reached the dark part of the forest, still filled with determination, but as soon as he glimpsed the tree he became frightened again. For there was never a more terrible sight than that tree, dripping blood, as if it were wounded. And then he saw his ax lying beneath it, covered with blood, for the blood of the tree was dripping directly upon it, as if a murder had just been committed. Then the man ran forward and snatched up the ax, but the moment he did so, he felt a great force take possession of him. It was then, to his horror, that he realized that the ax held him in its power, and he felt it lifting, as if on its own, wrenching itself out of his hands. And at that very moment the ax cut him down.

Germany: Twelfth Century

The Demon in the Tree

t happened in the city of Worms that the rabbi's son was playing hide-and-seek with a friend, and he was looking for him in a hollow tree trunk. All at once he saw a finger emerge from the tree and, assuming it was that of his friend, he took off his ring as a jest and slipped it on the finger, pronouncing the words of the wedding vow. Suddenly the finger was pulled back into the tree, and a moment later the face of a strange-looking woman, with long black hair, emerged. Her smile was so evil that the young man jumped away, and then she disappeared back into the hollow trunk. At that the young man turned and ran away as fast as he could. Nor did he tell anyone what had happened.

Years passed, and the young man was wed. The night the bride and groom went to his home together for the first time, the bride lingered outside, looking around. At that moment the demoness emerged from the hollow tree and pulled back a branch that struck her in the face, killing her.

When the year of mourning was over, the young man was betrothed again, and the same thing happened when he returned home with his new wife, on the very first night.

Now the man was becoming afraid that he was cursed. So too did many fathers refuse to consider him as a husband for any daughter, causing great anxiety to his parents. What was worse was that no one could explain what had happened to the brides, and a cloud of suspicion hung over him.

His third bride was the daughter of a very poor man, who had been unable to give a dowry. This girl had always worked very hard to help her family get by. She was modest and yet wise in the ways of the world. This girl too took a walk around the house to explore it, and the demoness in the hollow tree came out to kill her, as she had done to the others. But the girl saw the branch that the demoness had pulled back, and quickly bent down, avoiding the branch. So too did she see the demoness run away and followed her until she saw her slip back into the tree.

That night she told her groom what had happened, and he was horrified. He recalled at once the demon in the tree, whom he had long ago put out of his mind. He turned very pale, and in a solemn voice he recounted the strange incident. But why would this demon harm only his wives, and not him? The girl understood at once: "Because she considers herself your true bride. Did you not, after all, pronounce the words of the wedding vow?" And the poor groom grew faint with fear.

All that night they debated what to do. When the young man recovered from his panic, he grew angry. It had been a jest, after all! And he wanted to take revenge. He insisted that they must burn down the tree. But his bride talked him out of it. She said, "That tree is her home, and if you deprive her of it, she might seek to deprive you of yours." And he realized that she was right.

Then the girl said, "Let me try to come to terms with her. It is said that demons love jam above all things. Let me take a plate of jam and leave it by the hollow trunk as an offering of peace." And because he could think of nothing else, except to move away and abandon his home, the young man agreed.

The next morning the young bride placed the plate of jam by the hollow trunk. All that day she stayed away from the tree, and the next morning she came back to see what had happened. There she found a gold coin on the plate, gleaming in the sun. She hurried in and showed it to her husband, who sighed with relief to know that they had appeased the demoness—at least for a while.

Every day after that the young bride left a plate of jam by the tree, and the next day she found a gold coin. The young couple were grateful for the gold, but they still lived in fear of the demoness.

The time came when the young bride found that she was with child. She knew all the tales about Lilith and how she liked to strangle children. Nor did she doubt that the demon in the tree was a daughter of Lilith. Therefore she felt that her unborn child was in danger.

So it was that the bride one day went to the tree and called for the demoness to come forth. At first there was silence, then at last the unearthly voice of the demoness was heard, demanding to know what she wanted. "All I want is to come to an understanding, for I know about the ring, and therefore I know that you feel that you are my husband's true wife." "Yes, that is right," hissed the demoness. "In that case," the girl continued, "let me be brief. I am willing to share him with you, if you will vow not to harm any one of our family, including any child. If so, I will let him come to you one hour a day, at sunset."

At that moment the head of the demoness emerged from the tree, still looking exactly as she had when the young man was a child. She looked directly into the eyes of the bride and nodded. Then she sank back into the trunk.

For seven years after that, the man was a free man all but one hour of the day, when he was the slave of his demon wife. And all that time the demoness did not bring harm to anyone, and it even seemed that she protected them from danger. At the end of seven years the man came to the trunk and there on the plate used for the jam he found his ring, the one he had placed on her finger. And he knew at once that the demoness had taken leave of them for good.

Germany: Sixteenth Century

Rabbi Samuel the Pious
and the Magicians

abbi Samuel the Pious, father of Rabbi Judah the Pious, was endowed with great powers, which were as well known abroad as they were in his own land. One day three magicians from foreign lands came to him. They offered to reveal all the secrets of their magic if Rabbi Samuel would divulge his secrets to them. Samuel first requested a demonstration of their powers and had them agree that if his proved to be greater, he would not have to reveal anything at all. Confident of their own powers, the magicians agreed to these terms. They even offered to let Rabbi Samuel make a demand of them, which they would then fulfill.

Rabbi Samuel thought carefully, then he said, "Rabbi Jacob, my teacher, lives far from here. It takes three months to travel there. I will write a letter to him, asking him to send me a certain book. If you can bring the book back in three days, I will accept that your powers are great enough to reveal my own." All of the magicians smiled, and one of them said, "This we will gladly do, for we have come here from a place farther than six months away in traveling time, and it took us only three days. We can travel to this rabbi and be back in the same time."

So the three magicians went with Rabbi Samuel into the forest and walked until they came to a clearing. There, hidden from everyone else, one of them drew a circle, and the other conjured the soul of the third one and sent it off on the task. Rabbi Samuel saw the man go into a deep trance, almost like death. So too did he see the man's soul as it departed from his body, for nothing of the supernatural was hidden from his eyes. And at the very moment that the soul departed, Samuel quietly pronounced a spell making it impossible for the soul to reenter the body.

At that the magicians turned to take their leave. Samuel asked them if they were not going to guard the body of their friend while his soul was gone, but they assured him that he was safe inside the magic circle, for nothing could enter it except for his soul, on its return. At this Rabbi Samuel smiled to himself.

On the third day they returned to the same place in the forest. Rabbi Samuel saw that the man's body was exactly as they had left it. That in itself spoke well of their powers. Not long afterward Rabbi Samuel saw the soul of the third magician returning, like a flaming comet. But this was visible to him alone, for the others could not see the soul, although they were able to conjure it. The soul reached the edge of the magic circle, but could not go beyond it. Thus, no matter how it tried, the magician's soul could not reenter his body.

The time for the soul to return had passed, and the magician's body still resembled a corpse. The other magicians began to worry, for the soul was required by the spell to be not a moment late. When they were beginning to panic, Rabbi Samuel asked them if they would acknowledge his powers as greater if he were able to assist the soul in returning to the body. They both begged him to do so at once and accepted his terms. And Rabbi Samuel pronounced a holy name and all at once the barrier that had held back the soul vanished, and the soul reentered the magician's body, and the magician opened his eyes.

Now whenever a soul enters a body, it forgets everything it ever knew. So it was that the magician who had sent his soul on the mission recalled nothing of how it had been prevented from coming back. And when the magician found the strength to sit up, he reached into his pouch and took out the book that Samuel had requested. In it was a reply to his letter from Rabbi Jacob.

Then the magicians told their companion how his life had almost been lost, but that Rabbi Samuel had saved him. And they all thanked him again for saving him and gratefully divulged their secrets to him, and afterward they went on their way. Nor did they ever hesitate to say that Rabbi Samuel's magic was greater than their own, for they had seen proof with their own eyes.

Germany: Sixteenth Century

The Dead Man's Accusation

wo builders were working in the house of a Jew in Regensburg. During their work they noticed gold and silver in one room and decided to rob the house when the owner left for the synagogue. This they did, and when they had taken everything of value and were about to leave, one of the robbers thought to himself that he would rather not divide the spoils, so he took a hammer and struck his partner from behind, killing him with one blow. Then he grabbed the bag of spoils and ran away, leaving the body behind.

When the man returned from the synagogue, he found the body in his house. Then he was very afraid, lest he be accused of having killed him. And that is what happened—when the police were called they took the Jew into custody, and when the rumor that a Jew had killed a Christian spread among the people, a restless mob formed in front of the house.

Learning what had happened, Rabbi Judah the Pious went directly to the mayor of the town and told him it was certain that the man had been killed by his partner, with whom he had worked in the Jew's house. And Rabbi Judah assured the mayor that he could prove what he said was true. He asked the mayor to first give an order that the gates to the city be closed, so that the murderer would not be able to escape, and then accompany him to the place of the murder. Although skeptical, the mayor agreed to do these things, and after giving the order he went with him to the house of the Jew, where the body still lay, and a great crowd had gathered. And among them was the murderer himself, who was not afraid of being there because the Jew had been jailed, and there was no one else to recognize him.

When they stood in the presence of the body, Rabbi Judah took out of his pocket a tiny scroll, on which he had written the Holy Name, and he placed it in the dead man's right hand and closed his cold fingers around it. Rabbi Judah stood back, and the others could see that the body was breathing again, and the man slowly opened his eyes. All those who saw this trembled with fear, for they knew they were witnessing a miracle.

Then Rabbi Judah said to the dead man, "Who killed you?" And the man raised his eyes, which were terrible to behold, for he had already glimpsed the punishments of Hell. He looked around the room and saw his partner, who was frozen with fear. The dead man said, "There he is! That is the one who killed me! He struck me on the head with a hammer!" All at once the murderer tried to run away, but the crowd grabbed him and began to beat him. They were already filled with hatred, and if they could not blame the killing on the Jews, at least they could exact some revenge. And when they finished with him, he was a corpse.

The dead man witnessed all this and saw that his death had been avenged. Then he turned to Rabbi Judah and said, "Free me, now, of the burden of living, for it is terrible to be brought back from the dead." And Rabbi Judah reached down and took the parchment from the man's hands, and at that instant his body slumped back to the ground. But none of those present ever forgot what they had witnessed. They told it to their children, and it is still spoken of to this day.

Germany: Sixteenth Century

Mocking Devils

he journey from the fair in the Moldavian town of Milaileni to the town of Banila was fraught with danger, as was the return trip. Any merchant not safely in an inn by nightfall had to face several unpleasant areas populated by spirits, demons, ghosts, imps, and devils, who would suddenly appear in strange forms.

Now one night the merchant Yehoshua set out in his wagon from Milaileni. The wagon was heavily laden with flour, grapes, watermelon, and wine. All around the darkness was heavy, but the road before him was straight. Here and there he came across wagoneers on their way back from the fair. The stillness of the night was broken at times by the barking of dogs. He passed village after village, each time picking up the calls of the cemetery watchmen saying, "Who goes there?"

He arrived unharmed around noon the following day in the city of Banila, where he delivered his goods, selling them to the grocers there. He spent several hours unloading and taking new orders, and before he could turn around, the day was over. He left the town at nightfall, determined to return home to Milaileni well before the Sabbath.

The merchant steered the wagon down the road, lost in thought. Suddenly he awoke from his daydreams: the horses were agitated and stood up on their hind legs, neighing and snorting as if there were wolves around. He was very afraid, for he did not doubt the instincts of the horses. So he took the torch from the ring beside him and held it up, looking for wolves, but instead he saw a fettered buck lying in the middle of the road. He assumed that it had fallen off the wagon of some merchant, and he jumped down to pick it up. But much to his surprise he could not. It was much heavier than one would have supposed from its size and appearance. He slaved and sweated, but he could not lift it off the ground. And it seemed very strange, even eerie, for he had lifted many a buck in his day, and none had been that heavy.

The merchant quickly jumped back onto the wagon and spurred on the horses. They kicked and stamped, but did not move forward. It was as if the wheels of his wagon had been bound with ropes. The horses neighed and whinnied and foamed at the mouth, but the wagon stood still. All at once he grew afraid again, took the torch, and looked behind him. And there, sitting on the goods of his wagon, was the fettered buck, smoking a pipe.

The merchant wanted to open his mouth and shout for help, but he was so terrified he could not make a sound. His hair stood on end and he panicked and became confused. Then he forced himself to get hold of his thoughts. He unbuttoned his coat, and with shaking fingers grabbed hold of the fringes of his prayershawl and started to pray.

A moment later he heard the barking of dogs and found that the cock had crowed and that the horses were once again trotting down the road. He looked behind him, and the buck and his pipe were gone. But he recovered his senses slowly, and he never forgot that night of horror.

Rumania: Nineteenth Century

The Demons' Wedding

ne day, not long after Passover, strange noises were heard in the house of the master Hasedaji Yohai, not far from the great synagogue of Galipoli. These sounds grew louder and more frightening, like a mass of bees swarming out of a hive. The master and his wife were startled and thought that the noise was coming from the street. The master called out, "Who is there?" When there was no answer, he called out again. Still there was silence. Then the strange noise resumed, and this time it seemed to be coming from upstairs. The master and his wife thought it might be thieves, so they quickly woke the servant, who lit a torch and reluctantly led the way up to the second floor. The hand of the servant shook as he unlocked the door and looked inside, but though they carried the torch to every corner of the room, they didn't see anything unusual. So they relocked the door and started down the stairs, when little stones suddenly began to rain down on them from the room above, sailing right through the locked door. Even stranger, the stones passed through their bodies as well, making them shudder, but there was no damage. Still, they were all so paralyzed with fear that they remained speechless, for they realized that demons had invaded the house.

Now they all understood that they would have to abandon the house. They knew what had happened to those who had tried to resist: the imprudent ones were now to be found in the graveyard, where flames could be seen burning from their graves at midnight, and a distant howling could be heard that sounded exactly like the voices of those buried there. No, the demons could have the house as long as they wanted it. And without uttering a single word, the master's wife and the servant started to pack personal belongings, while the master gathered together his most sacred texts.

An hour later they had finished packing, and by dawn the house was in perfect order. For if everything is in order, the demons will respect the house and leave it as they found it. But if it is not, the demons will wreck havoc to their hearts' content. The last thing the master's wife did was to put a white cloth on the table and set out a plate of jam, as a sign of welcome. For demons are said to love the taste of jam. Then the master and his wife sadly took leave of their house, and the servant pushed their possessions in a barrel to the home of their son, who was startled to see them and upset when he heard why they had come.

That day the master and his wife and son went to see the town rabbi and told him about the noises and the rain of enchanted stones. The rabbi listened to all they said in amazement, and then he replied, "Be assured, then, that you have done the right thing in abandoning your house. So too was it fortunate that you remained silent. That is why the stones did not harm you—for if you had protested, the stones would have struck you down. I once heard of such a case in the time of my grandfather. For three nights the demons hurled stones into a courtyard to force the owners to evacuate their house so the demons could take possession of it and celebrate a wedding there. The stones were harmless to those who said nothing, but one man who shouted in anger at the demons was struck in the head and knocked out. Then the people who lived there knew that they would have to vacate the house. They set up tables with candles, dishes, and tableware, and opened wide all the doors. After that they went out and locked the gate after them. For a full month nobody entered that courtyard. And when they finally opened the gate, they found that the demons had departed.

"That incident took place at this very time of the year, in the month after Passover, when no weddings are supposed to take place. It is said that every year at this time multitudes of demons gather together to get married. Then they are married off at a great rate, thousands every hour, and the weddings sometimes last more than a month!" The master and his family were shocked and saddened to hear that they might be exiled from their own house for that long, but at the same time they were greatly relieved that they had not tried to resist the onslaught of demons, for how could they have succeeded against such great multitudes?

Then the rabbi asked, "Did you, by chance, count the number of stones that the demons tossed at you? For it is said that in this way they reveal how many days they intend to stay." But the master and his wife had not counted the stones, although they vouchsafed that there were many of them, far too many if they were to suffer that number of days as exiles from their own home.

Still, the master and his wife remained with their son, along with their servant, and after a day or two sounds of loud singing and wild dancing came from the house they had abandoned. The next day, neighbors on both sides of that house said that they weren't able to sleep all night because of the noise, which went on until dawn. And even though everyone was frightened, one man was brave enough to look in the window, and he noticed couples cavorting in a dance. He also heard music that sounded like the love cries of cats. He reported seeing more demons crowded together in that one place than there were inhabitants in all of Galipoli, all of them flying around in a torrent of celebration, as one wedding after another took place, new demons pairing off in endless succession in ceremonies that did not last as long as the blink of an eye.

So it was to be for forty nights, as the revelries went on from midnight until dawn, and there was no sign that they were about to stop. By that time the master and his wife could not bear being exiled from their home any longer, and their neighbors were red-eyed from lack of sleep. At last the entire neighborhood descended on the rabbi and demanded that he do something to free them of this curse. For a multitude of demons is born every minute, and if such weddings take place only once a year, who knows how long they would last? The rabbi saw that the time had come for him to confront the demons and demand their departure.

So he went to the house with the rest of the rabbinic court and a scribe. There the scribe began to write an amulet in the shape of a *menorah*. But after he had written no more than one line, a large black cat suddenly appeared and sat down at his feet, staring into his eyes. The scribe became terrified and the members of the rabbinic court began to tremble. Only the rabbi found the strength to act. He made a vow in the Name of God, and the cat disappeared. After that the scribe was able to finish writing the amulet, and the rabbi hung it on the door of the house.

The next day the master and his wife and servant returned to the house and found that their home was silent. They stood outside and said, "We caused you no harm; now you too should cause us no harm." Then they took ashes and sprinkled them on the earth. Next they reached through the door and poured oil on the floor and scattered sugar on it, saying, "Peace be unto you! Peace be unto you!" Only then did they reenter their house. They found everything was exactly as they had left it, except that the plate of jam had been emptied. They went upstairs and opened the door. And there in the middle of the room they saw a large pile of golden coins, a present from the demons for the disturbance they had caused.

Turkey: Oral Tradition

The Hair in the Milk

nce there was a woman who felt that she was about to give birth. They called the old midwife, who had learned the secrets of her trade from her mother and grandmother before her. Not long after she arrived, one of the servants served the expectant mother a glass of milk. Just as she was about to drink it, the woman looked into the cup, put it down with shaky hands, and all of a sudden fainted.

The midwife picked up the cup and saw that there was a long black hair in the milk. She looked around, but none of the other women had hair that was so long or so black. Then she knew what to do. She quickly poured the milk into a jug, the hair along with it. Then she corked the jug and shook it with all her might, using both hands. All at once there was a scream from inside it. Another might have dropped and broken it then, but not the midwife. Instead, she listened. And from inside the bottle she heard a distant voice crying, "Stop! Please let me go! I beg for forgiveness!"

The first impulse of the midwife was to carry the jug to the sea and throw it as far as she could. Instead, she took it outside and when all the doors and windows of the house were locked, she lifted the cork, set it down, and peered inside the bottle. Then all at once the head of a woman popped out. And the first thing the midwife noticed was that her hair was very black and so long that it fell back into the bottle. "Lilith!" the midwife hissed, and she started to pick up the cork to replace it in the bottle. But she found that it had become so heavy that she could not raise it even one inch. And then, for the first time, the midwife became afraid.

"What are you doing here!" the midwife shouted. "Set me free from this bottle and I will do you no harm," Lilith replied, for that is who it was. "First tell me why you have come to this house," said the woman. "I have come for the mother or the child, of course," said Lilith. "You know that. But now I will forswear doing any harm to them if you will only let me go." "That is not enough," said the midwife. "What more do you want?" asked Lilith. "First, how did you know that a woman was here who was about to give birth?" demanded the midwife. And Lilith replied, "As I was flying past, I smelled the odor of a mother's milk. I wanted to steal the afterbirth—we feed it to our children." "And what happens then?" asked the wise midwife. "Then the woman dies," Lilith whispered.

In a sudden motion the midwife grabbed Lilith by the hair, pulling her out of the bottle at the same time. The demoness struggled to get free of her, but the woman held on with all her might, for she knew that a demoness is helpless when held by her hair. When Lilith stopped struggling, the woman said, "Know that you will not leave here until you tell us how to save this woman from you once and for all!" And Lilith, seeing that she had no choice, said, "Take saliva from the woman's mouth and put it in a bucket filled with water." They did this. Then Lilith blew on the foam of the water, and at that instant the woman awoke from her faint. The midwife then said, "How is it that you did not fear to approach this house?" Lilith replied, "The *mezzuzah* of the house is defective, and the people do not have an amulet against me hung on the infant's bed. Now, will you set me free?"

"Not yet!" said the woman, holding Lilith's hair just as tightly. "There is more that I want of you." "What is it?" Lilith asked. "That you serve this family in every way, especially the mother and child, and protect them from every danger for three years." "And what if I do not agree?" asked Lilith. "Then I will throw you and the bottle into an old trunk, lock it, and cast it to the bottom of the sea, with you still in it!" cried the midwife, ready to carry out the threat.

Lilith saw that the midwife was a formidable opponent indeed. Her voice grew calm and reassuring. "I vow to do as you say, and to serve this family for three years. Nor will any demons dare to approach while I am here, for I am their queen." Then the midwife demanded, "Swear in the names of the angels Senoy, Sansenoy, and Semangelof," and Lilith saw that there was no escape. For those were the three angels who had commanded her to return to Adam when she had left him and flown to a cave by the Red Sea. And she had vowed that whenever she saw or heard their names, she would do no harm. So Lilith swore in the names of the three angels, and after that she did indeed remain captive there and serve as a faithful servant. For the words of a vow are sacred not only among men and the angels, but among the demons as well. She pumped water from the well, cut wood, and guarded the woman and her child at all times so that no harm came to them.

Long before Lilith left, the text of the *mezuzzah* was repaired. And when she took her leave, she promised that she would never come back. Nor did Lilith or her daughters attempt to return to that house, and the family lived a life of peace.

Turkish Kurdistan: Oral Tradition

The Soul of Avyatar

 colt was born in the stable of Rabbi Eleazar Shehona. It was pure black and grew at an astonishing rate. Soon it was larger than its mother, then it surpassed the size of its father. Before long it towered above every other horse. The temper of the colt was very bad, and only in the presence of Rabbi Eleazar was it calm.

Not long after the colt was born, Rabbi Eleazar began to have strange dreams. In the dreams he witnessed terrible punishments taking place. Angels with flaming rods drove on the soul of a man riddled with sin. These dreams worried him, because they were so vivid. He wondered what they meant. He did not think they were warnings for himself, for he had always cleaved to the path of righteousness. And this was a mystery to him, as was the horse, which sprang up so rapidly.

One day as Rabbi Eleazar fed the colt, he heard a voice say, "Welcome." Rabbi Eleazar looked around, but he did not see anyone. Then the voice said, "It is I, the horse, that is speaking. Let me tell you my story." Rabbi Eleazar jumped back in surprise, saying, "Who are you?" "My name was Avyatar," the horse replied. "I was a scholar from a family of scholars and a Kohen from a family of Kohens. But I pursued a life of sin, and now I am being pursued by the avenging angels." "Why is it that you are so punished?" asked Rabbi Eleazar, frightened and intrigued at the same time.

"I sinned with a young boy and ruled his body and soul for twenty years. Then my punishment came with terrible suddenness. It happened like this: Three days before Yom Kippur a fiery snake with two heads poked through my stomach. All who saw it were horrified and ran away as fast as they could, for they had never seen such a thing. None would comfort me and I died on Yom Kippur in the throes of agony. When I was dead they refused to bury me, because the serpent was still writhing. Instead my body was cast out like that of a dead beast.

"When my soul fled my body, avenging angels chased me with burning rods, whipping me as often as they could. To escape them I entered into a rock. There I was safe but I was overcome with fatigue, and my memory began to grow faint. At last I fell asleep. I may have slept in that rock for centuries.

"When I awoke and remembered, the void of being there was like falling endlessly into an abyss. With all my strength I freed myself from the rock, but to my horror I found that the angels were still waiting. They had never even closed their eyes.

"Again I fled as fast as I could, and this time I escaped into a flower. There I was at peace at night, but during the day, when the flower opened itself to the sun, my soul writhed in pain.

"Now on the third day that flower was picked by a young boy. At the moment he picked it I took possession of him, more firmly than of the other boy whose life I had destroyed. It was a great relief to inhabit a human being once again, but for the boy it was agony.

"They brought sages and wizards to help him, but no one could find what ailed him until they brought Rabbi Nathan Yerushalmi. Using holy names that I could not resist, he compelled me to reveal my history and my sin. Then he forced me to take leave of the boy from under the nail of his little toe, which I did with great reluctance. Of course the avenging angels were waiting. They threw me into a pit of boiling semen, where my suffering was so excruciating it cannot be described or even imagined. The only way to escape was to enter a drop of sperm. This I did, and before long I was conceived as a horse, in your barn."

Rabbi Eleazar was amazed at these words, but at the same time he was angered, for the man's sin was very great, and he deserved no sympathy. And Rabbi Eleazar said, "Do not imagine that you have found a resting place here. You cannot remain in this horse either! I command you to go!" And Rabbi Eleazar pronounced a holy name, and at that instant the soul found itself wrenched out of the horse's body, and blows rained down from the flaming rods of the avenging angels. The lifeless colt fell to the floor of the stable and shrank until it was no larger than the pit of a peach.

At the same time Rabbi Eleazar's daughter had a terrible nightmare, from which she never awoke.

Persia: Sixteenth Century

Rabbi Shabazi and
the Cruel Governor

abbi Shalem Shabazi was one of the greatest sages and
poets of all time, and he was also a master of the secret
mysteries of the Kabbalah. One day he was plowing his
field when a soldier approached, calling out, "Jew, Jew,
leave your plow and oxen and follow me." Now the cruel governor had
ordered the soldier to bring Rabbi Shabazi to him, for he took great pleasure in tormenting the Jews, and now he had thought up a new edict that
would make their lives even more difficult.

Rabbi Shabazi knew well why the soldier was calling him, and he did
not intend to put up with the evil ways of the cruel governor any longer.
So he ignored the soldier and continued to plow. The soldier soon lost
patience and shouted, "Here is a Jew who acts like an ox and doesn't want
to obey!" At that moment Rabbi Shabazi pronounced a holy name and
the soldier turned into an ox. Rabbi Shabazi attached the new ox to the
plow and let one of his other oxen rest.

The next day, when the first soldier did not return, the governor sent
a second soldier to Rabbi Shabazi. The soldier found the rabbi in the field
and ordered him to leave his work and follow him. The rabbi ignored the
soldier and his order until the soldier said, "I see, Jew, that you behave
like a donkey. I speak to you and you pretend you do not hear." Then Rabbi
Shabazi looked up, pronounced a holy name, and turned him into a
donkey, which he loaded with things to carry.

On the third day, when the second soldier did not come back, the
angry governor sent yet another soldier to bring Rabbi Shabazi to him
in chains. This soldier insulted the holy man and called him a dog. So
guess what the rabbi turned him into? Whatever it was, it ran around in
circles, barking.

On the fourth day, when he had finished his plowing, Rabbi Shabazi
went to see the governor, to find out what he wanted. The governor sat
on the fourth floor of his palace, and in order to reach him a special pass

was required on every floor. The rabbi decided to eliminate these obstacles. So he stood next to the palace and put a peg in the ground. He struck the peg once, and the first floor of the palace sank into the earth, along with all that it contained.

When he struck the peg a second time, the second floor sank down. The third time he struck it, the third floor sank under the earth, and the fourth floor stood on level ground. The terrified governor looked out the window and saw Rabbi Shabazi standing before him. "Why have you done this?" cried the governor. "What do you want from me?" But Rabbi Shabazi just stared at him. Then the governor, who had planned to announce the evil decree, realized that the tables were turned. He said, "The inhabitants of the palace are yelling and screaming from the depths of the earth. Please, make the palace the way it was."

Rabbi Shabazi replied, "I will agree to do this, on the condition that you vow to eliminate all evil decrees against the Jews and promise not to make any new ones." "I accept," said the governor, "if you will also return my three soldiers." "I will return them," said the rabbi.

Then the rabbi pulled out the peg, and the palace returned to its former condition. And the ox, the donkey, and the dog turned back into soldiers and ran home as fast as they could. And the cruel governor never lifted his hand against the Jews again.

Yemen: Oral Tradition

The Elusive Diamond

here was a Jewish woman in Kurdistan who gave birth to a son. After the birth her husband reminded her that she must remain indoors for forty days. For when a woman gives birth, it is as if she herself has been reborn, and like a newborn child she is in danger from malicious demons and spirits, who resent her bringing new life into this world.

So it was that the woman remained at home, taking care of her infant, and when she had time to rest, she sat by the window and looked outside. Those were the coolest days of spring, and she would have loved to have gone out to enjoy the breeze and the scent of blossoms in the wind. But she had to remain inside, where time passed very slowly.

Now the fortieth day finally arrived, and it was the eve of the Sabbath. The woman dressed in her finest Sabbath dress and waited by the open door for her husband's return from synagogue. She imagined how fine it would be to walk outside the next day and work in the garden. And there in the doorway the winds tantalized her with rich scents, as if beckoning her to come out. Just then the woman glimpsed something glowing brightly in the hollow trunk of the tree just outside their door. At first she thought it was a star that only appeared to rest in the hollow trunk. But the more she stared at it, the more convinced she became that it was right there, only a few steps away. What could it be? It must be something precious that glowed so brightly, surely a diamond of immense value.

The more she stared at it, the more certain the woman became that it was indeed a diamond resting in the hollow trunk, glowing as brightly as any star. Such a diamond could change their lives completely. No more would they have to scrape a living from the earth, barely surviving from day to day. And with these thoughts in mind, the woman forgot about her husband's warning about not leaving the house.

So it was that the woman stepped outside the door and reached out to clutch the glowing jewel. But before she could grasp it, it vanished right before her eyes. Much amazed, she felt all around the hollow trunk, but the jewel was not to be found. Just then a light caught her eye, and when she looked up she saw the very same jewel perched on the gate where the goats were penned. This amazed her, for she could not imagine how it had gotten there, but all the same she hurried after it, determined not to lose it this time. And as she ran she kept her gaze fixed on the glowing object.

Even so, it was gone by the time she reached the gate. At first she thought it might have fallen to the ground. She searched for it on her hands and knees, but when she finally looked up she saw it glowing in the weeds by the road. Perhaps it had rolled there, she told herself, although it was a considerable distance away, and she hurried off to catch up with the glowing gem.

Strangely enough, every time she tried to approach the jewel it seemed to move away. The woman could not understand this, but she kept running after it, even though she was already short of breath. In this way the elusive diamond led her down the road to the river. The woman had begun to grow desperate, and nothing could have stopped her from trying to catch up with that glowing stone. Yet she trembled at the thought of going to the river at night, especially on the eve of the Sabbath, when demons and spirits were said to congregate there.

But the woman forced these fears out of her mind and hurried onward until she reached the bank of the river. There she saw the glowing gem hovering above the water near the shore, and her only thought was that she must have that diamond, no matter what. And she noticed that the diamond was no longer moving away, but remained in the same spot, an arm's length away. For the first time the woman saw the glowing jewel up close. It was indeed a diamond, glowing mysteriously, perfectly cut, only inches beyond her reach. Kneeling on the shore the woman leaned out as far as she could. It was then that she fell in the water, and as soon as she did, she was pulled down by mysterious arms, which held her in an unbreakable grip. And the last thing she saw as she sank like a stone was the diamond glowing before her, only inches away.

When the woman's husband returned from the synagogue, he was astonished to find the door open, the baby crying, and no sign at all of his wife. He alerted the neighbors, and they spent the rest of the night searching for her. But only at dawn did they find her body, floating face down near the shore of the river. And never did they find out what had caused her to leave the house on that, the fortieth night. But it was whispered in the village that demons had lured her to the river, and after that no woman among them dared to leave home after giving birth until the full forty days were over and the danger posed by the demons had passed.

Iraqi Kurdistan: Oral Tradition

Lilith's Cave

here was a house in Tunis that was said to be haunted by demons. Once it had belonged to a wealthy family, but demons had invaded the house to hold a wedding, and when the wealthy owner had resisted, neither he nor his wife had ever been seen again. After that the house was boarded up, and no one entered it.

At last the house was sold for next to nothing to a man who planned to tear it down and build another in its place. But before he did, his wife convinced him that they should examine it and take for their own any valuables that might remain there. Though reluctant because of the rumors of demons, he finally agreed that they would go there together and search for anything of value. When the old people heard of their plans, they warned them not to go, but they refused to heed them.

When they succeeded in opening the front door, the couple found that the expensive furnishings inside had molded; nothing of value had survived. But before they left, the wife insisted on opening the door to the cellar as well, and at last the husband kicked the door in, despite the fact that the demons were rumored to have made their home there. Much to their surprise they found the cellar furnishings in perfect condition; none seemed to have aged at all. They were worthy of a place in a palace, and especially valuable was a mirror with an ornate gold frame, which in itself was worth far more than they had paid for the house.

The wife brought the mirror and all of the fine furnishings in the cellar to her own home and proudly displayed it. She hung the mirror in the room of their daughter, who was a dark-haired coquette. The girl glanced at herself in the mirror all the time, and in this way she was drawn into Lilith's web.

For that mirror had hung in the den of demons, and a daughter of Lilith had made her home there. And when the mirror was taken from the haunted house, the demoness came with it. For every mirror is a gateway to the Other World and leads directly to Lilith's cave. That is the cave

Lilith went to when she abandoned Adam and the Garden of Eden for all time, the cave where she sported with her demon lovers. From these unions multitudes of demons were born, who flocked from that cave and infiltrated the world. And when they want to return, they simply enter the nearest mirror. That is why it is said that Lilith makes her home in every mirror.

Nine months after the wife brought those furnishings into the house, she was found dead one morning, having choked on a feather she breathed in from one of the silken pillows she had taken from the cellar. After her death her husband sold all of the furniture and gave the proceeds to charity. He only wanted to get rid of it. All he kept was the gold-framed mirror, for his daughter refused to part with it.

In the days that followed, things went from bad to worse. During the day the girl avoided her household duties, nor did she give her widowed father any assistance. Instead she spent her time before the mirror, admiring herself.

Now the daughter of Lilith who made her home in that mirror watched every movement of the girl who posed before it. She bided her time and one day she slipped out of the mirror and took possession of the girl, entering through her eyes. In this way she took control of her, stirring her desire at will.

So it happened that this young girl, driven by the evil wishes of Lilith's daughter, ran around with young men who lived in the same neighborhood. She started coming home later and later, and a time came when she sometimes did not come home at night at all. Her father suffered greatly over this, filled with shame. For he knew that once her reputation had been ruined, no worthy young man would marry her.

And in this he was right, for the daughter of Lilith that possessed the girl never let her come close enough to any one young man to feel love for him. For if this had happened, the power of the demoness over the girl would have been broken. Instead, she drove her on, commanding her roving eye to seek out yet another.

Once, when she had not returned home for two nights and her bed had not been slept in in all that time, her father was possessed by a great fury and uttered a curse against her. The curse was so severe that even he was surprised to hear it spoken: "May the Lord turn my unworthy daughter into a bat, flitting around from place to place, from one man to the next, without ever becoming attached to any one! Because she has chosen to abandon herself to the night, may she be doomed to live in darkness! And may she be fated to bear this curse as long as the shame lives in my heart!"

At that moment the young woman, in the arms of a young man, suddenly screamed and vanished from the room. And all that he saw in that instant was a bat that flew out the window uttering a terrible cry.

Tunisia: Oral Tradition

The Bridegroom

century ago, in the city of Botosani, there lived a very wealthy Jewish miller. Only the best wheat was ground in his mills, and his customers were legion. This miller had also been blessed with a lovely daughter, Hannah, who was as beautiful and delicate as a flower. He bought the finest silks and furs for her, as well as precious jewels. And he gave her the finest chamber in the house, which opened onto a beautiful balcony. Whenever she went out on the balcony, all those who saw her were astonished at her great beauty.

Many marriage brokers sought to make a match for her with sons of the wealthiest men not only from Botosani, but from other cities as well. But somehow none of these young men was good enough for the wealthy miller. Either their families were not rich enough, or the young men were not handsome enough, or learned enough in the Torah. In time Hannah grew tired of waiting for a match to be made and began to feel like a bird in a golden cage. If only her father had asked for her opinion, she would have been wed long before. But he had not.

Now despite his great wealth, the miller never helped a widow or an orphan or a needy beggar. The only time he opened his door to another was to admit the prophet Elijah on the night of the *Seder*.

One day a young man passing the mansion of the miller looked up and saw the daughter standing on the balcony, and he was so struck with her beauty that he fell in love at once. He began to be seen outside the house very often, as if he were courting the girl from there. And she, for her part, was seen on the balcony much more often, for if the truth be known she had fallen in love with him.

But when the miller heard about the young man, he went outside and asked him what he was doing there. The young man replied, "I am Yossel, the son of the water carrier. I study Torah and I earn a living as a scribe. I love your daughter and want to marry her." The miller fell into a fury and ordered the young man to leave and warned him that he would set his servants upon him if he were ever seen there again. His heart broken, Yossel left, never to return.

Some time later another young man fell in love with the miller's beautiful daughter. As a sign of his love he tossed up to the balcony a small shoe that he himself had sewn with gold and silver threads. The girl was moved by this sign of his affection, and the next day she dropped a rose at his feet. Soon after that the young man presented himself to the miller and asked for the hand of his daughter. When the miller asked him who he was, he said, "I am Pinchas, the son of the shoemaker. I study Torah and I make shoes. I love your daughter and want to marry her." Needless to say, the miller had him thrown out of the house, and so another love was lost from Hannah's life.

Several weeks after this a very strange man stopped beneath the balcony of the miller's daughter and called out her name in a very tempting voice. He was short, bent over, and his smile froze the blood of anyone who saw it. The miller, who was at home, heard him calling to her and became furious. He ran outside and said, "Who are you and how dare you call my daughter?" The strange, bent man replied, "I am her groom and I have come to take her with me." The miller could not believe his ears. In his fury he shouted for the man to get away from his house. Then the man got up to leave, but before he did he smiled at the miller, and that smile caused a chill to go up and down the miller's spine. And as he left he said, "Your daughter is rich and beautiful, and she will go away with me."

Not long afterward the strange man appeared again. This time he leaped from the ground to the balcony of the miller's daughter, then he opened his arms like black wings and embraced her. They flew away together and disappeared in the darkness, the miller's daughter and her groom, the Angel of Death.

Rumania: Oral Tradition

The Dead Fiancée

here once was a Hasid of the holy rabbi of Koznitz who was without children. Every few months he went to the Maggid of Koznitz and asked him to pray for him so that God would bless him with children. But the rabbi was always silent when the Hasid made this request and never indicated if he would assist him. As the years passed and the couple remained childless, the Hasid's wife grew bitter because of her lot. And when she could not bear it any longer, she cried out to her husband, "Go, now, to the holy rabbi. And don't leave his doorstep until he replies to you, for my life is not life without children." The man asked, "What if the rabbi tells me to divorce you?" And the wife answered, "We shall do whatever the rabbi tells us to do."

The man went to the rabbi once again and threw himself on his mercy. The rabbi listened, then said, "If you are willing to make a great sacrifice, to go on a long journey that will leave you impoverished, you may yet succeed in having a child." The Hasid saw that the prospect was a difficult one, but he was willing to undertake it. He told the rabbi, however, that he must first consult with his wife. And when his wife heard the rabbi's words, she said, "Wealth means nothing if I cannot leave a memory after me. Therefore do as the rabbi says, and perhaps God will have mercy on us after all."

The man returned to the rabbi and was told, "Go home, sell all of your possessions, and take the gold with you. Do not keep anything, or your journey will be in vain. Your wife will have to find a way to sustain herself while you are gone. Then go to Rabbi Yakov Yitzhak of Lublin, and tell him that I have sent you. Tell him what you are seeking, and then do exactly what he tells you to do, nothing more or less."

So the man journeyed from Koznitz to Lublin and sought an audience with Rabbi Yakov Yitzhak, known as the Seer of Lublin. But the rabbi was unable to see him for the first week, nor did he call him in for an audience during the second long week of waiting. Meanwhile, the cost to the man was considerable, for he had to pay an inn for his room and board. Still, he dared not repeat his request, for fear of provoking the rabbi's wrath. So he continued to wait even though other petitioners were often called in soon after their arrival. And at the end of the third week, just as the man was beginning to give up hope, the audience took place.

When the man came into the presence of the rabbi, he saw that the holy man was immersed in a text. Naturally the man did not interrupt, but waited for a signal to speak. The rabbi continued to read, however, and did not lift his eyes from the page. At last, after a very long silence, the rabbi said, "In your youth you were betrothed for four years to a young woman, Miriam Shifra, but when you came of age you broke this engagement on your own, without even informing her or her parents of your decision. She continued to wait for you until the news finally reached her that you had already been wed to another. This caused her great grief, and her father did not find another for her to wed. Now her hour of joy has passed, and you are to blame. Go to her and seek her forgiveness. For only if she forgives you will a soul from on high be set free to become your child."

The Hasid was staggered, for he had not even said why he had come, and yet the rabbi knew things about him that the man had never spoken of to anyone. And he realized that this must indeed be the reason he had remained childless, and he said, "I cannot imagine how you know this, but it is true, although I have put it out of my mind for many years. I had even forgotten the name of the woman. But now I will do exactly as you say." And the Maggid said, "In two months' time there will be a bazaar in the town of Balta, where she can be found. Go there, and don't leave until you have spoken with her."

So the man set out for Balta, and along the way he sought information about her everywhere he went, in hope that he might find her before he reached that town. But all his effort came to naught, as no one had ever heard of her. So he continued his journey until he reached Balta, where he took up residence in an inn. Each day he walked through the streets asking about her, but to no avail. And in the evening he returned to the room and spent the night in the study of the Torah and in prayer that he might fulfill his quest. That is how the days passed until the time arrived for the great bazaar. Crowds of people jammed the streets, and the man went everywhere among them, asking if they had heard of Miriam Shifra. But no one knew anything at all. The Hasid's frustration was very great, and many times he thought of leaving that town and returning home in defeat. And he stayed only because the Maggid had told him not to leave until he had found her.

When the bazaar was about to end, and the merchants were all packing up their goods, the Hasid realized that if he did not learn anything of her that day, there would be no point in remaining any longer. So he stood by the gate of the town, speaking to everyone who came or went, but to no avail. In the evening a cold rain began to fall, and the few remaining merchants quickly packed up and set out to find shelter. Soon the streets were almost completely empty, and the Hasid had a sense of despair far greater than anything he had ever known.

The cold rain had begun to chill him, and he sought refuge under the eaves of a store. But the owner told him to leave, and once more he found himself out in the rain. Looking around he saw two women taking shelter near a house, and he went there. When he reached the house he saw that one of the women was very beautiful, exceptionally so. She was dressed in embroidered silk and wore many jewels. He was astonished to see such a wealthy woman standing outside in the rain, but he assumed that she had been caught there when it had started. In any case, the Hasid stepped away from her, to keep his proper distance.

When the woman saw this, an ironic smile crossed her lips. She turned to her servant and said, "Do you see that man standing there? That man betrayed me when I was young, and now he's trying to escape from me again." When the Hasid overheard these words, he was staggered. Was it possible? Meekly he approached the woman and said, "What do you mean? Is it true that I was once engaged to you?" The woman replied, "Are you still pretending that it is not so? That is how you have acted all these years, leaving me forgotten like one of the dead. Tell me, do you at least recall my name?" And the Hasid spoke in a whisper, "Are you Miriam Shifra?" And when the woman nodded, the Hasid broke into sobs. When he found his voice, he said, "I have come here to seek you out. You have every right to despise me, and it is too late for me to right the matter, but I hope it is not too late for you to forgive me. For I have come seeking your forgiveness, so that my wife and I may have children of our own. The Seer of Lublin told me that until you do, we will never know the blessing of a child. Now I beg you to forgive my sin, if you can, and I would do anything to repay you."

The woman stared hard at him and saw that his repentance was true. And she said, "There is nothing I need that you could give me. But I have a very poor brother, a scholar of the Torah, who lives in the town of

Sublack. His daughter is of the age to be wed, but my brother does not have enough to pay for the dowry and the wedding. Therefore go to him and give him three hundred silver coins. And tell him that you are giving it in my honor and at my request. When the deed is done, I will forgive you with all my heart. Then, I am certain, God will bless you with children and grandchildren, all of whom will have a love of the Torah."

As the Hasid heard these words, a great weight was lifted from him. Then the woman said that she had to go, stepped out into the street, and went around the corner. But when the Hasid hurried after her to thank her, she had disappeared. Then, in a state of shock and relief, he made his way back to the inn where he was staying, and in the morning he set out for the town of Sublack.

When the Hasid located her brother, he found him very distracted. The Hasid asked him what was wrong, and the man said, "My daughter was engaged to the son of a master here in Sublack, and I promised a dowry of three hundred silver pieces, but I have not been able to save that much. Now I have received a letter saying that they will cancel the wedding if they do not receive the money in three days. So my daughter is sitting and crying and can't be comforted, and my soul is bitter because there is nothing I can do." And when the Hasid heard this, his heart leaped, because he had exactly three hundred silver pieces left of all that he had brought with him. He did not hesitate, but took out his money pouch, handed it to the man, and said, "Here, take this, and may the wedding be a great joy to everyone." And when the man saw that it was exactly the amount he needed, he was overwhelmed. "Why are you helping me like this? I have never heard of such generosity."

Then the Hasid said, "I am a messenger from your sister, Miriam Shifra. She directed me to give these coins to you for your daughter's dowry." A very strange look came over the man's face, and he said, "Where did you see my sister? When did she tell you that?" The Hasid replied, "I saw her in the marketplace in Balta about three weeks ago." Then the man shouted, "My sister has been dead for ten years! Come with me and I will show you her grave!" And when the Hasid heard this, a chill ran down his spine, for he realized that the woman he had met in Balta was not one of the living. When he stopped trembling he related everything that had happened and how the sister had promised to forgive him if he paid the dowry. And when the man heard this, he realized that his sister must indeed have come back from the beyond to help him, and he too turned pale. The two of them sat in silence for a long time, contemplating the miracle that had taken place. At last the man said, "Please, describe the woman you met, so I'll know if she resembled my sister." Then the Hasid described her great beauty and the way she was dressed. When the man heard this description, he broke into tears and left the room. And when he returned, he carried with him the very same dress that the woman had worn. He said, "This was my sister's favorite dress. After her death it came into the possession of my wife, but she has never worn it, in honor of my sister, whom she loved very much." The Hasid stood up and took the dress in his hands, and when he did, he felt that it was still slightly damp, as if it had been exposed to the rain. And in that moment he heard a distant voice whisper, "All is forgiven," but when he looked to see who had spoken, he saw no one. The Hasid felt the tears well up within him, and he began to cry like an infant, shamelessly and without restraint. And the man also broke into tears, for he too had heard the whispered words, and he had recognized the voice that had spoken—that of his sister.

After that the Hasid remained as the man's honored guest and was present at the daughter's wedding and shared in its joy. When he left that town, he first returned to Lublin, to tell the Maggid all that had happened. But when he arrived he found that the seer already knew. And the Maggid said, "The gates of repentance are open to all. Nor must the gates of forgiveness be closed to those who would truly repent." The Hasid asked for a blessing, so that he and his wife might be fruitful and multiply. The Maggid gave him a great blessing, that his lineage might live through many generations and that all of his children would have a great love of the Torah. And that is exactly what came to pass.

Eastern Europe: Nineteenth Century

The Kiss of Death

here once was a poor peddler who lived in the Jewish quarter of Prague. His trade barely yielded enough to support his family, and hunger was an almost daily guest in his house. After many years of the worst kind of poverty, the peddler could not bear it any longer, so he decided to set out on a journey to change his luck. He remembered his father speaking of a land on the other side of the sea where it was eternally summer, where roasted chestnuts grew on the trees, and where cherries were as large as melons. Gold and diamonds lay scattered everywhere like pebbles for whoever wished to pick them up. The people who lived there were so lazy, however, that they made no effort to learn the crafts, and as a result, gold and other treasures were not as valuable as pins, buttons, pots, and plates. Now these were the very objects that the poor peddler hawked on the street every day, and from which he could barely scratch out a living. If only he could sell his wares in that land of eternal summer!

Now the father of that peddler had once found that faraway land by accident, and there he had gained great wealth. But on his return a heavy gale had flung his ship against a cliff, and it had sunk, along with the man's entire treasure. He had returned home penniless and dressed in rags. Still, he had often told his son of the astonishing summer kingdom and its unimaginable wealth. But he had also harped on the dangers of the sea, which had deprived him of his fortune and had almost snatched his life as well, and he had implored his son never to set sail. But now, in his great misery, the son forgot his father's warning.

So it was that the poor peddler set out on foot for that abundant land, carrying with him a large supply of his wares. He took the way described by his father, and after several weeks he reached a port city, where he found a ship about to depart for that very land. The peddler, who had no money to pay for his passage, threw himself on the mercy of the captain, who was impressed with the determination of a man who would carry such a heavy load of merchandise for so many miles. Therefore the captain agreed to take him on board, on condition that he would pay double the cost of the voyage on his return. And this the peddler readily agreed to do.

For two months the ship sailed through calm waters, and one day the peddler was able to see from afar the blue shore of the summer land. Then a terrible storm suddenly sprang up, and in no time the ship had sunk with everyone on board, man and mouse. In mortal dread the peddler clasped a floating plank and was flung by the storm onto a small island. But when he began to explore that place, he soon cursed his persistent misfortune, for the island was barren; not a single bird or beast was to be seen, nor were there any trees or berries or food of any kind. In despair the Jew sank down to await his death. Just then a huge griffin flying overhead swooped down and seized him. It carried him high into the air and flew off toward its nest. The terror of the Jew was indescribable, and the will to live, which he had almost lost, came back to him in force, but there was nothing he could do to escape the claws of that great winged beast.

Suddenly the griffin released its grip, and the man tumbled through the air to a royal terrace. The adjoining palace was built of diamond stones and golden spires. The roof was marble, set with rubies. The gates were forged of silver, and all the stairways were covered with purple carpets. Dazed after the abrupt flight and sudden fall, the Jew lay there for a long time. When he finally opened his eyes, he was lying on a couch of soft silk carpets, and nearby sat a most beautiful girl with golden hair. Astonished, the Jew stared at the glorious being and wondered if he were dead or alive. But before he could ask, the girl said, "Who are you, stranger, that you came to this place in such a miraculous way? Never before has a mortal set foot in this palace on his own. It is a strict command of my father that every human who wanders into his kingdom be put to death. For you must know that this is the kingdom of the demons, and my father is their king!"

"Mercy, princess!" said the Jew in mortal dread. "You, who might well be an angel, save me from death!" The princess was silent for a long time, and the man knew that his soul hung in the balance by a thread. At last she said, "Perhaps there is a way to save you. Know that there are women among you—you would call them witches—who are in league with us. They steal human children and substitute changelings for them. Such a witch stole my mother when she was a small child and brought her to my father. He educated her in his palace and when she came of age she became one of his wives, his favorite one, because of her great beauty. But she died giving birth to me, and my father, in his grief, blamed me for my mother's death and banished me to this solitary palace, which he visits only once a year. I am allowed no other visitors, and I am suffering greatly from loneliness. Now that you have come here so miraculously, take me for your wife, and in this way you will save yourself. For my father would not put my husband to death."

Enraptured by the charm and beauty of the princess, and desperate as well, the Jew agreed to marry her, even though she was half-human and half-demon. He even forgot that he was already married and the father of children. Thus he let himself be drawn by the beauty that shone before him like a star. The wedding took place the same day, and they celebrated for seven days, although there were no guests. At first the Jew imagined that he was in love, and he erased his past life from his mind, as if he had died and been reborn.

But after a few months the man found that he was dreaming at night of his human family, so far away. In those dreams he kissed his children and held them and told them how much he had missed them. And when he awoke and found that they were still separated, he grew very sad, so that the princess could not help but notice. She saw as well how often he would cry out in his sleep. And when at last she recognized that he was homesick, she said, "I can see that your thoughts dwell in your native country. I do not want to hold you back, if it is your will to go. Soon the time will come for my father to arrive. You can depart with him and return home for one year, if you will promise to come back. For now that I have grown to love you, I do not think that I could bear the solitude any longer."

The man was overjoyed at the generosity of the princess and recognized that her love for him must be great. And he made a vow that he would indeed return at the end of the year. Then she presented him with a great bag of gold, so that he would not return home empty-handed and would lack for nothing.

Soon afterward Asmodeus arrived with all of his retinue, and he was amazed, to say the least, to discover that his daughter had been wed to a human being. But, as she had expected, he did not attempt to deprive her husband of his life. He was more reluctant, however, to agree to his daughter's request that the man should be given safe passage for one year, to return to his native land. For Asmodeus could not comprehend how his daughter's husband could be true to her and still long for his human family at the same time. But when his daughter implored him and told him of the man's vow to return, Asmodeus agreed at last, although he warned the man not to take his vow lightly, and to return when the year had ended.

The man assured Asmodeus that he would. And with that the King of Demons motioned to one of his demonic slaves, who seized the man with his mighty arms and took flight. On racing wings they traveled a distance that seemed to cover half the Earth, and before an hour had passed, the man recognized the towers of Prague. The demon flew the Jew to the roof of his house, dropped him down the chimney, and disappeared.

Now when someone suddenly fell out of the chimney, the terror of the peddler's family was immense. But the terror soon changed to joy when they recognized him. And when the man recovered from the shock, he embraced and kissed all the members of his family, showed them the bag of gold that he had brought with him, and began to tell of his adventures. But he avoided telling them that he had taken a second wife in the kingdom of demons. Instead he said that he had succeeded in selling his wares in the land of the eternal summer and that the bag of gold was what he had earned. They were amazed by all they heard, but because of the gold, they did not doubt the tale.

The Jew, who had always been more ardent to study the Torah than to ply his trade, now devoted himself to that subject the whole time. His knowledge secured him honor in the community, and his wealth made it possible for him to provide charity to many of those in need. In this way the year soon came to an end, but the man had forgotten the princess and felt no desire to return. She, however, still awaited her husband impatiently and was confident that he would fulfill his vow.

When he did not appear, she sent the winged demon to fetch him just as the man was on his way home from the evening prayers. The demon said, "The year away from your wife is more than over. It is time for you to return." The Jew was terrified, for he knew that the demon could snatch him away at will. So he said, "I am not yet prepared to return. Go back to your mistress and ask her if I may be given just one more week." The demon disappeared, and the man hoped that he had gained more time. But the next day, when he went to synagogue, he saw the princess herself. She showed her wedding contract to the congregation and called for a rabbinic court to be convened. This was done at once, and after hearing the testimony of both sides, the court ruled that because the man had previously been married, his marriage to the princess was invalid, and therefore he was freed from his vow.

The princess was devastated and burst into tears. Then a great anger took hold of her, and she decided to take revenge. But she hid her feelings, and instead she went up to her husband to kiss him good-bye. The man agreed to this, thinking to be finished with her for good. But no sooner did his lips meet hers than she snatched away his breath, and he sank down dead. Then the Princess of Demons disappeared, and she has never been seen on Earth again.

Eastern Europe: Nineteenth Century

Summoning the Patriarchs

uring the reign of Emperor Rudolf II, there lived among the Jews of Prague the great Rabbi Judah Loew, who was well versed in all of the mysteries and was a great master of the Kabbalah. Now it happened that the emperor heard of Rabbi Loew's reputation and sent for him with a strange request: he wanted the rabbi to invoke the patriarchs Abraham, Isaac, and Jacob, and the sons of Jacob, to summon them from their graves. Rabbi Loew was appalled at this request, but when the emperor threatened the well-being of the Jews of Prague if he did not comply, Rabbi Loew agreed to attempt to do as he had asked. The rabbi warned the emperor, however, that under no circumstances must he laugh at what he saw, and the emperor promised that he would not.

So it was that the day and place were fixed, and when Rabbi Loew and the emperor were alone in a secluded room of the castle, Rabbi Loew pronounced the spell that summoned the patriarchs and the sons of Jacob. And to the great amazement of the emperor, they appeared one after the other in their true form, and the emperor was amazed at the size and power of each of them, which far exceeded that of men in his own time. But when Naphtali, the son of Jacob, leaped with great ease over ears of corn and stalks of flax in the vision, the emperor could not contain himself and began to laugh. Suddenly the apparitions vanished and the ceiling of that room began to descend and was on the verge of crushing the emperor, when Rabbi Loew succeeded in making it halt with the help of another spell. And it is told that the fallen ceiling can still be seen today in that room, which is kept locked.

Eastern Europe: Nineteenth Century

The Cause of the Plague

uring the days of Rudolf II, a plague broke out among the Jews of Prague, which took as its victims only young children. The effects of the plague were terrible, ravaging the ghetto. Fast days were ordained, and special prayers were said, but to no avail, for the cause of the plague was not found.

One night Rabbi Judah Loew of Prague, the master of Kabbalah, prayed to God to reveal the cause of the disaster. Soon after this he fell asleep. He dreamed that it was midnight, and the prophet Elijah came to him and told him to follow. Elijah led Rabbi Loew to the Jewish cemetery, where he saw the spirits of children rising up from their graves. Just then Rabbi Loew woke up, convinced that the dream contained the secret behind the plague, although he was not certain what it was.

Then Rabbi Loew noticed that it was almost midnight, and he decided that he must go to the cemetery at once. He quickly woke one of his closest disciples, who followed him to the cemetery without question. They arrived at midnight and saw the spirits of young children float above their graves and begin a strange dance. The disciple was terrified and wanted to run away, but Rabbi Loew understood that the spirits had been revealed to them for a purpose. Just then Rabbi Loew saw that one of the dancing spirits had left its shroud lying across a tombstone. Rabbi Loew hurried there and took it, then moved back into the shadows.

When the ghostly dance ended, all of the spirits returned to the grave, except for the one who discovered that its shroud was missing. It went flitting about, trying to find it. Then Rabbi Loew stepped out of the shadows and told the spirit that it could have the shroud back only if it revealed the cause of the plague. The spirit begged and pleaded to be given the shroud, but Rabbi Loew insisted on knowing the secret cause. At last the spirit revealed the presence of an evil sorcerer living among the Jews, who had invoked demonic spirits, which, in turn, had caused the plague. And the spirit of the child also revealed the name of this sorcerer. Then Rabbi Loew returned the shroud, and the spirit flew back to its resting place.

When they left the cemetery, Rabbi Loew and his disciple went to the house of the sorcerer. They saw from outside his window that he had lit candles and was standing inside the Pentangle of Solomon. The sorcerer began a formula invoking the evil spirits, whom he sent to ravage the community, but before he could finish, Rabbi Loew shouted out a different conclusion for the magic spell, directing the demons to destroy the evil sorcerer instead. And all at once the sorcerer burst into flames, and his body vanished in a puff of smoke.

That very day the plague ended in Prague, thanks to the wisdom of Rabbi Loew.

Eastern Europe: Nineteenth Century

The Speaking Head

n the city of Prague there once was a wealthy merchant whose young son possessed knowledge and wisdom far in advance of his years. When the merchant discovered his son's remarkable gifts, he hired the finest teacher in Prague to serve as his exclusive tutor. And in the hands of this man the natural gifts of the boy, whose name was Mordecai, flourished, so that by the time he was twelve he was permitted to partake in discussions with some of the most learned rabbis in Prague.

Now young Mordecai's father intended that his son be wed to a maiden from one of the finest families. Therefore he announced that no offers would be considered unless they included a dowry so large that only a few of the wealthiest men in Prague could afford to pay it, and of these none had a daughter of marriageable age.

When Mordecai was in his twelfth year his father began to do business with a rich merchant from another country, who always purchased vast amounts of goods from him. While in Prague this merchant stayed at the home of Mordecai's father, and they enjoyed each other's company. At last a day came when the merchant sought to make a match between his only daughter and young Mordecai. And that was the first time that anyone had agreed to provide the huge dowry Mordecai's father had required.

This situation created a dilemma for Mordecai's father. After all, the merchant was one of the richest men in the world, and anyone marrying his daughter would one day inherit immense wealth. But on the other hand, the father was very reluctant to have his son depart from Prague, especially to such a distant land. Therefore he went to the rabbi who served as his son's tutor and discussed the matter with him. The rabbi agreed that such a match would surely be for the boy's benefit, although he too would hate to see him depart, for never before had he known such a fine student.

At last Mordecai's father told his son of the plans that were being made for him. Now Mordecai knew that his father would take great care

in making a match, and even though he was saddened to think that he would have to leave home, he agreed to accept his father's decision. Shortly afterward, however, Mordecai began to have disturbing dreams in which an old man, whose hair and beard were white, gave him dire warnings. But when he awoke he could not remember what the old man had said. At first Mordecai did not pay much attention to the dream, but when it kept recurring, he finally told his father about it. But his father did not consider dreams to be very important and thought that they merely revealed that his son was afraid to take leave of his family.

So it was that the match was made and the engagement contract written. And when the time came for the wealthy merchant to leave Prague and return to his land, he entreated Mordecai's father to permit him to take Mordecai along with him, to be introduced to the bride and the rest of the family. This Mordecai's father was very reluctant to do. But when the merchant continued to implore him, Mordecai's father finally gave his consent, with the understanding that Mordecai would return to Prague in time for his Bar Mitzvah.

Soon the day came for Mordecai to set out on the long journey with the wealthy merchant. During the trip the merchant continued to treat Mordecai with great deference and respect. And at last they reached the foreign land in which the merchant made his home. He took Mordecai to a great castle with an enormous tower, in which he said he lived. When they entered the castle the merchant showed Mordecai around it, and the boy was amazed to see that every room seemed to be even more splendid than the last. But as they walked through the castle Mordecai was astonished not to see anyone else, not even a single servant. Nor did he meet the merchant's wife or his intended bride.

For the first few weeks Mordecai said nothing about this, because he was a very polite and respectful young man. But in exploring the castle he discovered that the door at the entrance was locked, so that no one could enter or leave. So too did he explore every room of the castle, all of which were open, except for one room at the very top of the tower, which was locked. Mordecai wondered about this, but did not ask the merchant about it. Often he wished he had but a single text to study, so the passing of time would not be so oppressive. But, as far as he had seen, the castle was entirely barren of books. And each day he was alone except at meals, when he was joined by the merchant. Once Mordecai asked him who prepared the elaborate meals, and the merchant replied that he did so himself.

At last, however, when several months had passed, and Mordecai had not seen a single soul except for his host, he finally could not restrain himself and asked to know why he had not yet met anyone else. The merchant told him that his wife and daughter had left on a journey of their own, with all of their servants, and would be back before too long. This pacified the young man for a few weeks, but when he continued to spend day after day in the prison of that castle, he became worried. To relieve himself he wrote letters to his father, in which he confessed his confusion at the strange turn of events. He sealed these letters and gave them to the host, who promised they would be delivered. Meanwhile, he continued to await the first letter from his family, for in all that time he had not received a single one.

Meanwhile, in the home of Mordecai's family, where months had also passed without the arrival of a single letter, their anxiety grew until it became distress, and the distress grew until it became grief. At last Mordecai's father came to the conclusion that he had made a terrible error, and the heartbroken father became so distraught that he was unable to work. He went to the rabbi who had been Mordecai's teacher, and in his grief he accused him of having misled him into agreeing to the match. So too did the father recall, now that it was too late, Mordecai's terrible dreams, and he berated himself every hour of every day for not paying more attention to them.

At last Mordecai's father sent a caravan to seek out Mordecai in the city where the wealthy merchant had said he made his home. But imagine the father's horror when the caravan returned with the news that no merchant of that name lived in that city or had ever been heard of there! As the planned time for Mordecai's Bar Mitzvah grew near, his father's grief grew even greater, and he cried out to Heaven ceaselessly to redeem him from his error, fasting and weeping from Sabbath to Sabbath. And still there was no word from Mordecai.

Now when the evil merchant saw how Mordecai was becoming restless, he began to worry the boy might try to escape. For the boy was well aware that the time of his Bar Mitzvah was at hand, and he knew as well that they should have set out to return more than a month before.

That very day the merchant joined the boy for a walk through the castle, which was immense. There were doorways everywhere and a multitude of passages. Just to be on the safe side, the merchant had seen to it that every room in the palace was locked, except for one, where he planned to trap the boy. Mordecai noticed that all of the doors, which were usually open, had been shut. He sensed danger, but he feared that if he tipped his hand and let the merchant know of his suspicions, the danger would become imminent. Instead he remained alert at all times and watched for a way to escape.

The merchant led Mordecai up the tower stairs, acting unusually kind and friendly, and telling the boy that he wanted to show him the library, which was the one room that Mordecai had never entered, for it had always been locked. Now Mordecai was hungry for study and learning, and he let himself be swayed by the thought of reading once again. If only he were back in Prague, in the home of his beloved father, studying Talmud with his teacher!

When Mordecai entered that tower, he was astonished at how many dark bound books had been crowded together in one place. So many books! Not even in Prague, in the library of his teacher, had he seen such a collection. And as Mordecai peered in amazement at the books assembled there, he had the strange feeling that he had been in that dark, high-ceilinged room before, even though he knew that to be impossible. Surrounded by that sea of books, Mordecai did not notice the evil merchant slip out of the room and lock the door behind him. When he heard the key turning, Mordecai dashed to the door, but it was too late. The merchant had locked him in without a word. All that he had feared most had come to pass, or so he thought.

In despair, Mordecai drifted back to the bookcase, and randomly took down a book, which he saw was a kabbalistic text. Mordecai opened it and began to read, and a moment later he was horrified to see that in the place where God's Name had been written, the Name had been blotted out. A sense of terror descended upon him. He quickly turned through all the pages of the manuscript and saw that this abomination had been performed on each and every holy name in that book. Swiftly Mordecai returned that book to the shelf and grabbed another one, this time a prayer book. He turned to the Shema, the prayer that he said so often to himself, to give him strength. And there too the Holy Name had been obliterated. In great confusion Mordecai began to feel his knees grow weak. He put that book back and looked around for a place to sit down.

That was when he saw the head. It was the head of an old man, his hair pure white, a look of great pain on his face. That was all there was, only a head. It lay in the center of a round table, on black velvet. When Mordecai realized that the head was missing a body, he nearly fainted, for he had suddenly remembered him from his dreams. And that is when the head first spoke. It said, "So they have captured you as well. May God have mercy on you!"

These words, coming from the detached head, almost drove Mordecai to madness. Still, he found strength enough to cry out, "Who are you?" And the head replied, "I too was once a bright youth like yourself, with great promise. For I know who you are, Mordecai, and how proud all who have observed your learning must be. Yet know that the merchant who brought you to this place is not a man at all, but a demon, and this castle is, in fact, an illusion, created out of evil. And this realm is not that of men, but the kingdom in which the demons make their home. It is the side of Lilith you have reached, the dark side, from which it is dreadful to escape. But escape you must, for if you don't by tomorrow morning, the day of your Bar Mitzvah, your head will be severed from your body, just as mine was."

It was clear to Mordecai that his fate was far more terrible than anything he could have imagined. And in his anguish he cried out to the speaking head, "Why have they done this terrible thing to you, and why do they want to do it to me?" And the head replied, "These demons seek to know the ways of the future, which are forbidden to the living. By placing holy names beneath my tongue, they subject my soul to unbearable anguish, for these names compel me to pry into the future and reveal it to these monsters to serve their evil cause. But I can be used thus for only eighty years, and now that the time has come to pass, the demons have sought you out to take my place!"

Mordecai shuddered. Not only would his life be lost, but his soul soiled in the worst possible way. The sin was of such magnitude he could not even bear the thought of it. But suddenly Mordecai discovered unexpected strength, a certainty that he would outwit those malignant demons. And he begged the head to tell him if there was any way to escape. The head said, "Yes, but you must leave now. Not an instant must be lost. But the only way you will escape them and all the snares built into this palace of illusion is if you take me with you. For if you do not, they will compel me to tell them where you can be found. And my will, as you know, is not my own. No, take me with you, and I will guide you as best I can. If you succeed, you will bury me properly and say *Kaddish*, so that my soiled soul may be restored."

Mordecai vowed at once, with all his heart, that if only they escaped he would say *Kaddish* for him every day for eleven months and once every year thereafter, for as long as he lived. Then the head restrained a sob and said, "But we must hurry! There is a secret compartment in this room. Quickly, go to the last bookcase in the room, and take out the center book on the top shelf."

Mordecai hurried to the bookshelf and tried to reach the book, but found that he could not. He grabbed a chair and stood on it. Then he pulled down the center book, and all at once there was a creaking, and that very instant the bookcase began to move, revealing a hidden passage. That was when Mordecai felt his first glimmer of hope. He ran back to the head and took it under his arm, and he hurried into the passageway.

Soon after he had entered that dark place, Mordecai heard the bookcase close loudly behind him, and he suddenly realized that he was trapped. For an instant he feared that the head had not told him the truth, but was itself an illusion of the evil demons and had lured him to that place, where he would meet a terrible end. But at that very moment the head began to speak again, in a calm, reassuring voice. The head said, "This is the top flight of a long spiral staircase. There are ten flights in all. We must reach the last flight and escape this castle before the demons find out; if not, we will become ensnared in one of their traps. So hurry!"

When Mordecai heard the voice of the speaking head, his suspicions vanished, and he reminded himself that the head offered him his only hope. Yet it was so dark there that Mordecai was forced to cling to the wall of the staircase, so as not to tumble down those many flights. He cried out to the head, "How do the demons find their way in this dark place?" And the head replied, "They flourish in darkness. That is why we will be much safer once we have reached the light."

These words spurred on Mordecai to hurry even more, and now that he had become familiar with the turn of the spiral steps he was not afraid. Each time he completed one full turn, he took note of it. They had descended seven spirals when the head suddenly cried out, "The demon has just discovered that you are missing and that you have taken me along! He is rushing off to sound the alarm. For though the castle may have appeared empty to you, in fact it is overflowing with demons, who make their home in every nook and cranny. And any second now, all of them will rush out to capture you!"

At that instant Mordecai suddenly lost his footing and cried out. He very nearly plunged into a dark abyss and also very nearly dropped the head that he held under his arm. The demons had found out in time to dissolve the illusion of the remaining stairs, and at any moment Mordecai expected them to come after him from above. "We are lost!" Mordecai cried out in despair. "No, not yet," said the head. "As I told you, this castle is an illusion, a mirage thrown up by the demons to ensnare you. Up till now we have accepted that illusion, in hope that in this way we might escape it. But now the illusion serves us no longer. All that you need to do is have faith that what I am telling you is true, and then the demons will be unable to perpetuate the mirage."

In that moment of complete terror, Mordecai could barely grasp the words of the speaking head, but he forced his mind to consider what it would mean to be ensnared in an illusion. And no sooner had he done so than he grew angry with himself for permitting the demons so much power over him. At that very moment Mordecai suddenly found himself standing in a barren field with dozens of glowworms at his feet. And the first thing Mordecai heard was the jubilant voice of the head crying out, "You have broken the power of the illusion! Those glowworms are all that is left of it." "Does that mean we are safe?" Mordecai asked. "Only from that illusion," the head replied. "They will surely try to ensnare us in other ways. For once an illusion is shattered, it is gone for good, yet another illusion can easily take its place. You believe, for instance, that this is a wilderness. That is not true. In fact, we are at the bottom of an abyss, out of which you must climb. But in this abyss everything is upside down. That is why you believed you were ascending to the tower of the castle when the demon led you there, when in fact you were descending far into the abyss. For here every ascent is a descent, and every descent, an ascent."

Modecai tried to comprehend this notion, so strange to him. At last he said, "Would that mean we must continue to descend in order to escape this terrible place?" "Exactly," said the head. Just then Mordecai sighted a well in the distance, and asked, "Could that serve us?" The head said, "It's just what we need! Hurry!"

Mordecai ran with all his might. And when he reached the well, the head said, "Now climb into the bucket, and let it descend as fast as possible!" Mordecai climbed over the wall of the well, cradling the head in one arm, and stepped inside the wooden bucket. And his weight immediately caused it to slip downward, plunging into the darkness below. Yet, to his amazement, as they fell much farther than the depth of any well, the darkness began to lift, so that he could make out his hand in front of his face. Then Mordecai realized that all the head had told him was true and that in that descent they were somehow climbing out of that abyss.

While Mordecai and the speaking head were plunging through the seemingly bottomless well toward a distant light, the whole city of Prague was convulsed by grief at his absence. For the day of Mordecai's Bar Mitzvah had almost arrived, and he still had not returned; nor had any word of him been received in all that time. Of course the demon had consigned all of the boy's letters to the flames. Never before had Mordecai's father been torn by such grief, and above all he blamed himself for agreeing to let his son go.

Now during the days preceding the time of Mordecai's Bar Mitzvah, Rabbi Judah Loew of Prague, known as the Maharal, had a series of dreams that had come to haunt him. In the first dream the Maharal found a letter nailed to his front door, like a proclamation, that stated that the life of the boy Mordecai, whose soul could bring great blessing to the Jewish people, hung in the balance, and that only the Maharal could save him. The second night the Maharal heard the voice of an old man speaking, but he could not see him, nor did he know from whence he spoke. And the voice urged him to do all within his power to save young Mordecai, who was in mortal danger.

Then, the third night, the Maharal dreamed that he stood face to face with another old man, who told him that he was Mordecai's grandfather, who had returned from beyond the grave to seek help in saving his grandson. Even in the dream the Maharal felt determined to do everything he could for the boy Mordecai, whose grandfather had come from the other world to deliver this message. Then the old man revealed how Mordecai had fallen into the clutches of evil and was desperately trying to escape. And he told the Maharal that somehow the Gates of Heaven had become locked, preventing prayers for the boy's well-being from reaching on high. If only the Maharal could find the way to open those gates!

It was then that the Maharal awoke, filled with apprehension. He had heard of the wonders of the boy Mordecai, but they had never met. Yet the fear he felt for him was as great as if he were his own son. Without delay the Maharal hurried to the home of Mordecai's father and revealed the miraculous dreams to him. Then Mordecai's father had his first glimmer of hope and quickly sent out messengers to all the Jews in Prague, telling them to gather in the Old Synagogue of the Maharal the next day, that of Mordecai's Bar Mitzvah, for their help was sorely needed.

The Jews of Prague did not spurn this plea, but turned out in great numbers, filling every seat of the Old Synagogue, and standing in the aisles as well, so that it seemed as if every Jew in the city of Prague had crowded in there. Now there were ten times as many Jews in Prague as there were seats in that great synagogue, yet there are those who insist that some-how the synagogue miraculously absorbed everyone. Then the Maharal stood before the people and told them that only if their prayers unlocked the Gates of Heaven could the life of Mordecai be saved. And when they heard this, the people joined in the prayers with one voice, and they recited in full the first book of the Psalms. Among them spread the hope, still unspoken, that a miracle might occur. Yet when they had completed the first book of the Psalms, nothing happened, and somehow they knew that the Gates of Heaven were still tightly shut.

Then the Maharal asked them to recite the second book of Psalms in unison, and this they did. Somehow the Maharal perceived that the gates had begun to shudder, but were still locked. Then he directed the con-gregation to read with one voice the third and final book of Psalms. And this they began to do.

Meanwhile, Mordecai and the speaking head were still falling through the bottomless well. Mordecai's first hope had now given way to fear that they might fall forever. He asked the head why it was taking so long to reach the light of salvation, and the head replied, "The place we are fall-ing through does not change, because the fate of our souls still hangs in the balance." Mordecai begged to know if there was anything they could do, and the head replied, "All that remains is to preserve your faith, for the moment we lose it we are completely lost. If we despair, the Other Side will snare us."

Mordecai felt great frustration that there was nothing more to do, but he now trusted completely in the head to guide him. Then Mordecai remembered the holy names the demons had placed beneath the head's tongue. "But the future is supposed to reveal itself to you—surely you must know what lot awaits us!" And the head sadly replied, "No, this has never been permitted. No seer is allowed to see the future for himself, and because my fate and yours are bound together, your fate is also unknown to me." And when he heard this, Mordecai realized that there was noth-ing he could do but wait.

Back in the Old Synagogue, the Jews of Prague poured out their hearts and souls in the recitation of the third book of Psalms. Tears shown from every eye, and they prayed with all their might. For one and all were gripped by an intense desire to save their long-lost Mordecai, and all of them felt the grief of Mordecai's parents as if he were their very own son. As they prayed, a miracle took place—their prayers fused and ascended as one, unlocking the resistant gates, which suddenly swung open. And in that moment they heard a sudden knocking at the closed doors of the synagogue, and when they opened them, they saw none other than the boy Mordecai standing there, a strange object under his arm. It is hard to say who was more amazed, the boy or those who had prayed so hard to save him, and a thrill passed through them, one and all.

For at the very instant that their prayers unlocked the gates, the endless falling came to an end, and Mordecai found himself standing at the door of that synagogue, in the city he had been exiled from for so long. He had no idea how he had gotten there, but the relief he felt was monumental, and he knew that his fate, which had hung in the balance, had somehow been redeemed.

That Bar Mitzvah was the greatest ever held in the city of Prague, and the only one where every single resident later claimed to have been present. Then Mordecai revealed all that the speaking head had done to save him from the dangers of the Other Side, and Mordecai's father saw to it that the head was buried with great honor. So too did Mordecai remember to say *Kaddish* as he had promised, and he never forgot how the head had helped him in his hour of direst need.

As for Mordecai himself, he had a wonderful reunion with his father and mother, who had feared for so long that they would never see him alive again. Soon afterward he became first the pupil and later the disciple of the Maharal. In time he became betrothed to the Maharal's daughter. And when Mordecai's father saw how happy they were, he knew that this had been his son's destined match from the first.

Eastern Europe: Nineteenth Century

The Chronicle of Ephraim

ong ago in Poland lived an upright man, Rabbi Aaron, who leased land from the duke of the village of Luntshitz. His payments to the duke were considerable, and as time went on he grew exceedingly poor, until he could no longer pay. During this period the duke dunned him continuously, and finally he grew so furious that he ordered Rabbi Aaron and his household to be cast into a deep pit, neither to be freed nor sustained with bread or water, so that they would die of starvation and thirst. Moreover, he ordered that the garbage of the entire courtyard be thrown into the same pit along with them.

The duke's servants reluctantly obeyed his orders, casting Rabbi Aaron and his family into a dark and gloomy pit. Rabbi Aaron's wife was pregnant at the time, and he prayed to God and wept and pleaded. His voice rose up from the depths of the pit and reached the highest circles of heaven. And God saw to it that the spirit of the departed father of one of the duke's officers delivered a dream to him in which he revealed that the child of Rabbi Aaron's wife had an extraordinary destiny and that the officer's help in saving them was required. When the officer awoke the dream was imprinted on his memory, and out of honor to his father he decided to see to it that the family was secretly fed.

Every day the officer rose early, took bread, and went to the pit. When he saw no one looking, he tossed it inside. So too did he lower jugs of water and see to it that the garbage was dumped elsewhere. In this way Rabbi Aaron and his wife remained alive at the bottom of the pit. When they had been there for five months, the same dream came to them both on the same night. And in the dream it was revealed to them that the destiny of their son, who was soon to be born, had been foretold in heaven, and that he bore a great blessing. So too was it destined that they would lose him for a number of years, but they would finally be reunited with him.

And it came to pass that the rabbi's wife gave birth to a son of such great beauty that his face radiated an aura, which illumined the pit for them. So too was he born circumcised. Not since the time of Moses had such a miracle occurred. Rabbi Aaron named his son Shlomo Ephraim, and he gave thanks to God and prayed that they should somehow escape that terrible place.

One day, as the officer leaned over the pit to throw down the food and water, he glimpsed the light cast from the face of the infant boy. And when the officer saw this, he remembered the dream of his father, and he was moved to pity.

Soon afterward the duke happened to ask, "Who knows when Rabbi Aaron and his family met their end?" The officer spoke up and said, "Sire, much to my amazement I passed by the pit the other day and saw a light shining from it. I looked down and saw Reb Aaron, his wife, and their infant son, whose face gave forth light, like that of a shining star." "Can this be true?" shouted the duke. "How could anyone live without food or water for a year?" The officer replied, "It is beyond my understanding, sire, unless what has occurred is one of the miracles such as those recounted in the books of the Jews. Did not the sea split before them and manna fall from heaven to feed them in the wilderness? Perhaps a similar miracle has taken place."

The duke got up at once to see for himself. He went with his wife to the pit, which he had avoided for more than a year, and when they looked down they saw, indeed, that a great light glowed there. He called out, "Aaron!" And the reply came from the bottom of the pit, "Here I am, sire." The duke said, "How are you?" "My family and I are alive and well," he replied. Then the duke said, "Show me your child." And Rabbi Aaron held out the child, and the duke saw with his own eyes that it was the source of the light glowing in that dark place.

Then the duke said, "You know, Aaron, that your life and that of your family is in my hands. Somehow you have lived until now, but that can be changed whenever I will it. I am, however, prepared to pardon you and let you and your family live if you will give me this child. For my wife and I are childless, and we would raise this child as our own. What is your answer, Aaron? Think carefully before you speak."

And Rabbi Aaron realized at once that what the duke said was true and that their lives were in his hands. So too did he recall the dream that had come to both him and his wife and the prophecy that they must lose the child for some time. And he understood that this was destined in order to save their lives. But he clung to the prophecy that one day they would be reunited.

In the years that followed, the young boy, Shlomo Ephraim, was raised by the duke as if he were his own son. Because the boy had been an infant when he had been taken away from his true parents, he assumed that the duke and his wife were his true father and mother. Nor did the duke even hint to him that he was a Jew. So too did the duke order his servants to keep silent on the subject. And the duke forgot how he had obtained him and thought of him as his own.

Before long it became apparent that the boy was very intelligent, and the duke saw to it that he received the best tutors, both in study and in music, and he himself began to reveal some of the secrets of magic to the boy. For the duke was himself a sorcerer, who had long been immersed in the Black Arts. In fact, he had been born a common man, but by using his magic he had murdered the true duke and transformed his own appearance so that he was able to take the duke's place. And not even the lovely wife of the duke had realized that the man with whom she lived was not her real husband.

The duke always told the boy to keep the lessons in magic secret, and the boy obeyed, so that no one else in the house, not even the wife, knew anything about them. But the duke revealed a great many of his powers to the boy, for he hoped that one day they would practice evil together and that the powers of the two of them would be even greater than his own.

When the boy was ten years old, the duke held a feast, to which he invited all of the other nobles, and they were astonished at the boy's great learning, but when he played the flute and violin for them, they were even more astonished at his musical accomplishment. Afterward one of the nobles said to the duke, "I have just returned from Paris. There I saw a musical instrument that none of the best musicians could discover how to play. For the secret of how to do so has been lost. If you would like me to, I shall obtain this instrument for your son. It would serve as a fine challenge for him." The duke agreed at once to this, for he wanted his son's talents to become known to the world. And a month later the noble brought back the instrument and gave it to the boy.

The boy found himself fascinated with the mystery of the strange instrument. No one knew its history, although it was rumored to have come from the East. It had been carved from a very rich wood and engraved with intricate designs and various signs and symbols. There were ten holes in it, but the secret of how to use its reed baffled even the greatest musicians. The first time Shlomo Ephraim tried to play the instrument, however, a beautiful burst of music came forth, much to the amazement of everyone. He took to the instrument as if it had been destined only for him, and it seemed as if he could draw a thousand notes from it. By the time of his twelfth birthday he was already acclaimed as a master of it.

Later that year, a few months before his thirteenth birthday, Shlomo Ephraim had a dream in which a strange man came to him who somehow seemed very familiar. The man embraced him in the dream and then told him that he, and not the duke, was his true father. So too did this man reveal to the boy that he was actually a Jew and that the time drew near when he would have to accept the yoke of the Law.

When Shlomo Ephraim awoke, he recalled this dream, and it haunted him throughout the day. He had noticed some time before that he did not resemble either the duke or his wife, but he had not thought much about the matter. Now the dream raised the question again, and he told the duke of it. Although deeply shocked, the duke hid his feelings and quickly dismissed the dream—all dreams, in fact, he told the boy, were nonsense.

The dream occurred again, and the man who said he was the boy's true father was more insistent and told him that he must leave the duke's household before his thirteenth birthday to join his true family and tradition. This time, however, the boy did not tell the duke about his dream. For he had seen that the duke put no store in dreams, and besides, the boy had begun to suspect that the duke might not be his true father. So he kept his thoughts to himself. And during that time the only consolation he found was with that instrument, which he alone knew how to play.

Soon the dream recurred more frequently. And each night the man who said he was Shlomo Ephraim's father became more insistent. Then, on the night before the boy's thirteenth birthday, Rabbi Aaron again came to his son in a dream and took him away from the home of the duke. He brought him to a synagogue and left him on the step outside it. When the boy awoke, he found himself at the door of that same synagogue, exactly as he had dreamed. And at that moment a man ran up to the synagogue, and it was none other than Rabbi Aaron, the true father of Shlomo Ephraim, who shouted with joy and kissed and embraced Shlomo Ephraim and led him inside.

The first thing that the boy asked was how he had come to be there.

Rabbi Aaron replied, "Ever since the duke stole you from me, I have prayed every night for your return. In this last year before your Bar Mitzvah my prayers have intensified, and in my dreams I have gone to the house of the duke and talked to you. And last night, in the most vivid dream of all, I brought you with me back to the synagogue. I ran here when I awoke this morning, for the dream had seemed so real. And I found you on the doorstep, exactly where I left you in the dream!"

Shlomo Ephraim shivered when he heard this, and both father and son knew that a great miracle had occurred that had brought them together. Then Rabbi Aaron told the boy that there was no time to spare, for he was to have his Bar Mitzvah that day. Rabbi Aaron then revealed to his son for the first time the sacred scriptures that were his own, and much to his amazement, he found that the boy was already fluent in Hebrew, which he apparently recalled from hearing his father pray when he was only an infant in the pit. And by the time the Bar Mitzvah took place that day, Shlomo Ephraim was able to pray as well as any other man in that congregation, and he was welcomed into the fold of his true people.

Soon after that, Rabbi Aaron revealed to his son how the duke had sought to extinguish their lives by throwing them into the pit and how the birth of the beautiful child had saved them, but had cost them their beloved son. And now that they were reunited, the boy realized that he had been missing the love of his true parents all that time. So too did Shlomo Ephraim realize how evil the duke was and how dangerous was his involvement in the Black Arts, which the duke had taught him. And both father and son wondered if the duke still posed a danger to them, now that Rabbi Aaron had taken back what was rightfully his.

As for the duke, when he discovered that Shlomo Ephraim was gone, he was enraged. After all, the mansion in which he lived had many guards, including one stationed outside the boy's door. How could anyone have gotten in to take him? It was impossible! Only magic could have accomplished it. It was then that the duke decided that the boy must have done it himself, using the magic that he had taught him. He remembered the dream of which the boy had spoken and realized that in the end the boy had come to believe it and had chosen Rabbi Aaron as his father rather than himself.

And in that moment of terrible revelation the duke vowed to revenge himself on the boy and on Rabbi Aaron as well.

A few days later the duke's wife, in going through the boy's possessions, found the rare instrument that they knew he so loved. The duke was astonished to see it, for he had assumed that the boy had taken it with him. That is when the duke decided to hunt down the boy to find out if he had left of his own volition. If it turned out that he had been kidnapped against his will, he would take him back and raise him as his own, while punishing those guilty of abducting him. But if the boy had used the magic that the duke had taught him in order to return to the Jews, then the boy would die, along with the rest of his family.

At midnight that night the duke went into his chamber and pronounced a spell that turned him into a black wolf that leapt over the walls of the mansion and set out for Prague, where the duke knew that Rabbi Aaron now lived. The wolf found his way to their home, pushed the door open, and entered the room in which the boy Shlomo Ephraim slept. Then he approached the bed, growling softly.

At that very moment Shlomo Ephraim was having a nightmare, in which he dreamed that the duke had slipped into his room and was standing above his bed with a knife in his hand. Shlomo Ephraim wrenched himself awake, sobbing, and his sudden outburst startled the wolf, which quickly ran from the room and jumped out an open window. So it was that Shlomo Ephraim glimpsed the wolf as he awoke, and Rabbi Aaron saw it leap out of the window as he rushed to the boy's room to see what was wrong. And that was how they learned that their lives were in danger and that the duke had decided to seek revenge.

Then Rabbi Aaron went to the Maharal, as Rabbi Judah Loew was known, and sought his help. For he knew that only the great power of the Maharal could protect them from the duke's Black Magic. When the Maharal heard the whole story, he was truly amazed and realized that Shlomo Ephraim must have been very blessed to have escaped from the duke in that miraculous way. And he recognized as well that the boy was in grave danger.

So it was that the Maharal sent up a dream question, in which he asked to know how he might protect the boy. In reply the Maharal learned that one night soon the duke intended to cast a spell outside the boy's window that would lure him outside. And the Maharal sent four of his disciples to spend the night with Shlomo Ephraim. He told them to go to the House of Study, lock all the doors and windows, and immerse themselves in learning all night long with him, never closing their eyes to sleep, for only in that way would they be able to protect him from the evil powers of the duke.

Now after the duke had glimpsed the boy and had returned to his mansion, he realized that he still wanted, more than anything else, to have him back again. So he resumed the duke's form and decided to find a way to capture, rather than kill, Shlomo Ephraim. Then he came up with an evil plan to set out for Prague, taking with him the instrument that the boy so loved. For he assumed, correctly, that the boy greatly missed it.

That night Shlomo Ephraim and the four disciples of the Maharal poured over texts in the House of Study with great intensity, while unknown to them the duke was hidden nearby, working his magic. The duke had found them, using his crystal ball, and then conjured up a bird, whose cry was identical to the sound of the instrument that the boy had played with such love. (For despite his powers, the duke was unable to produce a single sound from the instrument itself, which still refused to work for anyone but Shlomo Ephraim.) When the boy heard the sound of this bird, he was overcome with longing for that instrument, to which he had confided his soul. All at once Shlomo Ephraim broke away from the others and rushed to the window, searching in the night for the source of that melody, so painfully familiar. The others insisted it was a bird he heard, but he refused to believe it, convinced, instead, that someone else had taken possesion of his prized instrument and had learned how to play it. And only with great effort did the others pull him back to their studies. After that he seemed distracted and unable to concentrate, much to the distress of the others.

Now the duke, from his hiding place, saw Shlomo Ephraim come to the window, and he thought that he had him in his grasp, but then the others dragged him away. Thus the sorcerer decided to cast a sleeping spell on the students, which spared only Shlomo Ephraim. When the four students dropped off to sleep one by one, despite a great effort to stay awake, the duke had the supernatural bird repeat its song.

This time Shlomo Ephraim, with no one to hold him back, was overcome with longing, and he opened the window as far as it would go and leaped out—right into the waiting carriage of the duke, who had them quickly driven to a nearby inn. Now the duke wanted to leave Prague immediately, but the city was locked at night, and there was no choice but to wait until morning. Meanwhile the duke and his driver had a great deal of wine that night and got drunk, both rejoicing over having recovered the boy at last, while Shlomo Ephraim, to whom the duke had given the precious instrument, forgot about the presence of the duke and his cohort, and lost himself in the melodies of his beloved music. For he was fully under the duke's power, and his will was not his own.

Meanwhile the Maharal found that he was unable to sleep, and he began to worry about Shlomo Ephraim. So he got up in the middle of the night and went to the House of Study. There he found his disciples deep asleep, much to his dismay. He woke them and found that they knew nothing, only that they had fought off sleep, but had found it impossible to resist. And the Maharal knew that he must act quickly and trap the duke and Shlomo Ephraim in Prague before the gates were opened. So he hurried to the home of the governor that very night, woke him from his sleep, and told him that one of his students had been kidnapped. So it was that the governor ordered that all of the gates of Prague remain locked, except for one, which the Maharal himself would stand by, watching for the missing student. And when he had found him, the guards were to take him back.

So it was that when the duke awoke early the next morning, still half-drunk, he decided that he should depart with the boy at once, for the farther he was from Prague, the safer he would feel. He found it impossible to wake the drunken driver of his carriage, so he took the reins himself. He drove with Shlomo Ephraim to the closest of the city's gates, but found it locked. So he drove to the next one, but it was locked as well, as was the third gate. The duke began to fear that he was trapped in the city until he reached the fourth and final gate and found that it was open, although there was a long line of wagons and carriages waiting to depart.

The duke was greatly relieved to find the gate open, although he still wondered why the others had been locked. Before long he reached the head of the line, and the moment he did, the Maharal recognized him, from the aura of evil that shone from his face. And the Maharal informed the guards, who stopped the carriage, opened the doors, and carried out Shlomo Ephraim, who was still clinging to the instrument, much to the fury of the duke, who shouted that the boy was his son. The Maharal told the duke that as soon as he could prove that this was so, the court would return the boy to him—but meanwhile he would remain with them. And the duke shot the Maharal a look of hatred. "It is you, I know, who has done this. Don't think I won't take my revenge on the boy as well as on you!" And the duke whipped the horses of the carriage and rode off through the gate alone, without Shlomo Ephraim, and the fire of anger and hatred burned in his heart.

Now revenge became the central obsession of the duke's life, and he put all of his efforts into conceiving a plan worthy of his fury. In this way the duke delved further into the powers of evil and found a way to conjure up not only the demons of Hell, but Satan himself. And when he had learned how to accomplish this, he set about to undertake his diabolical scheme.

In the meantime, the Maharal decided that the best thing to do would be to send Shlomo Ephraim as far away as possible. So he sent him to Pressburg and gave him a letter to give to the head of the *yeshivah* there, stating that he was the best of his many students. For by then Shlomo Ephraim was already perfectly versed in the entire Torah. And in his letter the Maharal cautioned the rabbi to watch over him, lest he be snared by the forces of evil. So too was the boy taken into the home of a wealthy man, who wined and dined him and took care of all of his needs. For he meant to betroth him to his daughter, his only child.

The duke, meanwhile, had already located Shlomo Ephraim and knew of both the house in which he lived and the *yeshivah* in which he studied. He also knew of the garden in which Shlomo Ephraim walked each evening, because he had sent spies to observe him.

Thus the duke came to that garden, and there he invoked the evil plan he had waited so long to use, conjuring up all of the forces of the underworld and, finally, Satan himself. That evening, as Shlomo Ephraim sat on a garden bench, he was lost in his thoughts as usual. There were strange omens in the air, however, and strange rumblings in the earth, and at last Shlomo Ephraim looked up and saw that it had grown very dark. Suddenly he sensed the near presence of evil, and he grew afraid. Then he recalled what he had learned about the power of the magic circle, and he quickly drew one around himself, using his staff. And no sooner had he completed drawing it than the nearby chimes struck midnight, and Shlomo Ephraim saw a great company of demons coming in his direction. He became very frightened, yet he knew he must not run, but should remain within that enchanted circle.

Moments later a horde of demons descended on him, but found that they could not cross the circle. The demons tried to terrify and taunt him to drive him out, but he remained in the very center of it and did not move an inch. Finally Satan himself came and said, "Look, you are in my hands, to do with as I please. But I do not wish to destroy you. All I ask is that you read the book that I am going to give you, one page every day. If you will make a vow to do that, I will depart, with all my company. But if you refuse, your life and your soul are as good as lost!"

Shlomo Ephraim heard these words and shivered, for he did not know if the magic circle could withstand the powers of Satan himself. Nor did it seem that the demand of Satan was impossible to accept—to read one page of a book every day, that was a minor matter for one who immersed himself in texts as he did. So Shlomo Ephraim made the vow, and at that instant Satan and his company vanished, leaving the book behind as the only sign that they had been there. And the evil duke, who had witnessed everything from his hiding place, reveled in his success, for his plan had worked out exactly as he had hoped.

When he returned that night, Shlomo Ephraim did not reveal to anyone what had happened. For he knew that if he did, they would take the book away at once, making it impossible for him to honor his vow. And Shlomo Ephraim could not bring himself to break any vow, even if it was made to Satan. That day he opened the book as he had promised and read one page, and instantly he lost all desire to study Torah.

The next day he studied another page, and all at once the sight of the holy books, which he had always loved, became repulsive to him. On the third day, after he read another page, he stopped attending the *yeshivah*. The wealthy man in whose home he lived noticed that he, who had always immersed himself either in the Torah or in his music, had become a different person. He started to watch him in secret, and that is how he learned that he was reading from a book that he kept hidden.

A few days later, when Shlomo Ephraim began to stop practicing some of the *mitzvot*, the man in whose house he stayed secretly brought the book to the rabbi and told him of Shlomo Ephraim's strange behavior. The rabbi opened only one page of that book, read a few lines, and slammed it closed. He was staggered by what he had read and terrified that such a vile text had fallen into the hands of such a pure vessel as Shlomo Ephraim. He ordered the boy to be brought to him at once, and when he came in, the rabbi held out the book. When Shlomo Ephraim saw that he knew about it, he burst into tears. Then, at the rabbi's urging, he revealed all that had happened and of his unfortunate vow.

The rabbi did not hesitate, but called for a rabbinic court to be assembled at once. He brought forth the book and the boy and presented them to the court, with an account of all that had happened. Then the court called upon Satan to testify if the truth had been told. A partition was put up in the court, and when the question was directed to Satan a great rumbling was heard from behind it, and the House of Study began to tremble. But the court stood fast, and when no voice came forth to defend

Satan, the court declared the vow null and void, as it had been made under coercion, and they freed Shlomo Ephraim from every requirement of it. And they also ordered that the evil book be destroyed. At this judgment the growling behind the partition grew even louder, and the foundations of the building started to collapse. But the rabbis appealed to the Holy One, blessed be He, to protect them, and the walls held in the end and did not fall. Then the court departed from the House of Study and cast the book into a bonfire outside, and as it struck the flames it vanished, without leaving a single ash. And at that very moment the duke, who had put his life at risk by bringing the evil book into this world, dropped dead, and at the same time his soul started burning and still burns to this very day.

As for Shlomo Ephraim, he came back to the embrace of the Torah. He was a constant source of pride to his parents and lived out his life as a God-fearing Jew. And when the time came for the Maharal to depart from this world to take his place in the rabbinic court on high, Shlomo Ephraim was appointed to take his place, for there was none other whose soul was as pure or whose ways were as righteous.

Eastern Europe: Nineteenth Century

Rabbi Loew and
the Angel of Death

ne night, not long before the Holy Days were to begin, Rabbi Loew glimpsed a light in the synagogue across the way, and he wondered who might be there at that hour. He left his house, and as he approached the synagogue he saw through the window a strange figure standing at the pulpit. The closer Rabbi Loew came, the more sinister did the figure seem, and suddenly Rabbi Loew realized who it was—the Angel of Death—and at the same time he came close enough to see the angel sharpening a knife over a long scroll on which many names were written. Rabbi Loew was pierced with terror and resisted a powerful impulse to run away. But a moment later he became calm and self-possessed, and he knew what he had to do. As silently as possible he opened the door of the synagogue and came up behind the dread angel. All at once he snatched the long list out of the angel's hands, tearing it away from him, and ran from the synagogue to his home, where he threw the list into the flames and watched until every scrap of it had burned to ashes.

Now the plague had begun to spread in the city, and that was the list of victims the Angel of Death had come to take in one fell swoop. Now only those on the piece of the list left in his hands fell victim to him; all the rest were spared. But among those on the list was Rabbi Loew, and it was he, above all, that the deadly angel was determined to capture.

Rabbi Loew, who could read the lines of the future, knew that the angel would try to snatch him to seek revenge. But Rabbi Loew used his powers to avoid the angel, much as King David had done, studying Torah day and night. For the Angel of Death is forbidden to take a man while he is engaged in the study of Torah. Yet even so, the angel found a ruse by which to capture him. He hid in a rose of great beauty that grew in the garden of Rabbi Loew's grandson. One day the boy plucked the rose as a gift for his grandfather, and as he held it in his hands to present it to Rabbi Loew, the rabbi perceived the presence of the dark angel, hidden in the rose. Then he did not hesitate, but accepted the gift from his grandson, for he knew that if he did not, the boy's life would be endangered. But no sooner did Rabbi Loew take it in his hand than the Angel of Death struck him like a serpent and snatched his soul.

Eastern Europe: Nineteenth Century

The Other Side

he kingdom of Satan is measure for measure like the kingdom of man. Every male child, when born, already has a double in the kingdom of demons. So too does every female, when she is born, have her shadow born there as well, in her precise shape and image, not unlike that seen in a mirror. And at the hour that a heavenly voice goes forth to announce that this one will be married to that one, a partner is also prepared at the same time in the spirit world. She sits and waits for him there from that time forward. And the man who is fortunate marries his partner from the family of man, but less fortunate is he who is found alone on the fourth night of the week or on the night of the Sabbath. For then he is in danger of being kidnapped by the sons of Satan, and led to a place that no man's feet should ever enter.

In one city in the Diaspora lived a pious man of great wealth who was respectful of everyone. He knew the Torah and taught it to his sons and educated them to love the ways of knowledge. He had two sons who were married, but his youngest son was not. This young man was a model of virtue and was very clever as well. In the entire congregation there wasn't a lad smarter than he. The rich man betrothed his son to a fine maiden, and the happiness in both houses was very great.

One day not long after his engagement, the young man went alone to the river to wash, and he was very happy, for the time of his marriage was not far off. It happened to be the fourth night of the week, and no one else was to be seen on the shore or in the water. The young man did not wonder about this, but got undressed and jumped into the river to swim. Later, as he returned to shore, he saw another man also emerging from the water. They greeted each other and as both of them dried off and dressed, they conversed. The young man didn't recognize the other, but he appeared to be an honorable gentleman, and they started back to town together. As they walked along and discussed various matters, the young man failed to notice that they took an unfamiliar path. All of a sudden they stood before an immense mansion. A great many lights shone from within it, and the young man was astonished, for he had never seen it before. From the mansion emerged an old man of great bearing, who said to both of them, "Come in and rest a little before you continue your walk." They agreed to this and entered a very large hall, where the walls and the chairs were made of ivory.

The old man spoke with gentleness and charm, and then he asked the young man about himself. And while they were sitting and talking, they heard the lovely voice of a girl singing from another room. Never in his life had the young man heard a voice so enchanting. After half an hour the door opened, and the maiden who had been singing came to serve them wine and pastries. She carried these on a golden tray, which she placed on the table before them. The girl was as charming as she was beautiful, and the young man thought that there was no one like her among all the maidens of the world. And once he lifted his eyes to her, he found he could not turn his eyes away.

So it was that the hours passed in delightful conversation until midnight, when the young man got up to leave. The old man rose and said, "Don't worry. You are welcome to stay here tonight. Tomorrow I'll have my servants accompany you to the house of your father. And if he is angry with you, he can come to me and I will explain." The young man promptly agreed to stay, for, if the truth be known, he was having a hard time leaving that house.

They gave the young man a special room of his own. The walls were pure marble, and the pillows and the sheets on the bed were white as snow. He slept like a prince that night and was delighted by dreams in which he was united with the maiden with the beautiful voice. After what seemed ages, morning came. The sun shone into the room and pleasant feelings came into his heart, unlike any he had ever known. He got up, washed, dressed, and went into the chamber of his host. The old man welcomed him with affection and suggested they say the morning prayers together. And afterward the old man said, "Sit down, my son," and a servant came and brought them each a drink. That morning they spoke of wisdom and Torah, and the young man thought to himself that the old man was wise indeed.

The young man stayed in that beautiful house the whole day. He no longer remembered the house of his father. He ate and drank and enjoyed the company of the old man and the young man he had met at the river. The old man showed them his beautiful mansion and possessions. They went from one room to another, from one hall to another, and there was no end to the treasures the young man saw there.

When evening came the three of them joined together in the beautiful hall, and once again they heard the delightful voice of the singing girl. This time the young man was even more fascinated with her. And once again, after she had finished singing, the girl entered the hall. She brought them rare and exotic fruits and seemed even more beautiful than the day before. The heart of the young man beat strongly, for she stood close to him, her face shining, and his spirit belonged to her.

By the third day the young man felt as if he had become a member of the family. The man he had met at the river spoke to him when they were alone. He suggested that the young man ask to marry the daughter of the owner of the mansion, and the young man agreed at once, for he was deeply smitten with her. He didn't recall that he was already engaged to a different girl, nor did he remember her at all.

Later that very day his newfound friend brought him the news that the maiden's father had agreed to the match. Indeed, her father had suggested that the marriage be consummated at once. The young man readily agreed to this, and soon servants brought out princely garments, dressed him as a bridegroom, and led him to a large hall, which stood on seventy posts. Its walls shone from the golden tiles mounted there, as in the palace of a king. Never had the young man seen anything like it. Through every doorway came guests dressed in silk and jewels. The hall was completely full, and they all stood crowded together, waiting. And soon the bride appeared with a golden crown on her head. She was wearing the jeweled gown of a princess, and the radiant splendor of her beauty illuminated the entire hall.

The bride was led to the place of the groom, and as she approached him, the young man felt as if he were about to faint. First they gave him a silver ring, with very distinctive markings, and he placed the ring upon her finger. After that they told him to say, "With this ring you are consecrated to me," and he repeated the vow three times. Following that he repeated word for word whatever they asked him to say, for by now he no longer knew his own soul. Then he heard the cheers of those assembled rising up, mixed with mocking laughter, but when he looked around him all that he saw were pale shadows. He turned back to see his bride, but she was no longer there. Just then the ground began to tremble, the door to the room seemed to circle around him, and suddenly the hall disappeared completely, along with everyone there, and he found himself alone, lying by the edge of the river, greatly confused. Standing up, he saw that it was already very late, past midnight, and he went in a daze back to the city. Only with great effort did he reach the house of his father. He barely managed to open the door, then collapsed in the entrance. There were screams from inside the house, and the neighbors came running to see what was wrong. They poured water on him, tore off his robe, and carried him to bed.

After an hour the young man opened his eyes and found, to his horror, that he was unable to explain what had happened, for he had lost the power of speech. In the days that followed, many doctors came with many remedies, but none could cure him. And in every home there was mourning over the disaster that had struck that family. All were especially sorry because they did not know what had caused it.

Now there was one rabbi in that city who was engaged in the study of Kabbalah, and he suspected that the forces of the Other Side had something to do with the evil fate that had befallen that young man. Therefore every day for seven days, in the morning and in the evening, he immersed himself eighteen times, and on the seventh day, before he went to sleep, he offered up a dream question, in which he prayed to learn the truth about what had happened. And in the dream that came that night, the terrible truth was revealed from on high, through combinations of words and letters. Alarmed by what he had learned, this rabbi vowed to try to set free the young man who had become imprisoned by the sons of Satan.

So he went to the rabbinic court and revealed the secret that had been conveyed from on high, and the rabbis of the court agreed that the young man had an account to settle with the kingdom of demons. Therefore they made preparations for a trial and blew the *shofar* to announce it to the demons and commanded them to attend. So too did they put up a partition in the court, which the representatives of the kingdom of demons could remain behind.

When the time set for the trial arrived, the young man who had been struck dumb came, along with his father. The first witness to step forward was the Kabbalist, who repeated to the court all that he had learned in his dream. And he argued that the demons of the Other Side didn't have the right to deceive the young man into marrying one of their own, because he had already been betrothed. For marriage, in such a case, is forbidden. The rabbis of the court asked the demons to reply to this, but all that was heard from the other side of the partition was a terrible din. Those assembled there found this very frightening, but they refused to be intimidated.

Then the rabbis of the court asked the father of the young man to bring forth the engagement contract for his son. It clearly stated that the engagement could not be broken without the approval of both parties, and it listed as well the names of the witnesses who had been present when it was signed. Once again the judges turned to the partition and asked the demons to present their defense. But the din grew even louder. Then the judges consulted together and at last announced the verdict: the boy was freed from his vows and the false marriage was canceled. The *shofar* was sounded three times, and each time all the people there repeated, "You have been freed." Then a great storm arose from the other side of the partition, as if to tear down the building, and a voice was heard to cry out in the distance, "Free me of this man!" And after that everything became silent.

That evening the boy's father bought a fish from a passing fisherman, and when his wife cut it open she found a silver ring in its belly. When the young man was shown that ring, he recoiled in horror. It was the very ring he had placed on the finger of his demon bride. His father grabbed the ring and threw it into the fireplace, where it vanished in a sudden burst of flames. And at that very moment the young man found that he was able to speak again, and he began to recover from the terrible ordeal.

Eastern Europe: Nineteenth Century

The Cellar

here once was a wealthy goldsmith in the city of Posen who had to travel to another town for urgent business. In order to get there in one day he decided to take a shortcut, following a rarely used path through the forest. The goldsmith intended to leave at dawn, but he was delayed, and the sun stood high in the sky before he was able to depart. At last he entered the forest, riding at a leisurely pace. He was filled with thoughts about his powerful horse and his high position when he noticed that it was already growing dark, and he still had not reached the town. All at once he grew afraid. What was he going to do? Was he to spend the night in such a lonely place?

One thought after another swirled through his mind, and at last he decided to light a torch and continue on the path even after it grew dark. That way he might be out of the forest in an hour or two, while if he stopped until morning he would have to spend the whole gloomy night there.

He dismounted and gathered some sticks to build a fire. Then he picked up a fallen branch and lit a torch. Carrying it high above his head, he quickly remounted his horse and continued to ride as the darkness descended around him.

Now it had been some time since that path had been used, so that it was difficult to follow, especially at night. In some places it was so dense that the goldsmith could only guess where the path was, and he soon lost his way, far from human habitation.

The goldsmith rode on, more and more frightened, until almost midnight. But no matter which way he turned, he could not find the path, and at last he realized that going on would only make matters worse. So he reluctantly dismounted and tied his horse to a tree. He gathered sticks again and was about to use the torch to light a fire, when a sudden wind extinguished it. The fury of the man would have been terrible to behold, if there had been anyone there to see it. But wait, there was someone out there, whose laughter chilled the man to the bone. "Who's there?" he

screamed out. And a very strange voice replied, "It is I." "Who are you?" the man cried out, his voice cracking. "Why I am your old friend, the horse," came the reply.

Now the man grew so afraid that he almost fainted. When he finally was able to speak, his voice was strangled, and he said, "A talking horse?" "Not really a horse," was the reply. "That much is for certain." "What are you then?" cried the man. "A demon, of course," was the answer. "And what do you intend to do with me?" the man whispered. "Why, I want to kill you," the demon said. "That's why I led you here. Where do you think the foolish thought of riding through a forest after dark came from? And now that you have crossed the boundary from the forest of men, you are my victim in the forest of demons, where it is always night!"

At that moment, as hopeless as it seemed, the poor goldsmith found enough strength to plead for his life. He promised to give the demon anything he asked for, if only he would let him live. And when the demon knew he held the man completely in his power, he said, "In that case I will spare your life on one condition—that you marry my daughter and give her the honor due to a wife."

Now the man had not expected this demand, but he was willing to agree to anything in order to escape the clutches of that demon. And he did not even consider that he was already married and had children as well. The only thing he knew was fear, mixed with a faint hope that he might somehow escape with his life. So the man agreed to take the demon's daughter as his bride. Then the demon said, "Take off your wedding ring!" The man obeyed at once, and suddenly the ring was snatched away. "Now," said the demon, "repeat this after me." And he began to say the words by which a man and woman are wed, and the poor man, in a daze, spoke as he was ordered, until he had repeated the vow three times.

At that moment there was an uproar all around him, hideous laughter mixed with obscene cheers, and the man knew that he was indeed in the clutches of demons. When the noise subsided the hidden demon spoke again and said, "Now that you are the husband of my daughter, know this: in a moment you will find yourself back in your own house, safe in your own bed. For this you have me to thank. And I will be there— as your horse—to be certain that you behave properly to your new wife. You will find her awaiting you in your cellar, where you have your workshop. Go to her every day, and treat her with honor and respect. If you do not, I will know soon enough, and your life will be as good as lost!"

These last words were chilling, and the man's knees grew weak. Suddenly he lost consciousness and slipped to the ground, and when he opened his eyes he found himself sleeping in his own bed, beside his true wife. He could not believe his eyes. He leapt from the bed and ran to the window, from where he could see the barn in the light of the newly risen moon. The door to the barn was open, and the head of the horse peered out of it, with a mocking look in his eyes. Then the man quickly looked at his hand and saw that his wedding ring was gone. He was staggered. It was not a dream after all. Oh, he thought to himself, if only it had been.

Then, with great trepidation, he made his way down to the cellar and opened the door with the key. When he went inside and lit a lamp, he saw that the room had been completely transformed, so that it now resembled the chamber of a palace. And there, in the middle of the room, which seemed ten times larger than before, was an enormous feather bed, and reclining on it was the most beautiful woman the goldsmith had ever seen. She smiled at him and beckoned to him with her finger. Like one in a daze, the goldsmith went to her and knew her as a husband does a wife. And afterward he returned to the bed he shared with his true wife, who was still asleep.

So it was that the life of this man was transformed, and he came to spend most of his time in the cellar. His family assumed that he was working hard on his craft, because, in any case, their wealth had noticeably increased, and the jewelry made by the goldsmith was in great demand. But if the truth be known, the goldsmith had completely abandoned his trade. Instead the daughter of the demon brought him gold, finely crafted and even embedded with diamonds, and left it for him on his workbench. So how did the goldsmith spend his time? In the embrace of the demoness, whom he lusted for day and night.

Now the goldsmith had the only key to the cellar, and he always kept it on him, because he stored his gold there. At least that is what he told his wife, and he never permitted her to enter there. So it was that the goldsmith was able to conceal the presence of the demoness for many years. During that time she bore him three sons, half-human and half-demon, and they also made their home in one of the many rooms that magically fit into that small cellar. In time his demon wife and children became as important to him as his human family. Nor did anyone know his secret, although his wife wondered why her husband's ardor for her had waned. But it did not occur to her that he might be unfaithful. On the contrary, she regarded him as immune to such temptations, because he was alone in his workshop so often, while many other Jewish men were merchants, traveling from place to place.

That all changed one Passover, on the night of the first *Seder*. As the family joined together in the reading of the *Haggadah* and reached the passage *He went down to Egypt*, the goldsmith was suddenly overcome with lust for his demon wife. At first he tried to repress it, but it was the most powerful desire he had ever known, and his will had already been so weakened by his ongoing passion for the demoness that he got up in the middle of the reading and left without a word of explanation. His family was alarmed, and his wife was afraid that he was feeling ill, so she followed after him. She saw him descend to the cellar and knew he surely would not work at a time such as that. From the top of the stairs she saw him take out the key and unlock the door and heard him relock it after he stepped inside.

Seized by a curiosity as great as her husband's passion, the wife descended the stairs to the cellar and knelt down to peer through the keyhole, something she had never done before. And what she saw there caused a tremor to pass through her body, for the cellar was not the dank place she recalled from the days when they had moved into that house. At first the wife thought that it must be an illusion, but then she glimpsed her husband in the embrace of a beautiful woman, as beautiful as any princess, whom he held naked in his arms. The sight almost caused her to faint, but she crept back up the stairs and returned to the *Seder* table, pale and trembling. When her family asked her what was wrong, she said that their father had not been feeling well and had asked them to continue without him. And so they did, while the goldsmith sated his lust in the chamber below.

Even when he came back later that night, after the *Seder* had ended and the meal had been eaten, his wife said nothing to him about what she had seen. He lied to her, claiming that he had been overcome with memories of his departed parents, and this angered her even more, but still she kept silent. The next day, however, she went to Rabbi Sheftel and told him all that she had seen. The rabbi realized that the man must have lost his soul to that she-demon; a daughter of Lilith—only one such as this would dare to seduce a man in his own house. And the cellar's transformation into a palace chamber confirmed this. The rabbi knew that the man was in grave danger, with his very soul at stake.

Rabbi Sheftel told the wife to continue to act as if she knew nothing, and that day, after the evening prayers had been said, he approached the man and asked if he might speak to him. The man agreed, and they returned together to the rabbi's house. When they were alone, the rabbi told him that he knew of his strange behavior at the *Seder*. Then the man repeated the lie he had told to his wife, and Rabbi Sheftel grew angry and shouted at him, "Do you dare to take the honored names of your departed parents in vain! I know exactly where you went!" The man grew pale and began to tremble, for he realized that his secret was out. Suddenly all the remorse he had held back for so many years washed over him, and he confessed to the rabbi about how the demon had threatened to kill him if he did not marry his daughter. He confessed as well that he had lost his will to his demonic wife. And the rabbi was amazed at what he heard and found that it was even worse than he had feared. For should the man turn against the demoness, her father would take revenge against him.

Then Rabbi Sheftel took out an amulet that was very old and precious, one that had been handed down in his family for generations. It was an amulet against the demoness Lilith and her daughters and contained the words *Out, Lilith!* The rabbi gave the amulet to the goldsmith and told him to wear it at all times and especially when he came into the demoness's presence. The amulet, the rabbi assured him, would protect him not only from the demoness, but from his own lust as well. And he told the goldsmith not to attempt to expel the demoness and her offspring, but simply to cut himself off from them. He would have to set up a workshop elsewhere. For it was sufficient to separate himself from her to end the state of sin, while if he attempted to drive the demoness away, he might provoke her wrath or that of her father.

Thus warned, the goldsmith placed the amulet in his pocket and vowed never to be parted from it. The next day he discovered, to his amazement, that his lust for her had waned, and he did not feel tempted to lose himself in her embrace. For two more days he restrained himself from temptation, but on the third night the demoness, suspecting that something was wrong, visited him in a dream and embraced him there. And when the man awoke, he found himself gripped with passion for her, and then and there, in the middle of the night, he went down and gave himself to her. For the amulet that had protected him so well had remained in his coat pocket, and when he had undressed for bed he had lost its protection.

The next day, however, when he again wore the amulet, he was filled with remorse. He realized that he could not separate himself from the demoness if she remained in his house. And with the power of the amulet inspiring him, the man returned to the cellar and confronted the demoness, despite the rabbi's advice. She knew at once that he had changed, and she knew why. She backed away from him and did not argue with anything he said. But when he finished, she said, "Have you forgotten that my father is still present, watching everything you do? How long do you think he would let you live if you expelled me from here, along with the sons I have borne for you. Not more than a minute, let me assure you! But I see that you have polluted yourself with holiness and that you no longer desire me. Then let this be our understanding: I will leave you and your kind alone and protect you from the wrath of my father as well. But you, in return, must vow to turn this cellar over to my sons and me, to be our home for all time. For our sons are not pure demons, nor are they men. The other demons will reject them, just as men will. Therefore you must let us remain here, for we have nowhere else to go."

The man saw that this was the best he could hope for, and he gladly swore, giving the cellar to her and her offspring for all generations. So too did he feel sympathy for the sons he had procreated with her, even though they were partly demonic, for they were still his own. And he hoped that in this way the matter would be settled, and he would be free of her, but not at the cost of his life.

That day the man hurried to the rabbi and reported the bargain he had struck with the demoness, and the rabbi agreed that it was the best he could do under the circumstances. And the rabbi recorded the entire tale in his diary, for it was an exceptional case, but he revealed nothing of it to anyone, lest it bring the man's life into danger.

So it was that the years passed, and the man never ventured into the cellar again. In fact, he sealed it with seven locks and seven seals, and he set up his workshop in another room of the house, where he resumed his craft for the first time in many years. His fingers had not forgotten the secrets of his trade, and it was a great joy to work. Only once in a while did he slip into melancholy, when he remembered the demons living in the same house and knew that his own sons were among them, sons he had never seen since that fateful day.

At last the man, now grown old, lay on his deathbed, and when he was about to take leave of this world, he saw his demon wife standing by his bed, weeping along with his human wife and children, and he understood that she was invisible to them. So too did the dying man see his demon sons standing there, and he heard them sobbing over him. With this vision the goldsmith departed from this life and entered the

World to Come. There he found that he was not punished because of the sin he had committed with the demoness, for his repentance had been complete. And so his story came to an end, but that of the demons living in his cellar did not.

Now when the children of the goldsmith came to inherit that house, they honored the tradition of keeping the cellar locked. Even though they did not know why this had been done—for their parents had been silent on the subject—they recognized that something terrible must lurk there, for both their father and mother would become upset if the cellar was even mentioned. So too did their children avoid the cellar, for by then strange stories had grown up about it, tales involving demons, imps, and goblins; tales so frightening they never even went near the door.

In this way several generations passed, and eventually the house was sold and passed on to other hands. The new owners needed to store things in the cellar, and they wondered why it had been locked so securely—for the seven locks, now rusted, and seven seals still remained. They too had heard the rumors about it being haunted, but they were skeptical of such tales and sent a workman down to unlock the door. He knocked off the locks, broke the seals, and pulled the door open. But the moment he did, a terrible scream was heard, and when the owners ran down to see what had happened, they found the workman lying dead outside the door.

The incident so frightened the new owners that they moved out of the house at once and put it up for sale. But all Posen had heard of the workman's strange death, and nobody wanted to live there. At last it was abandoned and boarded up, with the cellar door still unlocked, for no one was willing to secure it.

After that the house became known as haunted. Children were warned to keep their distance from it, and everyone who had to pass it walked on the other side of the street. And in the months that followed the abandonment of the house, strange events began to take place in that part of town. Ashes would appear out of nowhere and fill up pots that had held the finest food. A layer of dust was found on all the holy books in the vicinity of the haunted house, and when it was swept outside it formed dust clouds, which rose above the roofs of the houses and obscured the sun. The best vintage wines were found to have turned to vinegar, and the milk went sour after only one day. So too did the weather turn strange. It snowed in the summer and rained in the winter, and, needless to say, caused a great deal of anguish.

Reports of these disasters, major and minor, all centered on the area of the haunted house, and it did not take long for the people to conclude that the demons had escaped from the cellar and were trying to take over that part of the town. This rumor put the city in an uproar, and the rabbinic council met to decide what to do. They sent a messenger to summon Rabbi Joel ben Isaac, who was known as the Baal Shem of Zamosc. Rabbi Joel came at once and went to the abandoned house. There he ordered the boards to be removed. This was done, and the rabbi went inside by himself. He went into the living room and blew the dust off an old wooden chair, one that had belonged to the goldsmith himself. Then he pronounced the holy names that gave him power to invoke the demons present there, and they were compelled to appear.

So it was that Rabbi Joel soon found himself in the presence of three demons, whom he commanded to identify themselves. They revealed that they were the sons of the goldsmith and insisted that they had the right to remain there. Then they told the rabbi the history of the goldsmith and his demon wife and how he had vowed to give them that cellar for all time. Rabbi Joel listened to the tale in amazement, and then he asked to know if any other demons inhabited that place. Then the demons revealed that now there were legions of demons who made their home there, for they had multiplied many times. But all those present were descendants of the three demon sons of the goldsmith and therefore had the right to remain.

When Rabbi Joel had heard the account of the demons, he told them that he could not decide this matter by himself, but that it would have to be brought before a rabbinic court. And he ordered the demons to appear there when the time came for them to testify. Then he got up and left the house.

Three days later the *Beit Din* met to hear the case. The man and wife who had abandoned the house were called upon to prove their ownership, which they did. So too did they testify how the workman had lost his life. Then other witnesses were called to describe the plague of demons that had infested that neighborhood. After that the court called upon the demons to testify, from behind a partition. They told their side of the story and then requested that the rabbis read in the diary of Rabbi Sheftel, to whom the goldsmith had confided his secret. The court sent for the diary to be brought at once, for it was known to have been preserved. And when it was brought, they read the tragic history of the goldsmith and the she-demon and all about the agreement the goldsmith had made with her to save himself from harm. After that they consulted among themselves for many hours, and the demons, assembled behind the partition, were heard to rustle as they waited for the verdict to be announced.

At last Rabbi Joel announced it. He said, "It has been proved beyond doubt that the goldsmith intended to leave the cellar of his house to his demon wife and family, although he was forced to do this under duress, because he feared for his life. In any case, the area was to be restricted to the cellar itself, and not include the rest of the house, and certainly not extend to the other houses in the neighborhoods. By spreading beyond the area to which you were entitled, you have lost your right to remain in the cellar. This, then, is the court's decision: every demon who counts himself to be among the offspring of the goldsmith and his demon wife is hereby commanded to abandon that cellar and house for all time and to depart from our midst at once and to dwell only in forests and in the wilderness, for that shall be your home!"

And when this verdict was announced, there was a great noise heard from behind the partition, like thunder, and the building began to shake. Then Rabbi Joel ordered that the door be opened, and a swarm of demons was seen to depart from there. They passed over the city like a dark cloud and soon were gone. And that was the last anyone heard of those demons in the city of Posen, for the court had spoken, and they could not go against the Law.

Eastern Europe: Seventeenth Century

The Werewolf

n his youth the boy Israel ben Eliezer, who would one day become known as the Baal Shem Tov, spent a great deal of time in the forest. It seemed impossible for the elders of the town of Okopy to convince the orphan to remain in the House of Study. So they decided to put his love of the forest to good use and assigned him the task of bringing the children through the forest each day to school. This work transformed the boy Israel from a solitary young man to one who joyously led the children, singing with them as they went. And the songs they sang were so sweet that the melodies drifted into the highest heavens and were heard even before the Throne of Glory.

Then Satan, the Evil One, grew afraid that the innocent and pure singing of the boy Israel and the schoolchildren was so sacred that it might accomplish what no one had since the exile from Eden—cause the Holy One to release the Messiah from the chains that hold him back. And Satan knew that he must bring the singing to an end.

So Satan decided to take possession of a woodcutter who made his home in the forest. Now this man had called upon Satan to witness his sins many times, for he was not even ashamed of his sinning. And of course Satan had come to him, for he, more than any other, comes as soon as he is called. So Satan took possession of the soul of this man and made it his own, to do with as he pleased. To accomplish this he called down the evil soul of a sorcerer that had been hovering in the Other World, and he had this soul take possession of the soul of the sinful woodcutter. And into the mind of this evil being Satan put but one thought: to bring to an end the pure song of the children who accompanied the boy Israel into the forest.

This sorcerer, who now possessed the woodcutter's body, knew a spell that turned a man into a werewolf. So three days before the rising of the full moon, the sorcerer pronounced the words of that spell, knowing that on the night the moon was full he would turn into a beast.

Now the boy Israel led the children to school shortly after sunrise, and they returned home in the late afternoon. But it had already grown dark by then, for this was the heart of winter. So it was that on the night of the full moon the boy Israel led the children through the snowy forest to their homes. And suddenly, out of nowhere, the most terrible beast imaginable leaped out at them, howling in an unearthly voice, and frightening all the children. Then, as quickly as it had appeared, the werewolf dashed off into the dark woods, and the children, one and all, started sobbing. Even the boy Israel was stunned and barely understood what had happened, but still he gave thanks to God for having saved them from that wolf, more terrible than any wolf in the world. So too did he calm the children, and he led them home and told their parents what had happened.

Now many of the children were so upset that they were afraid to go to school the next day, or the next, or the next, just as Satan had hoped. In fact, a few of them started having nightmares of the worst kind, in which they saw that terrible wolf leap out at them again and again. They cried out in their sleep and shed many tears. And their parents decided that they themselves must lead the children through the forest, for they thought the task too dangerous for young Israel.

Israel was very sad about this, for he knew that the singing of the children was the purest form of prayer. And he grew angry that such a beast should lurk in that forest, driving out those who would enter there. He decided to see if he could find this wolf's den, so that hunters might be able to rid them of this curse. When Israel returned to the place where the beast had leaped out at them, he found the huge tracks of the wolf and followed them through the forest. But all of a sudden, the tracks of the wolf disappeared, and in their place Israel saw the tracks of a man.

Israel was much amazed by this. He realized that the wolf was supernatural—a werewolf—and he grew even more angry that something so evil should exist. Then Israel continued to follow the tracks until at last they led him to the hut of the woodcutter. Israel knew of that hut and knew the woodcutter was not a pious man, but he had not imagined that he was a sorcerer capable of such an evil transformation.

Thus Israel hid himself in the woods, day after day, and observed the woodcutter. Occasionally the man departed from his hut, but Israel never saw him cut wood. Yet smoke was always to be seen rising up from within. And Israel wondered how this was possible, for the hut itself was too small to store that much firewood. Then one day as Israel watched, a flock of birds happened to fly above the hut, and those passing through that smoke fell dead to the ground, one after another. This incident much amazed Israel, so he crept up and touched one of the fallen birds. Then he pulled his fingers back in horror, for the bird had been burned to a cinder in a single instant. That was when Israel realized that the fire, too, was supernatural. And he shuddered at the thought of the evil source of those flames.

Now three weeks had passed since the attack of the werewolf, and during that time Israel had not been seen at the House of Study even once. The rabbis again began to worry about him, and they asked the parents of the children to give Israel another chance. Israel was delighted when he learned that the parents were again willing to entrust him with their children.

Once Israel knew that the wolf was actually a werewolf, he knew that the beast posed a danger to them only on the night of the full moon. And he vowed that he would rid the forest of this recurring evil, but he did not know how. Then, three days before the full moon rose, on the same night that the sorcerer pronounced the spell to make himself into a werewolf again, the boy Israel had a dream that he was never to forget. In the dream an old man came to him who said his name was Elijah. He revealed great secrets to the boy, secrets of how the evil beast could be defeated once and for all. And when Israel awoke, he recalled every detail of this dream and was filled with certainty that he would prevail, for the Holy One wanted him to.

So it was that on the day of the full moon, Israel led the children to school as usual, shortly after sunrise. That day he sang with more fervor than the children had ever heard, and when they joined in, their song reached to the highest of the heavens, sailing above even the prayers offered up that day. The angel Sandalphon gathered those songs together and wove them into a garland to be worn by the Holy One as he sat on his Throne of Glory. And the Holy One, blessed be He, sent the angel Gabriel to Earth to guard over the boy Israel and shield him from all danger.

After Israel had brought the children to school, he himself returned to the forest. He went to the very place where the wolf had attacked them, and there he cleared a place and built a fire. He waited until the fire had burned down, and when all that remained of it were embers, he banked them with ashes, leaving little holes for air. Then he returned to the House of Study in time to lead the children home. And again, as they went together, they sang in the sweetest voices that ever were heard. Satan shuddered in terror at their purity and vowed that this time he would do whatever was necessary to silence their songs forever.

Now Israel and the children arrived at that place in the forest just before dark, and Israel quickly uncovered the embers and fanned them into a great blaze, warming them on that cold night and casting a great light. Then Israel told the children to stand by the fire, and he used his walking stick to draw a circle around them in the snow. And as he did, he whispered some words that the bewildered children could barely make out. Then Israel turned to the children and told them that no matter what happened, they were not to run outside that circle, for within it no harm would come to them. After that he began to sing, and the children, despite their fear, sang with him.

By then it had grown dark, and the full moon was seen rising in the sky. And as soon as it shone down upon them, the children heard the most terrible howling from the forest. One and all they began to cry out in fear, for they recognized the howling of the werewolf. But Israel told them not to be afraid, for God would protect them as long as they remained within that circle. And when the children saw how calm Israel was, they stopped crying, though they still shivered with fear.

Then Israel took his walking stick and put the end of it into the fire. Now Israel was very fond of that staff, and the children were perplexed, for they could not imagine him burning it. But the staff did not burst into flame. Its end just glowed brightly when Israel lifted it up. And at that very moment they heard the sound of branches breaking nearby, accompanied by another terrible howl, this time so close that the children started screaming. That is when Israel suddenly swung his walking stick around and around, so that it seemed as if a burning circle hovered there. And when the terrible werewolf leaped toward them, he was surrounded by that glowing circle. It grew smaller as the wolf passed through it, and those who dared to watch saw a great miracle take place: for as the wolf passed in one side and out the other, he was transformed into the sorcerer. And although this happened quickly, several students later insisted that for a moment they had seen a being half-man, half-wolf, suspended in that flaming circle, before the body of the woodcutter crashed to the ground.

When the children had become calm, Israel cautiously stepped outside the circle. Just then, much to their amazement, the woodcutter's body began to smoke. Then it suddenly turned to ashes, and then even the ashes disappeared. And Israel knew that somewhere the evil soul was being punished for what it had done and that it was burning in the fires of brimstone even then.

So Israel gathered the children together and led them back home beneath the light of the full moon, which seemed to cast a path before them. Satan knew the bitterness of his defeat and he knew as well that in the boy Israel he had an adversary far more powerful than any man he had opposed since the days of the Maharal in Prague. The angel Gabriel, who had witnessed all that had taken place, reported on high that the boy Israel had accomplished the deed without his help, exactly as Elijah had foretold in the dream. And in the palaces of Heaven that was a time of great celebration, for they knew that the era of the Baal Shem Tov had truly begun at last.

Eastern Europe: Nineteenth Century

The Beckoning of the Besht

s the time of Easter approached, the Baal Shem Tov, known as the Besht, grew tense. On the Sabbath preceding Easter Sunday he paced back and forth in his home, and his Hasidim wondered what was wrong. At the end of the Sabbath he had the wagon made ready and told three of his Hasidim to accompany him. They traveled all night in the wagon, and in the morning they reached a large city. There they came to a stop before one house in the Jewish quarter. All the windows of the house were barred, and the shades were drawn. The Besht got down from the wagon and knocked on the door, but no one came to answer it. The Besht knocked again, and a voice whispered from behind the door, "Are you crazy? What are you doing here today? Don't you know that the Bishop is about to speak? Don't you know what will happen when he finishes? They will burn down the Jewish quarter! Our lives are as good as lost!"

"There will be no slaughter of the Jews today," said the Baal Shem Tov. And when the rabbi who lived in the house heard the Besht say this with certainty, he was suddenly filled with confidence and opened the door. Then the Besht and the other Hasidim hurried inside, and they saw how everyone in the house was huddled together in fear. For the evil Bishop had made very clear his intention of bringing destruction upon the heads of the Jews that day.

Without even introducing himself, the Baal Shem Tov went directly to a window in the study. Then to the horror of those in the house, he opened the curtain and raised the window. Outside, across the way, a great mob had assembled and a platform had been erected. And just at that moment the Bishop ascended the platform, to the wild cheers of the spectators. Now the platform faced that window, and the Besht looked directly at the Bishop, whom he saw clearly in the distance, raised his right hand, and beckoned with his forefinger. Those who saw this thought that he must be mad and that he was intent on bringing about a disaster. And they could barely believe their eyes when they saw the Bishop suddenly begin to descend the platform, in front of all of the amazed spectators, and walk directly toward their house.

A moment later there was a knocking at the door. With trembling knees the rabbi opened the door and saw the Bishop standing there, a look of confusion on his face. He said, "I have come as he has commanded. Please take me to see him." The rabbi, also confused and bewildered, directed the Bishop to the study, where the Besht sat in a chair, reading a book. He did not even raise his eyes to look up at the Bishop. Now just before the entrance to the study there was a mirror, and as the Bishop passed it he glanced into it, and what he saw staggered him. For he did not see the reflection of himself. He rushed up to the mirror and stood directly in front of it, but still all the mirror reflected was the empty room. And a great darkness descended upon the Bishop, for he realized that he must no longer be among the living.

Then the Bishop raised his eyes and saw the Baal Shem Tov seated in the next room, his eyes focused on the page he was reading. The Bishop went there and stood directly before him, but the Baal Shem Tov did not look up. The Bishop first spoke quietly, with difficulty, begging the Baal Shem to save him. But the Besht showed no response whatsoever. In fact, it appeared as if he did not see the Bishop at all. The Bishop grew hysterical and fell to his knees and pleaded with the Besht, promising never to harm even a single hair of any Jew, but rather to be their most devoted protector and patron. When the Bishop said this, the Besht looked up and met his eyes for the first time. And the Besht said, "Aren't you expected somewhere?"

Then the Bishop suddenly remembered that a great crowd was waiting for him. He started to run from the room, and as he passed the mirror he peered into it with a look of foreboding and terror, but to his great relief he saw his image reflected there, and he knew that the Baal Shem had brought him back from the dead. With a glance back at the Besht, the Bishop hurried from the house. He climbed the stairs to the platform, walked to the podium, and began to speak. And the words he spoke were filled with admiration for the ways of Israel and the need for love between Gentile and Jew, for the truth was that they were brothers, whose roots were the same.

Naturally these words astounded the mob, who had come prepared for bloodshed. But the Bishop was so convincing that the anger of the people was dissipated, and when he finished speaking the crowd peacefully went on its way. And from behind the shades in the houses where they had barricaded themselves, the Jews observed all this with complete amazement. Nor did they turn away the Bishop when he showed up at the House of Study the next day and expressed the heartfelt desire to become a Jew. Instead they took him in and taught him and made him one of their own. And all who met him felt that his spirit was one of the most mild of men and most loving.

Now when the Hasidim of the Besht learned of this transformation in the character of the Bishop, they asked him about it. The Besht said, "The truth is that the Bishop does not appear to be the same man because he is not the same man. The evil spirit of the Bishop is now wandering among us, invisible to one and all, crying out for our forgiveness. In the place of the evil spirit there is the wandering spirit of a fellow Jew, who had done evil in his life and was punished for it, but whose spirit was at last purified and made ready to return to this world. And that is why the Bishop has now become a Jew, for this is the true identity of the spirit that inhabits his body."

Eastern Europe: Nineteenth Century

The Black Hand

man who was childless came to the Besht and begged him to intercede on his behalf so that his wife might bear a son. The first two times the man came to him, the Besht neither agreed nor refused to grant his request, but left the matter unresolved. But the third time the Besht assured him that his wife would indeed bear a son. The man was elated by this prophecy, but he saw that the Baal Shem seemed sad. Indeed, a few moments later the Baal Shem began to weep. "What is it?" the man asked, very worried. And the Besht replied, "Everything that comes to pass is first announced by a heavenly voice. It was from such a voice that I heard the birth of your son announced when you first asked for my help. But at the same time I heard the rest of the prophecy: that your son is destined to drown on the day he turns thirteen."

These words cut like a knife to the man who only moments before had reveled in the news that he would indeed be blessed with a son. He was about to weep, when he pleaded, "But tell me, Rabbi, can this fate be altered?" The Besht replied, "On the destined day a fog of forgetfulness will descend on everyone, and you and your wife will forget this prophecy, no matter how hard you try to remember it. That day there will be only one sign to remind you of the danger lurking: you son will put two socks on the same foot. When you see this, you must recall these words at once. For as soon as he puts his shoes on he will go outside to swim, and once he is in the water he will be in the hands of death, and nothing will be able to bring him back!"

The man vowed to the Besht that he would never forget the warning and that he would guard his son from that grave danger. He thanked the Besht many times for what he had revealed, and he set off to return to his wife. Now the prophecy came true, exactly as the Besht had said. Nine months later the man's wife gave birth to a fine son. The man took great pride in his child, who was so precious to him, and he and his wife often reminded themselves of the prophecy that the Besht had made. But on the day of the boy's thirteenth birthday, a fog rose up from the lake, which surrounded the house, and all memory of the Besht's warning was blotted out.

Now that was a very hot day, and the boy, who loved to swim, wanted more than anything else to cool off in the water. When he awoke he started to dress, and when he was putting on his socks his father came into the room and noticed that his son had put both socks on the same foot. Then a strange chill went down his spine, for he suddenly recalled the words of the Besht as if from a great distance. And without wasting an instant he slammed the door of the boy's room and locked it from the outside. His son, very startled, asked him to open the door, so that he could go swimming. But no matter how much he pleaded, his father refused to open it even a crack. And he sat there beside it the whole day, praying.

As the afternoon came to an end, the boy seemed to become possessed. He banged on the door and demanded to be let out. But his father guarded the door, and held his breath, waiting for the sun to set.

That afternoon many in the town hurried to the river to swim, for it was one of the hottest days of the year. And it was reported by many witnesses that a black hand the size of a tree trunk had risen up out of the water, made a fist, and cried out, "What's mine is missing!" Then the fist had struck the water so hard that the waves were three feet high. And at that very moment, the boy, who had been so delirious with desire to cool off in the water, fell asleep. And when his father finally came into the room and saw how his face was peaceful and calm, he knew that the danger had passed.

Eastern Europe: Nineteenth Century

A Combat in Magic

ne night the Baal Shem Tov dreamed that a strange star could be seen glowing darkly above a small town in Poland that was a day's journey from where he lived. And when he awoke, the Baal Shem had a dread feeling that the presence of evil was to be found there. Then he woke three of his Hasidim, who were living with him at that time, and they set out at once, even before dawn, at the Baal Shem's command. Nor did they ask him where they were going, but they followed their master faithfully, for they trusted him completely.

The Baal Shem and his Hasidim rode all day, and it was growing dark when they arrived at an inn in the small town. The Baal Shem indicated that they would stop there, so they dismounted and led the horses to the stables. Then they followed the Baal Shem to the door of the inn, but he hesitated before entering, and he peered up at the sky. And there, directly above that inn, shone a dark star whose presence was invisible to others, but which the Baal Shem, with his pure vision, was able to perceive. The other Hasidim also looked up into the night sky, but they saw nothing unusual and did not know what it was that the Baal Shem was staring at, nor did they dare ask. Then the Baal Shem opened the door of the inn and stepped inside, followed by the three Hasidim.

Inside they found the innkeeper sitting dejectedly by the fire. The Baal Shem approached him and said, "May we lodge here for the night?" And without looking up, the innkeeper said, "No." "Is that because all the rooms are taken?" asked the Baal Shem. "All of the rooms are empty," said the innkeeper. "In that case," said the Baal Shem, "surely there is a place for us?"

At last the innkeeper raised his head, and when he looked into the eyes of the Baal Shem, which held great power, he suddenly felt less dejected, for he recognized that he was in the presence of a holy man. Then he said, "Yes, you may stay."

The Baal Shem signaled the Hasidim to bring in the bags, and after they left he turned to the innkeeper and said, "Tell me, why are you so sad? Perhaps I can help you." "Tonight is my Watch Night," said the man. "For tomorrow my infant son is to be circumcised. I have little hope for him, however." "Why is that?" asked the Baal Shem. "Because this is my seventh son, and all of the others died at midnight of the eighth day after they were born, although there was no sign that anything was wrong with them. No, I am afraid that some evil force, some demon, must hate me for some reason, although I do not know why. For it has robbed me of my sons, every one, although my wife and I are honest, God-fearing people. And I believe that tonight it will try to take its vengeance again."

"My students and I will be glad to help you during the Watch Night," said the Baal Shem. Then the Baal Shem called to his three Hasidim and told them that they should take their places next to the cradle of the child, and for the rest of the night they should study the Law without ceasing. Above all, they must not close their eyes, for if they did all would be lost. He brought them a sack and told them that if they saw anything suspicious, to hold the sack open above the child, and if anything should fall into the sack, to tie it securely at once, and to call him. Then, after warning them one last time about not falling asleep, the Baal Shem left them and went into his chamber.

Now the three Hasidim did not doubt that the life of the child was in their hands. And during the night they kept each other awake by chanting prayers out loud, and whenever they heard eerie noises in the night, they shivered, for they did not know what awaited them. At midnight the candles in the room began to flicker as if blown by a powerful wind, and suddenly they went out, despite the best efforts of the Hasidim to keep them lit. Then a strange gloom filled the room, and the only light that remained was that from the fire, which was tossed to and fro as if by a mysterious wind, causing the shadows of the Hasidim to dance grotesquely on the walls. Suddenly the fire in the fireplace went out, and the room was pitch black. The Hasidim were terrified, but they kept to their posts beside the cradle and kept the sack open, as the Baal Shem had told them to do. All at once they saw two large green eyes glowing before them in the dark, and their blood ran cold. The creature made a hissing sound and suddenly sprang at the cradle, but the disciples held the sack open above it and felt something fall inside. Then the Hasidim wasted no time, but tightly secured the sack with a rope, and one of them hurried to the Baal Shem's chamber to awaken him.

When the Baal Shem arrived he was carrying his staff, and without any hesitation he began to beat the creature in the bag mercilessly, as it hissed and howled. The Hasidim watched in amazement, for they had never seen the Baal Shem so angry, nor did they understand what it was that the creature had done, although it had certainly given them a terrible fright. After he had given it a sound beating, the Baal Shem told his Hasidim to carry the sack out into the street and there to set the creature free. And when they did, a huge black cat jumped out and limped away as fast as it could.

The next day the child was still healthy, unlike the six brothers who had preceded him, and the circumcision could take place. The innkeeper was very grateful for the help the Baal Shem and his Hasidim had given him, and he made the Baal Shem the *sendak*, who has the honor of holding the child during the ceremony.

Following the circumcision there was a joyous celebration, with many happy toasts. Afterward the innkeeper happened to comment that it was strange that the duke had not joined them, because he had come to each previous celebration, only to learn, in those cases, that it had been canceled because of the child's death. And now, ironically, he was absent when the child was alive. The Baal Shem, however, did not consider this ironic, but deadly serious. He kept his thoughts secret, however, and said to the innkeeper, "Let me take some of the wine of the celebration to this duke, so that he will know you have not forgotten him. Perhaps he is not feeling well, and that is why he was unable to attend." The innkeeper thought this was a fine suggestion, and so the Baal Shem set off with a bottle of wine in his hand.

Now when the Baal Shem arrived at the home of the duke and announced his purpose, he was taken at once to the duke's chamber. There he saw the duke covered with bandages that could not conceal all his bruises. He stared at the Baal Shem with hatred in his eyes and said, "Do not imagine for even a moment that I do not know who was responsible for what happened last night." And the Baal Shem replied, "I too know exactly what happened."

Then the duke said, "The only reason you succeeded last night was because you caught me unaware. But that will never happen again. When you face the wrath of my power, yours will seem like nothing." The Baal Shem replied, "If that is a challenge, then let us meet in a magical combat and see whose power will hold sway." And the evil wizard, for that was what he really was, was astonished that the Baal Shem had not shrunk from the challenge and wondered just how great his powers were.

Then the two of them set a date and time for the duel. And when the day arrived, every man, woman, and child in that province had heard about it, and a great crowd had gathered in the open square where it was to take place. But not a single Jew was to be found there, for they had gathered in the synagogue to pray that the Baal Shem might not be defeated. And among them was the innkeeper, who owed his child's life to the Baal Shem Tov, and he prayed more intensely than anyone else.

Now the wizard had delved deeply into the realms of evil, using the powers for his own satanic purposes, such as killing the infant sons of the innkeeper. He saw his combat with the Baal Shem as the opportunity for a demonstration of these powers that would frighten all those in the province, so they would let him work his will as he saw fit. And the first thing the evil wizard intended to do upon his victory was to destroy the Jews of that city, who had brought about his severe beating at the hands of the Baal Shem. Yes, the wizard was delirious with the thoughts of power and revenge. But the Baal Shem was ready for him.

The combat began at dawn. The evil wizard jumped up and pronounced a spell, and a furnace appeared behind him, of great size, with huge swirls of smoke billowing from it. All who were watching stood in awe, except for the Baal Shem, who seemed to pay it no heed. Instead he used his staff to draw seven circles in the dust, one inside the other, and then he stood in the innermost circle. All at once the wizard threw open the door of that furnace, and a great flame leaped out that took the shape of a fiery lion. It gave off a terrible roar that shook the earth and ran straight for the Baal Shem Tov.

Everyone expected the Baal Shem to take flight, but instead he stood calmly in the center of those seven circles, words of prayer on his lips. And the moment the lion passed through the first circle, its flames burned out, as if they had been doused with water, and the lion vanished. The people were amazed to see this, and the wizard was furious, for that lion had possessed a great deal of his power. Then, once more, he opened the door of the furnace, and this time a fiery tiger sprang forth, which charged toward the Baal Shem Tov. But it broke through only the second circle before it disappeared.

After that the sorcerer called upon his powers yet again, and this time a great wolf leaped out, with its teeth bared, and charged toward the Baal Shem. But just as it entered the third circle, the Baal Shem lifted his staff off the ground, and all at once the flaming wolf turned to smoke and vanished as had all the rest. The wizard could not believe it, and at last he drew upon the most terrible spell he knew, which even he was afraid to pronounce, and when he opened the door whole herds of wild beasts came running out, not only lions, tigers, and wolves, but leopards, griffins, and wild boars. And among them were some creatures that looked like they had crept right out of Hell, and that indeed was where they had come from. For the powers the evil wizard drew upon were those of the Evil One himself, who had hoped to use the wizard to defeat the Baal Shem Tov.

But the Evil One could exercise his power only in the face of evil. And the Baal Shem's soul had a kernel so pure it did not even share the blame for the Fall of Adam and Eve. It was one of the Innocent Souls that had fled before the Fall had taken place. Thus all the powers of the evil wizard and of the Evil One himself were futile. When the beasts roared toward him, the Baal Shem faced them calmly. Some disappeared when they crossed the fourth circle, others when they passed through the fifth and sixth, but none breeched the seventh and innermost circle where the Baal Shem stood. In the end the evil wizard had drained himself of all his strength and power, and when he opened the furnace door one last time, the fire that leaped out suddenly consumed him, so that nothing more than ashes remained, which were shortly scattered in the wind. That was the end of that evil wizard and a great defeat for the Evil One in his struggle to gain power over our souls. And it was all because of the Baal Shem Tov and his faith in the Holy One, blessed be He, who had never abandoned him for a single second.

Eastern Europe: Eighteenth Century

The Perfect Saint

here once was a righteous man who wished to perfect himself. He regarded sexual desire as the primary temptation to sin, and he vowed to rid himself of it. First he withdrew from his wife and became celibate. Soon, however, he found that this was not enough. Lustful thoughts still haunted him, for even though they slept apart, his desire for his wife remained. Therefore he made a vow to fast one day for each lustful thought. This, however, turned out to be impractical. After a week of fasting, he decided that he must try something else.

The only solution, it was clear, was to move out of the house. So he moved outside to the *sukkah*, and it was there that his wife brought his meals. He entered the house only for important reasons, such as finding a book in his library. Otherwise he was alone, away from temptation. And yet, even in the *sukkah* impure thoughts pursued him like demons swarming around him, polluting the sacred presence of its shelter.

At last it became clear to the man that he couldn't be anywhere near his wife at all. He would have to go far away. Yet he knew that if he left his home to wander in the world, he might glimpse other women, who might also awaken his lust. And that would be an even greater sin than desiring his own wife. No, the only answer was to become a hermit, and that was what he decided to do.

Other men might think such thoughts but never carry them out. But this man desired to be a perfect saint. So it was that he set out, alone, taking the remote byways and little-used paths and made his way into the forest. Yet even there he could find no peace. The animals were too noisy and too full of lust for life. So he kept on his way, until he finally reached the desert. And he realized that this was the place for which he had been searching.

The first days in the peace and quiet of the desert, the man was free of the desires that had clung to him for so long, but soon he began to dream. And the dreams were dreams of desire. Even there in the desert

Lilith had not abandoned him! The man was overcome with grief. Was there nowhere, nowhere at all, that a man could be free of lust?

Out of his great disappointment the man began to fast. Not on purpose, but simply because he had lost his desire to live. He fasted for so long that his body grew light, and one day he simply ascended. He rose above the trees, above the clouds, and even above the stars. He ascended to the highest heavens. There he saw a pot filled with flesh and bones. It was a terrible sight to see. "What is this?" he asked. And he was told that the flesh and bones in that pot had once been an extremely beautiful woman. But she was a sinner who had warmed up her body to sin. Therefore, as a punishment, she was being warmed in that pot.

This explanation was most astonishing, and the new saint was very curious to know what that woman had looked like. When he asked about her, he was given a Divine Name with which it was possible to reassemble her as she was during her life. He pronounced this name and suddenly she stood before him, naked, and he saw that she was indeed a very great beauty. His lust for her grew until it was overpowering, and all at once he reached out to embrace her. And as he did, he fell from that high place. Some say he is still falling.

A Tale of Rabbi Nachman of Bratslav
Eastern Europe: Nineteenth Century

The Tale of a Vow

n a certain town lived a rabbi and a landlord who were as close as brothers. Because their friendship had lasted so many years, they hoped to remain friends in the World to Come as well. Therefore they made a sacred vow that the first one to die would return and tell the other what life in the Other World was like. Now it happened that the rabbi was the first to depart this world, and for a long time his friend the landlord waited for some sign from the beyond, but none came, and eventually he gave up hope that one might be forthcoming.

Ten years passed, and the time came for the landlord to take leave of this world. And before he died he told his son of the vow he had made with the rabbi, in case the rabbi's soul should seek out his son instead. Such a contact from the Other World never took place, however, and ten years later the landlord's son also departed from this life. But he too let his son know of that sacred vow, should it be fulfilled in his generation.

Then it happened, eight years later, that the soul of the rabbi did indeed approach the grandson of the landlord, reporting in a dream all that had happened to him in the Other World. And this is what the rabbi's soul told him:

"When they put me in the grave, I imagined that I was still strong and healthy, and I could not comprehend why they would take a man and bury him alive. But what could I do? I was helpless to protest, because no one seemed to hear any sounds I made or notice any of my movements. But after they had all departed from my grave, I decided to test myself, for I hoped that I might somehow escape from my coffin. So I made a great effort, and finally I succeeded in opening the coffin, thus escaping from the tomb.

"At first I was ecstatic, for I was still under the delusion that I was alive. But then it occurred to me that I could not enter the town dressed in a shroud, for if I arrived at my house that way, I might scare the mourners to death. So I decided to wait until nightfall, and then to enter my house when everyone was asleep, change my clothes, and seek a way to gently break the news that I was still alive.

"When nightfall came I quickly made my way to the town in the distance, which resembled my own in every respect. I was terribly afraid of being seen, however, because of the shroud I was wearing. But soon I saw the wagon of a clothes seller coming down my very path. With excitement and trepidation I approached him and asked if he would exchange clothes for a shroud that had been worn only one day. To my surprise, he agreed, nor did he seem to think it strange that I was wearing a shroud. Imagine my delight when I found among the clothes he carried those of a rabbi, not unlike my own! So we traded clothes and I entered the town.

"Yet when I was walking down the streets of the town, I was distressed to discover that it was not, in fact, my own. Then I became confused, thinking that I had taken the wrong path. But while I tried to get my bearings, time passed, and soon it was night. And as I looked around, I saw that all the candles in all of the houses had been extinguished, except for one, in which a flame continued to glow. That was when I realized that it had been a long time since I had eaten and that I was starving. So I went to that house and asked for food. But when they learned I had no money, they turned me away, for it was an inn.

"By the time I walked outside I was surprised to discover that dawn had arrived; it was the summer and the nights were short. And in the distance I saw two men who were discussing something. I went closer and discovered that they were debating a matter of the Law. And because I had often served as a judge, I offered to assist them in reaching a judgment. They each agreed to abide by my ruling, and both were greatly pleased by the fairness of my decision, and one of them gave me two gold coins for my wisdom. Then I returned to the inn and ordered food, because I then had money to pay for it. And just as I was about to sit down to a fine meal, two messengers came running in and approached me and told me that the rabbinic court of that town had sent for me and that I had to leave at once.

"When I stood before the court I discovered that I was on trial. For someone had reported that I had served as a judge, even though I was a stranger in that town and had not presented my credentials to the court, as required. The judges looked at me very sternly and ordered that I be searched, in case I had accepted a bribe. For the Law requires that a judge serve without payment from the parties whose case he has decided. And when they searched me, they found the two gold coins. Then the judges ordered that I be stripped of my rabbinical robe and had me pushed outside, naked. And I ran away from there as quickly as I could, for I was greatly ashamed of all that had happened. I was so downcast that I decided I would be better off to return to the grave, because death was better than a life like that.

"But how could I return to the grave without a shroud? And I pitied myself because I was so impoverished that I lacked a shroud and thus could not find a home even in the grave. Just then I heard a loud debate taking place. I approached carefully so that I could not be seen, and from behind a tree I observed a man arguing with the judges of the court who had sentenced me. And I was greatly astounded to discover that they were talking about me! Before long I understood that the man speaking to the judges desired that I be permitted to return to the grave in a proper manner. But the judges insisted that I could not, because of the holy vow I had made to the landlord so many years before. For I had never fulfilled the vow I had made to return and tell him of my life in the World to Come. And the judges argued that because the landlord had died, it was now impossible for me to fulfill the vow, and I would be condemned to become a wandering spirit, cursed to roam the world endlessly. But the man argued that the vow could still be fulfilled, because the landlord had told his son about it, and his son had in turn reported the vow to his son, and therefore I could fulfill it by going to the landlord's grandson and telling him all that had happened to me. And that is why I have come to you in a dream, twenty-eight years later, for I have been wandering all this time, although it appears to me to have been only a few days."

At that the grandson of the landlord awoke, with the dream vividly imprinted in his memory. He wrote it down and took it before the rabbinic court. When the judges had read it, they ruled that the rabbi had at last fulfilled his vow and was now free to return to the peace of the grave. And so his soul was at last set free.

A Tale of Rabbi Nachman of Bratslav
Eastern Europe: Nineteenth Century

A Tale of Delusion

nce Satan decided to tempt and torment a man. He disguised himself as a merchant and created the illusion of a magnificent horse, upon which he rode. Then it happened that he met this man, as if by accident, on the road. The man could not help but admire the fine horse, and he was amazed when the merchant offered to sell it to him for a mere pittance. He thought the man must be weak in the head, but he was not about to ignore such a bargain. So he paid the amount, mounted the horse, and rode off, feeling like a king.

The next day the man rode the horse into the market, and all who saw it turned their heads in admiration, for they had never seen a finer horse. And when the man announced that the horse was for sale, a great crowd gathered, for they wondered how much it would bring. The price offered for the horse rapidly increased, but the man turned down every offer, thinking to himself that the horse was worth twice as much. And when he had turned down the highest offer, it became apparent that the only one in the kingdom who could afford the horse was the king.

Therefore the man rode the horse to the palace, and when the guards saw how magnificent it was, they recognized that it was fit for a king, and they quickly gave the man the royal audience he requested. Yet although the king offered the man a huge amount of gold for the horse, the man turned the offer down, for he kept thinking that the horse was worth still more.

After he left the palace, the man decided to give the horse some water, for it was a precious possession, and he wanted to keep it in good health. He took it to a place where there was a pump for horses, but as the man raised the handle to pump water, the horse appeared to be sucked inside the pump and it disappeared. Now such a thing cannot happen, and yet it did, even though the man did not believe his eyes. But his precious horse was nowhere to be seen, and there was no other explanation. In great distress the man began to scream, as if someone were trying to murder him. Soon a crowd had gathered, and when he calmed down enough to explain that the horse had disappeared into the pump, the people became disgusted and took him for a fool. And when he continued to insist that this had happened, they began to taunt and beat him, because the hole of the pump was very narrow and certainly could not fit a horse.

Since no one believed him, and he was in danger, the man decided to escape. But just as he was about to run away, he glimpsed the head of the horse emerging from the pump. He screamed for the others to look, but when they did the head of the horse disappeared, and they began to taunt and beat him all over again. Again he thought only of escaping, but just before he tried to, the head of the horse reappeared, just long enough to drive him into a frenzy. And this time he was hit even harder than before.

Thus by the time the man returned to his home, he was black and blue all over. As for the horse, he never saw it again, except in the nightmares that tormented him afterward for a very long time, in which the head of the horse emerged from the pump and seemed to be laughing at him.

A Tale of Rabbi Nachman of Bratslav
Eastern Europe: Nineteenth Century

The Bridegroom
Who Vanished

n the town of Shargorod there were two *yeshivah* lads who were loyal friends. They spent all of their days in the House of Study and immersed themselves in the Torah and Talmud with great devotion. They even spent their spare time together and were seldom separated. For they were as close as brothers.

Then it happened that one of the lads took ill and died. This unexpected event grieved his friend greatly. Still, he remained as devoted to the Torah as before.

In time his grieving subsided from his heart, and when he thought of his friend he was able to smile at the memories of how close they had been. After a few years this lad became known throughout the region for his great knowledge of the Torah. Men of wealth and distinction began to visit his poor dwelling, hoping to bring him home as a groom for one of their daughters.

Eventually a match was made. The wedding day arrived and the entire household was occupied with preparations for the wedding feast. As for the bridegroom, he was isolated in a room, waiting for the ceremony to begin. Now he became restless in his isolation and stepped outside for a moment. Empty fields stretched before him, and on the horizon he saw a figure walking his way.

When the young man first observed the figure, he was barely curious to know who it was. But as the figure drew closer, it looked strangely familiar. All at once the young man recognized who it was—his friend, who had left this world for the other one, the *Yenne Velt*. A long chill took possession of him, but at the same time a terrible longing. All the love he held for his friend returned twofold, and he stood as one rooted until the other arrived. The two friends embraced, and the young groom saw that his friend looked exactly as he used to, as if he had never aged.

It was then that his long-lost friend spoke for the first time, his voice exactly as it had been. "Tell me," he said, "do you remember what point of the Law we last discussed?" It had been ten years, and the young man had completely forgotten. But his friend reminded him, and suddenly the whole discussion came back to him. He had not thought of it since then, but now it mattered to him as much as before. And they launched into a long debate, like those they had had in the *yeshivah*, sitting at the same table, reading the pages of the Talmud together.

As they spoke, lost in their words, the two friends wandered in the field, until they were far from home. The young groom, only hours before standing beneath the bridal canopy, forgot all about his wedding. Indeed, he forgot about everything, except for the fact that he was immersed in the Torah once more with his friend. How such a thing was possible did not occur to him at that time, so natural did it seem.

At last the two young men arrived at a small hut deep in the forest. They went inside and there the Talmud lay open to the very passage that they were discussing. The young man and his friend read it out loud together, as they had done so often in the *yeshivah*. And almost at once they were lost in the *pilpul*, where one idea led to another, and yet another, and still others beckoned.

Time flew past. The young man forgot whether it was day or night. The Law, after all, was infinite, and he was lost in its complexity, as he had been in the happiest days of his life, sharing insights with his friend.

Their rambling discussion led them, by one route or another, to the laws concerning the obligations of the bridegroom to the bride. At that moment the young man remembered that it was his wedding day. He looked outside and saw that it had grown dark, and the time of the wedding was at hand. Then he embraced his friend and hurried off as fast as he could, hoping that he would not provoke the fury of his new father-in-law or the disdain of his new bride.

When he reached the town, he found himself confused, for it seemed changed from what he remembered. Nor could he find his father-in-law's house, and he began to grow fearful that he would be late to his own wedding. At last he asked an old woman he met about where the house could be found, and she looked at him very strangely. For no such house existed.

The young groom was at a loss to understand. He told the old woman his story, that he had walked away from the house for only a few hours, and now it was the time for his wedding. And she replied, "When I was a girl I heard of how such a thing once happened—one hundred and thirty years ago. How the groom had left the house a few hours before the wedding and had never been seen again." "And what was the name of the unfortunate groom?" he asked in desperation. She thought long and hard and all at once she remembered it. And the name she recalled was his own.

Eastern Europe: Oral Tradition

The Exorcism of Witches from a Boy's Body

here once was a chest hidden in an attic in which four witches had been trapped by a rabbi. The descendants of that rabbi were all warned not to unlock it, and so it remained there, year after year, for there was nothing else that could be done. If it were burned, the witches would escape. If it were sunk into the sea, it might break open on the bottom, and they would emerge, seeking revenge. And if it were buried, the elements might cause its lock to rust, until it could be broken open from within. For no one doubted the danger those witches posed, and all kept their distance from them.

Now a young boy in this family had been warned many times not to open the chest, but one day curiosity overcame him, and he pried it open. The witches came swarming out of the chest and took possession of his body. Sometimes they came up from his belly into his neck, until he thought he would die, so stretched did his neck become. And sometimes they went into his back, and it became round like a barrel. But most of all they inhabited his stomach, which became swollen to an immense degree.

When all attempts to exorcise the witches had failed, his father brought him to the city of Brody, to the House of Study of Rabbi Eliyahu Gutmacher, who was well known for his mastery of practical Kabbalah. Rabbi Eliyahu was studying with his students when the thirteen-year-old boy was carried in by his sobbing father. The rabbi told him to take the boy from his shoulders, and when he did they saw how dreadful was the boy's condition.

The rabbi examined him and asked that he be taken to the rabbi's home. When this was done Rabbi Eliyahu called in two of the city's judges, and the father showed them the boy's belly, the breadth of which was amazing. The boy could say nothing, but only crept on his hands and feet like a beast. And his voice was sometimes like the bark of a dog and sometimes like the bleating of a calf.

The rabbi ordered that the boy be seated before him on a chair. He took hold of his hand, picked up a book of psalms, and opened it at random. Then he read the prayers with complete concentration, paying particular attention to the roots of the letters and especially to the mention of the Holy Name. For he was well versed in *gematria* and the mysteries of the Kabbalah, and that was why the father had brought his poor son to him.

This was repeated twice daily, but still the boy made no progress. Then one day when he returned from the ceremony of the Redemption of the Firstborn, the rabbi thought to himself that this would be the day the poor child would be redeemed from his troubles as well. So he ordered the boy to be brought before him. Then the rabbi recited a verse of Psalm 91 secretly, with great intention, and suddenly the boy emitted a startling sound and pointed to the end of his little finger. The rabbi ordered the window to be opened quickly, and it was done. And the boy spoke coherently for the first time, saying, "One of the witches has left me!"

Then the rabbi and the others present looked at his belly and saw that the left side looked empty, although the rest was as full as before. And the boy said that three witches were still inside him. The rabbi decided that because it was a propitious moment he would pray again. After he had recited the same psalm to himself three more times, the boy again screamed loudly, startling everyone there. And he cried, "Now they've all left!" And so it was, for his belly was shrunken, and he immediately acted as if it had never happened, taking his father's hand rather than walking on all fours.

So it was that the witches were expelled from the boy's body, and they fled as far away as they could go. And for this everyone gave thanks to the Holy One, blessed be He, who had saved the boy in that time of dreadful danger.

Eastern Europe: Nineteenth Century

The Demon of the Waters

n a village in the district of Radziwillow there lived a Jew whose name was Azriel Brisker. For many years he had rented the mill near the river and from this business he made a respectable livelihood. He was generous, his house was open to everyone, and he was very careful to fulfill the commandments in all ways. All the Jews who lived in the area came to pray on the Sabbath in the house of Azriel, who had set aside one room for use by the *minyan*. He had also arranged a hut near the river for the *mikveh*, the ritual bath.

In the next village in another part of that district there was a Jew whose name was Yakov Reiff. He was the owner of a tavern, and his livelihood was also quite secure. For years he and Azriel had lived in friendship and peace. Then, however, it happened that the friendship between the two was destroyed because of a dispute over a match. Yakov proposed a match between his eldest daughter and Azriel's eldest son, but Azriel refused because he felt that Yakov was not fully observant according to his standards. And from this matter they became angry at each other, and the matter festered until they became enemies and Yakov decided to take revenge.

So Yakov went to the district office, and he convinced the official to rent him the mill in which Azriel worked and lived. The man was unwilling at first, for Azriel had made his home there for many years and had the right to remain. But by slandering Azriel and offering to pay a rent twice as high, Yakov eventually convinced the man, who finally wrote a contract, transferring the rights to the mill to Yakov. Then the district official sent an announcement to Azriel that he had to move from the mill at the end of the year because the mill was going to be rented to someone else. When the announcement was received in the house of Azriel, everyone was in tears, for if they were expelled from the mill, their livelihood was lost.

Azriel sought the district official, but he refused to meet with him, and he was told to go to the district manager. Azriel went to this man, who told him that because the contract had been written, there was nothing that could be done. He suggested, however, that Azriel go to Yakov and ask him to change his mind about renting the mill. And even though Azriel knew that Yakov was stubborn, still he and his wife went to the house of Yakov and begged him not to take their livelihood. But Yakov and his wife, Feige, hardened their hearts, turned their faces away, and shut the door behind them. And Azriel told his wife that because Yakov and his wife had closed their ears, they must turn to God for help.

Now the rabbi most admired by the Jews who lived in that part of Russia was the Saba Kadisha Mishipoli, the holy grandfather of Shipoli. Azriel and his wife arrived in Shipoli shortly before Shavuot and remained there for the holiday to meet with the rabbi.

On the first day of Shavuot they sat at the rabbi's table. When Azriel's wine glass was filled, he opened his mouth to say *L'hayim*, but his eyes filled with tears and his voice was choked. The rabbi became angry that Azriel was dampening his spirits on the blessed day of Shavuot. And when Azriel saw the rabbi's anger, he grew terrified. The rabbi saw this, and he said, "Do you remember about six years ago a poor man knocked on the door of your house on a cold winter night? And you opened the door to him and let him come in? Then you prepared something hot for him to drink and gave him a place to sleep?" "Yes, I remember this well," said Azriel. "I asked the poor man what he did, and he said that he was a scribe. And I asked him if he would examine the *mezzuzah* on my door, for the wind had been howling loudly outside, as if some evil forces sought entrance there. He checked it for me. In two places the parchment was blank, and he said it was probably the work of demons. The man wrote a new parchment for my *mezzuzah*. And after that we did not hear the wind howling at our door." Then the rabbi said, "I am that poor man you helped. Therefore, have no fear, for God, blessed be He, will turn the curse into a blessing, and no man will be able to move you from the place of your livelihood."

After this Azriel became like a different man, and he ate and drank with a happy heart. At the end of Shavuot Azriel and his wife went to depart from the rabbi. Then the rabbi took a letter he had written and handed it to Azriel to read. It was addressed to Yakov and said, "I have heard that you, Yakov Reiff, desire to encroach on the boundary of your neighbor Azriel Brisker. Let it be known that I am giving you warning that you will not be permitted to do so, whether you learn this earlier or later. If you have a claim to bring against Azriel, call him before a rabbinic court, according to the ways of our people. You don't punish first; first you warn. If you listen to my words, you will be blessed. But if you don't listen to my words, you will live to regret it." And he signed it.

The rabbi gave the letter to Azriel and told him to go to Yakov and give him this letter. And he said, "If Yakov will listen it will be better. But if he won't, rent a house for yourself in a nearby village, until he himself comes to you and begs you to take back the mill." And Azriel and his wife took their leave of the rabbi with many thanks.

Azriel and his wife did as the rabbi had instructed them, but Yakov ignored the warning. He threw the letter in Azriel's face and said, "The rabbi you went to has no power here; in our village we have our own rabbi." So Azriel left and got a house in the next village, as the rabbi had told him, and when it was time to leave the mill, he moved. And Yakov moved into the house of Azriel.

It wasn't long before Feige, the wife of Yakov, went to the hut near the mill to dip in the waters of the ritual bath, because she didn't want to travel to the city. Feige took her eldest daughter to guard her clothes. And the daughter sat at the entrance of the hut, looking outside, while her mother went inside to wash and dip. But this time something terrifying happened to Feige. As she went down the stairs, the stairway collapsed and she fell silently into the waters, for she had fainted out of fear at once.

So it was that one of the daughters of the demons who exist in rivers, and especially in the rivers near mills, who resembled Feige in her height and in her face, came out of the water. And when Feige's daughter looked inside to see if her mother had finished, she saw her getting dressed. Soon she emerged with a scarf covering her face, but the girl didn't pay attention to it, for she thought it was only to protect her from the wind. Nor did the girl ask her anything, and they didn't speak all the way home. Then the daughter went outside to play. That left only the little children in the house, for Yakov was at work in the mill. The children thought the demon was their mother, and when they asked for something she drove them away. Then she went to the kitchen and took all the food that had been cooked for the whole family and ate directly from the pots with her hands. And when the children saw that their mother was eating, they asked to be fed as well. But instead of feeding them, she kicked and shoved them until they started screaming.

When the eldest daughter heard the cries of her brothers and sisters, she rushed in to see what had happened. And how frightened she was when she saw the strange behavior of her mother, who was standing in the kitchen, her face covered with a scarf, wrapped in the same robe she had worn from the *mikveh*, eating from the pots with her hands. She cried, "Mother, Mother, that food is for the whole family!" and when she didn't get any answer, the daughter tried to pull the scarf from her face, but the demon pushed the girl away with great force, so that she fell on the floor and hit her head, which began to bleed. When the little ones saw that their sister was hurt and crying, they started crying as well, until one of them went and called their father from the mill. And Yakov greatly wondered what had happened, for the boy was so terrified he could not speak.

When Yakov came to the house, he saw that everyone was crying and that his wife was wearing the robe of *mikveh*, and in her hand was a pot that she had emptied. He started yelling, "Feige, Feige, what did you do?" But when he saw his daughter crying, "My head, my head," he lifted her from the floor and wrapped her head with a handkerchief dipped in cold water. And he spoke to his wife and tried to lift the scarf in order to look in her face. But she pushed him with such great force that he fell on the floor. When he got up he begged her to listen to him and to tell him what was wrong, she made a growling sound, like that of a beast, which left him terrified. Then she went up the stairs to the attic and lay down on the straw mattress there.

When Yakov recovered from the shock, he decided to try to talk to his wife again. It was already night, so Yakov took a lamp to light his way up to the attic where she was still resting. But when he reached out to lift the scarf from her face, she knocked the lamp from his hand and ran into a corner, and he was afraid to go after her. He left her alone that night, and early in the morning Yakov returned to the attic and found her deep asleep. Nor did he wake her, for he hoped that if she got enough rest her mind would come back to her. He went downstairs quietly and went to the hut, and the first thing he noticed was that the stairway had broken and that the whole floor of the bath was rotten. And Yakov said to himself, "Now I understand. When she went down to dip, the stairs broke under her, the floor collapsed, she fell into the depths of the waters, and she lost her mind." Yakov returned and told his daughter what he had learned. And they comforted themselves that the doctors would find a cure, now that they knew the reason for her illness.

Then, before the family even sat down at the table, the woman came downstairs and took all the food that had been prepared and ate everything and threw the pots in the hall. Then she went back to the attic and they were too frightened to follow her. And this happened again at lunch and at dinner. She came, ate everything she saw, and went back upstairs.

Three days passed in this way, and they had to cook every meal twice, for she took everything they made and didn't leave anything for them. Soon it became known in the whole village that Feige, the wife of Yakov, had lost her mind. And on the fourth day of this, the daughter said to her father, "Maybe this is a punishment for us for taking the livelihood of Azriel. Perhaps we should give the mill back to him, and because of this my mother will recover." She cried loudly when she said these things, but her father had a hard heart. He said to his daughter, "Nonsense. We know she is sick because the stairs of the bath collapsed under her. What does the business of the mill have to do with it? People go crazy for different reasons. Tomorrow I will fetch a doctor from town, and we will listen to what he says."

So the next day Yakov went to town and came back with a doctor, along with four strong men to hold his wife until the doctor had examined her. They waited until she came down for lunch. Then one of the men jumped out and tried to hold her, but she took the boiling pot and poured it all over the man. His face and hands were badly burned, and he let go, crying out in pain. Soon enough the other three grabbed her, but she started spinning with the pot in her hands, hitting them and burning them until they ran from the house, screaming. There they waited until she took the bread and the other pot and went upstairs to eat.

Then they returned to the house to try to find a solution to this terrible problem. Yakov told the doctor what had happened in the bath, and the doctor agreed that this terrifying experience had caused her illness. And he said, "Usually for the first few weeks crazy people go wild, demonstrate great strength, and eat in an unnatural way. So the only thing to do is to give her less food until she becomes weaker. Then we'll be able to hold her in order to examine her." And Yakov said to his daughter, "See, I was right. This happened to her because she was frightened. It is not as you thought." Then the doctor said, "Make her some thin soup from bones and a few potatoes. For yourselves, don't cook in this house, but cook at your neighbors and eat there, so she won't take your food." The advice of the doctor pleased Yakov and he gave him a good fee for his work.

The next day they did as he suggested, and they made only watery soup for her. And when she saw how little there was, she smashed all the dishes and took a knife and cut the pillows and threw all the feathers out the window. Many people came by to watch, but they were afraid to approach her. When she finally went upstairs again, Yakov and his daughter returned to the house and saw all the destruction. Then they realized that the doctor's advice had not worked, and they decided to prepare the next meal as usual, so that she would not cause even greater harm. And at noon she ate the food and returned to the attic without doing any more damage. But they were afraid to go near her.

Meanwhile Feige, the true wife of Yakov, had fallen into the river and had been carried away by the currents. Now that river was not far from the great river Danipper. Many merchant ships passed there, and along its banks were many villages, but also many places where there are only forests and fields. And when Feige fell into the river and fainted, she floated on the waters until she reached the big river, which carried her a great distance and cast her on a deserted shore, near a forest. There she sustained herself on nuts and cherries and wove garments for herself out of grass. So too did she weave little baskets, into which she placed notes written on leaves, giving her name and that of her husband, saying that she was lost there. She cast the baskets into the river, and in time some of these notes were retrieved, and her plight became known, and the case became a famous one, spoken of in many circles.

Now when one man who lived in the village of Yakov Reiff heard about the woman lost on the river, he remembered that a man of that name ran the water mill, although he didn't know the name of his wife. Still, he decided to call on him. And when he did so, Yakov told him that although his wife's name was also Feige, she was living in that house, and he told of how she had lost her mind. The man was very surprised at the strange story and asked to return the next day to see her with his own eyes.

Now in that village there was a shepherd who was said to be a sorcerer. The man told the shepherd about the madwoman and asked him to accompany him to the home of Yakov Reiff.

The next day they came to the house and hid. And at noon, when she went to the kitchen, the shepherd jumped from his hiding place and lifted her scarf. But when he did, he saw that she had a very strange smile, which struck terror in his heart, and he backed away.

Then the woman turned away from him and ignored him as if he were not there. She took the pots and pans and the bread and went back upstairs. And after she left, the shepherd said to her husband, "This woman is not your wife. She is a demon of the waters. If she were an earth demon, I could control her and expel her. But because she is a water demon, I have no power over her." And Yakov said, "This must be the work of Azriel. He must have gone to a sorcerer and brought down this curse upon us." Then the shepherd said, "This is not the work of a sorcerer. There is no earthly sorcerer powerful enough to invoke the demons of the water—or to send them away. For they are among the most powerful and dangerous demons of all. Whoever is responsible for this demon is much more powerful than any sorcerer." The shepherd also warned Yakov to prepare the food on time as she desired, for she had the power to destroy the house and wreck the water mill. Yakov asked how long this would last. And the shepherd replied, "Only the one who sent her here can send her away."

Yakov said, "This must be the doing of the *Tzaddik* who warned me not to trespass the border of Azriel." "In that case," said the shepherd, "then you have no other choice but to go to this Azriel and to beg him to accompany you to this *Tzaddik*. For he alone can release you from this curse." And the shepherd warned him to go as soon as possible, for he knew what might happen with such a demon living in the house.

That same day Yakov went to Azriel and surrendered to him. He cried tears and confessed that he had sinned against Azriel and his family by taking away Azriel's livelihood. He came in complete repentance and told him to take the mill back. Azriel accepted his confession and agreed to forgive him, for he saw that he was suffering greatly. And they went together to Shipoli.

After Yakov greeted the *Tzaddik*, he begged for him to banish the demon from his house and restore his true wife to him. The rabbi told him, "I want you to know that the woman in your house is known as the demon of the mill. And because you took the mill from this man, the demons took your wife." Yakov said, "I accept all that I have been charged with, and I am prepared to accept the punishment." And the rabbi said, "It is true that repentance is very powerful, and everything can be repaired with God's help."

Then the rabbi had the verdict written on the paper: "Yakov Reiff will give the contract to Azriel Brisker and will repay all the damages that he has caused. He will also give a written contract, signed by himself, which states that the rights to the mill belong to Azriel and that he renounces any claim of his own over it." And he added, "When you return, each of you should load all your possessions in wagons at night, and early in the morning Azriel will return to his original home, and Yakov will go to the house where Azriel now lives. When you meet halfway, you will descend and make peace and each will ask for forgiveness from the other. And from then on you will be friends, loyal as before. In addition, your children will marry one another, because it is destined from Heaven that this should take place.

"If you listen to all the things that I have said, you will find your livelihoods restored, and God will help you. So too will Yakov's wife return safely and the trouble in the house disappear."

Then both Yakov and Azriel took their leave of this holy man and returned home. When they reached the village of the mill, they went to the shepherd and told him the rabbi's verdict and of his assurance that the demon could now be expelled. And the shepherd said, "I hope that this will happen. Still, Yakov should remain at the mill in the morning until I arrive, so that I can be present at the time the demoness is supposed to depart." And Yakov agreed that he would wait for him.

That night both Yakov and Azriel loaded all their possessions, as the rabbi had told them to do, and early in the morning the shepherd came to Yakov at the agreed upon hour. Then Yakov ordered the wagon to depart, and at the very moment the wagon began to move, the demoness left the house and followed after them. And when they saw this, Yakov and the shepherd both became terrified. The shepherd said, "How cruel is your fate that she is walking after you! What good did the rabbi do if this is the case!" And as he watched her following the wagon, Yakov shivered. But when the wagons passed near the hut of the ritual bath, the demoness entered the hut and disappeared within it. Yakov was afraid to go inside, but the shepherd went in after her. He opened the door slowly and cautiously, peered in, and saw to his surprise that she wasn't there. Only her clothes were to be seen, on the floor. And the shepherd ran back to Yakov and told him that she had returned to the place from which she had come. Yakov was overjoyed, and he became a true believer in the powers of the *Tzaddik*.

Then the shepherd told Yakov that the best thing to do would be to burn the hut and clothes, for surely no woman would ever want to immerse herself in the waters of that *mikveh* again or dress in clothes that had been worn by a demon. So Yakov burned them and took his leave of the shepherd, greatly thanking him for his help.

After that Yakov returned to his own wagon and departed from the mill, which had brought such disaster upon him. On the way he lifted his eyes to Heaven and thanked God for removing the evil demon from his life. He begged with tears that his wife be returned safely to him and that God forgive him for all his sins. While these thoughts filled him, Yakov met Azriel, driving the wagon of his possessions toward the mill. They both got down and cried, and they forgave each other. And so they dissolved the knot of hatred and anger that they had known. And they vowed to wed their children to each other with God's help, once the wife of Yakov had safely returned. Then they said good-bye, and each went on his way.

Meanwhile, Yakov's wife was still lost in the forest. For even though some of her baskets had been found, no one knew where to find her, for the river ran a great distance. Then it happened that three nobles went out to hunt in that part of the forest, and, as fate would have it, Feige fell into their trap.

The dogs of the hunters were chasing after two foxes, and when Feige heard the barking, she climbed a tall tree. Now when those dogs reached the tree, they started howling, and the hunters looked up and saw a woman dressed in woven grasses. They didn't know if she was human or a demon, for demons were said to dress that way. They questioned her and she told them her tale. And after that they helped her down and gave her shelter, and the next day the three men accompanied her to the village where she lived. When she got there, the whole village came out to see her, for she had been missing for three months. And there she learned that her husband and her children were no longer living in the mill and that Azriel was.

It is not difficult to imagine everyone's happiness when she was reunited with her family, and they told the whole tale from beginning to end, and none of those gathered there that day ever forgot it all the days of their lives. And they told it to their children, and it is still repeated to this day.

The next day Yakov's eldest daughter was wed to the eldest son of Azriel, and the happiness was great in their homes. After this the two families, including the bride and groom, traveled to the rabbi of Shipoli, and they told him all that had taken place. The *Tzaddik* shared their joy and blessed them, and they went back to their homes very happy. And after that both Yakov and Azriel succeeded in all that they undertook and became wealthy. From then on the heart of Yakov became like that of a different man, filled with kindness for one and all, and he was counted among the righteous of his time, whose good deeds were impossible to count. And all who met him saw how he believed in the power of the *Tzaddik* of Shipoli and in that of the Holy One, blessed be He.

Eastern Europe: Oral Tradition

The Underwater Palace

ong ago, in the city of Prague, not far from the river Moldau, there lived a wealthy merchant whose name was Kalman. He had but a single child, a daughter, whose name was Haminah. So beautiful was she that many thought she resembled a princess. Her adoring father had betrothed her to a young man who was a fine match, except that she could not bear the thought of marrying him. For if she did, she would lose forever her true love, the one who came to her from across the river every night. But no one knew of this, for she had kept it secret.

Every evening at twilight the maiden Haminah would go down to the bank of the river Moldau in Prague, unobserved by anyone. There she would wait in a ramshackle hut until it grew dark. Then she would go outside to the old dock and peer out over the river. At last the boat she was waiting for would come into view, and a young man of striking appearance would step out onto the shore. They would embrace for a long time, and before parting he would always say, "Let us leave together tonight." And as hard as it was for her to say, she would always reply, "Not yet."

Now as the time of the wedding approached, the secret lovers began to grow desperate. When only a few days remained, and Haminah had replied "Not yet" still another time, the young man rowed away in silence, and beneath the light of the full moon Haminah saw his boat stop, as if it had dropped anchor. Then the young man stood up in the boat and cried out, "If you truly love me, follow me!" and he dived into the waters and disappeared.

When Haminah did not return home that evening at the usual time, her father and her fiancé went out looking for her. They found her standing on the muddy riverbank, staring out over the waters, as if in a trance. They called out her name, and at that moment she made her decision. They saw her run into the river, where she soon vanished, carried off by the currents. Her father ran into the waters after her, but it was too late.

Nothing was to be seen on the surface of the water except for the reflection of the moon.

In the days that followed, fishermen searched for the body of the young girl, but in vain. And every day the broken-hearted Kalman sat at home, waiting for the news that she had been found. But the river refused to surrender her body. Only when the time of mourning came to an end did Kalman resign himself to the fact that he would never see his daughter again, dead or alive. And after that he became a different man, losing all interest in his possessions. He became known for his generosity to the poor, but it gave him no pleasure, for he was walking toward the grave without offspring.

Now Kalman had a sister, whose name was Shifra. She lived in a narrow lane of Prague with her husband. Although she had no children of her own, she had brought many into the world in her role as midwife. She would often visit her brother Kalman, who seldom left home, preferring to remain in isolation with his grief.

One day when she was visiting him, her brother stood at the window and stared out at the river. He was thinking of Haminah, and he relived for the hundred thousandth time how his beloved daughter had run out into the water and had been carried off by the currents. So too did he know again the bitterness of his loss. Then he turned to his sister and said, "How long has Haminah been gone?" And she replied, "Soon it will be a year."

Just then Frau Shifra became aware of a black cat sitting on the wall outside the window. It stared at her with green eyes full of sadness and wisdom and looked as if it were trying to speak to her, to beg her for something. "Look at that cat," she said to Kalman, hoping to distract him from his grief. He looked down at the wall and at the same time the cat looked up at him, and for a long time they stared at each other. And it seemed to him that he recognized the cat from somewhere, but he couldn't remember where. Then the cat suddenly jumped down from the wall and disappeared.

During the night a sharp wind blew from the direction of the Moldau, and all the weather vanes and merchants' signs were creaking. Frau Shifra was unable to sleep. The wind howled through the narrow lane, and the raindrops clattered as they fell in the chimney. Once she raised her head and peered out the window, and she saw that same black cat sitting outside, looking as if it wanted to come in. When Frau Shifra finally fell asleep she dreamed that she opened the window, called to the cat, and it was about to enter. Just then Shifra was awakened by the sound of knocking at the door. It was the middle of the night, but such things were not unusual for her, because she was a midwife.

Already exhausted from her lack of sleep, she got out of bed, walked to the door, and looked out the peephole. "Who is there?" she asked. "Someone who needs your help," came the reply. So she opened the door.

There stood a servant, elegantly dressed. Frau Shifra was very surprised, for she assumed that he served a nobleman, and those who came to her were all Jews. She tried to elicit some information, but he was in a great hurry, so she dressed quickly and left with him. He led her through the rain to the Moldau, where he had fastened a boat to the dock. As soon as Frau Shifra realized that she was expected to cross the river on such a stormy night, she wanted to turn back. The servant turned to her and said, "What are you afraid of?" And she replied, "The wind and the waves." But no sooner had she spoken than the wind calmed down and the water became smooth. Much amazed, Frau Shifra sighed and entered the boat, and the servant began rowing. Soon the bank receded into the distance, and Frau Shifra again became fearful. She closed her eyes and decided not to open them until she reached land once more.

When the boat finally bumped another dock, she opened her eyes. To her great astonishment she saw before her a palace more splendid than that of the emperor. Its spires and curving walls were green and blue and glistened like a waterfall. All things around her glowed with a soft light, that of neither night nor day, and she did not know whence it came. Strange plants grew in the palace garden, and it appeared that a faint breeze was constantly fanning them.

Frau Shifra finally took heart and climbed out of the boat. That was when she discovered that she did not walk in that place, but floated, as if lifted by an invisible power at every step. In her confusion she looked up, and above her she saw schools of fish swimming about, and she realized, with great amazement, that she must be beneath the river. She was breathing, but how was that possible? She did not have long for such musings, however, because the servant hurried off, and she followed as quickly as she could.

The servant knocked on the palace door, and a splendidly dressed young man opened it, who Frau Shifra knew at once must be a prince or king. He was dressed in a green coat and green pants, and his buttons, rings, and buckles were all made of gold. The young man smiled at her and said, "We have been expecting you, good woman. Please follow me."

Then he turned to go and she hastened after him, floating through the halls, which were illuminated by a mysterious light the color of pearls.

At last they arrived at a glowing green door, and when the prince opened it, Frau Shifra had the shock of her life. For there, lying on the bed inside, was none other than Haminah, holding out her hand to greet her aunt. The room glittered with gold, pearls, and diamonds, and the curtains that floated behind the bed had been embroidered with the colors of the rainbow. When Frau Shifra saw the miracle of Haminah, who was not only alive, but ready to give birth, she began to feel faint. But she pulled herself together, for she knew that she must not fail her niece. Haminah said, "Will you stay and help me?" And Frau Shifra said, "Of course."

Frau Shifra wished to ask questions but there was no time, for Haminah was well advanced in her labor. And before long a fine infant was born, a son. Frau Shifra gave the news to the young man, who was filled with joy, and happiness radiated from all corners of the palace.

Before long, lovely singing and harp playing were heard, although the musicians kept themselves hidden. Frau Shifra listened with pleasure to this supernatural music, then turned to Haminah. "Tell me, my child, how did you come to be here? For your father thought you were drowned on that terrible night, and he has never stopped mourning."

Haminah held her baby close and said, "I had a secret love whom no one knew. We met at night on the bank of the Moldau. When I refused to elope with him he dived into the waters and I thought that his life was lost. At the time my father reached the river I decided to follow my love into the grave. I descended farther and farther into the depths, certain that my life was lost, when I saw a green light glowing from the river bottom. Suddenly I was embraced, and I knew that I had been reunited with my loved one at last. He brought me to this water palace, for it is from here that he rules the river. And it was here that we celebrated our wedding."

Frau Shifra heard this explanation, but if she had not been in that very palace, she would not have believed it. And for the first time in her life, Frau Shifra found herself speechless. Haminah continued: "You must know that my husband is not a human being. He is the ruler of the river Moldau, but the king of all waters cursed him and condemned him to live on the land. He had to wander throughout the world until he found someone who loved him so much that she would be willing to sacrifice her life. Only then would the spell be broken. Throughout the ages he was engaged to many maidens, but none were willing to follow him into the realm of the deep. Only I did and thus redeemed him from that terrible curse. Now he once more reigns over the river, and our love for each other is strong.

"Yet," Haminah continued, "there is pain in my heart for causing grief to my father, and I long for him and the rest of my family, including you, my dear aunt. And when this longing begins to overwhelm me, my husband permits me to take the shape of a black cat and to visit the world above." And suddenly Frau Shifra realized that Haminah had been the black cat outside her brother's house and the one of which she had been dreaming when the knock had come on her door. And she said, "Your father felt there was something familiar about that cat, and I did too. Wait until I tell him!" But Haminah grew pale. "No, my aunt, you must not, for if those in the world above should learn of this kingdom, our existence would be endangered. As much as I would like to let my father know, I cannot."

Frau Shifra understood, and she vowed to keep all that she had learned secret. But she also became afraid that she would not be trusted to remain silent. "Will your husband let me go back?" she asked. And the girl replied, "As long as you do not eat or drink anything here, or accept any of the rewards that are offered to you, you will be free to leave. But if you do accept anything, you will be forced to remain here for the rest of your life. All that you may safely accept are some pieces of coal you will find lying outside the door of the palace. Take a handful of these with you, and be careful not to lose them."

At that very moment the ruler of that kingdom entered the room and beckoned for Frau Shifra to follow him. She said a fond farewell to Haminah, knowing that she might never see her again, at least not in human form.

As they floated down the hall, the ruler told her that she was welcome to dine with them, but she replied that it was still the middle of the night for her, and she was not hungry. Then he led her into the treasure room, where she saw great heaps of gold, silver, pearls, and jewels. "Take whatever you like," said the ruler. But Frau Shifra replied, "No, thank you, what my husband and I possess is sufficient for us. And I have been rewarded enough to learn that Haminah lives and that her life here is a happy one. My only desire now is to return home."

Then the ruler thanked her for all her help, and he called the servant who had brought her there. As she left the palace, Frau Shifra noticed pieces of coal sprinkled on the ground, and she bent down and picked up a handful, wrapping them in her apron. Then she climbed into the boat and closed her eyes once more, in order to forget just how far beneath the surface she really was.

Some time later the servant informed her that they had arrived at the riverbank. Frau Shifra opened her eyes and gave thanks when she saw the familiar shoreline of Prague before her. She climbed out of the boat and took leave of the servant. And when she turned around to watch him go, she saw that the boat had already disappeared, and there was nothing to be seen except circles on the surface of the water, as if someone had thrown a stone into it.

As she walked along, yawning, Frau Shifra began to realize just how exhausted she was. And she held her apron carelessly, not even thinking about the pieces of coal she carried in it. When she reached her home, she crawled into bed beside her husband and was sound asleep in no time.

In the morning she was awakened suddenly. Her husband was holding a large lump of gold in his hand, and he was jumping for joy. "Look," he shouted, "at what I found at the foot of the bed!" Frau Shifra rubbed her eyes. Was the visit to the underwater palace not a dream after all?

A moment later a great commotion was heard outside the house. Frau Shifra and her husband ran to the window, and they saw that people were streaming from all directions along the path to their house. Some of them were running around, scuffling and chasing each other, and others were hiding something in clenched fists. "They must have found gold too," her husband said. "Let's go outside and search with them. Perhaps gold has rained from the heavens instead of manna."

"We shall do no such thing," said Frau Shifra. But suddenly she thought of the apron, with the pieces of coal, and when she untied the knot she found a heap of gold glittering there. Her husband danced around the room and gave thanks, for never again would he have to worry about making a living.

Frau Shifra smiled but she remained silent. She knew that the gold on the path had fallen from her apron as she had returned from the river. And she thought of her niece Haminah with gratitude, and she recalled her promise not to reveal what had happened. So too did she keep that promise until the day she stood by the deathbed of Kalman, Haminah's father, and then she whispered the truth to him about his beloved daughter, so that he departed from this world with a smile on his face.

In the days that followed, the narrow lane outside Frau Shifra's house became known as Gold Lane, because of all the gold that had been found there. And from time to time a black cat would walk down it to sit outside the midwife's window. It was said that Frau Shifra always let it in so that it could hear all that was said inside. And the eyes of that cat were always melancholy, as if there were something it wanted to say. And there are those who insist that same cat can still be seen wandering the streets of Prague.

Eastern Europe: Nineteenth Century

SOURCES AND COMMENTARY

The kinds of Jewish tales of the supernatural collected here are a subgenre of Jewish folklore. They have been drawn from Hebrew, Yiddish, and German sources. The biblical account of the witch of Endor is probably the earliest such tale, and other tales are found as early as the first century, in texts such as *The Testament of Solomon* and *The Book of Tobit*. (See *The Apocrypha and Pseudepigrapha of the Old Testament*, edited by R. H. Charles and *The Old Testament Pseudepigrapha*, edited by James H. Charlesworth.) Several accounts with supernatural themes are also found in the Talmud, including "The Rabbi and the Witch," included here. Refer to the Bibliography for additional information concerning these and other books available in English and in English translation that are mentioned in these source notes. Full citations to the books mentioned in the following discussion (pp. 239–277) will be found in the notes to the Introduction and the stories.

The most frightening Jewish tales of the supernatural are found in *Sefer Hasidim*, a Hebrew text dating from the thirteenth century, which records the teachings of Judah the Pious and his followers, known as the Hasidim, or Pious Ones. (These Hasidim are not to be confused with the Hasidim of the eighteenth and nineteenth centuries, whose founder was the Baal Shem Tov.) The worldview of these Hasidim was bleak and oppressive, for it involved contending with swarms of demons and other evil spirits. Their tales tend to be short and their morals fiercely drawn. Among the tales from *Sefer Hasidim* found here are "The Haunted Violin," "The Knife," and "The Bleeding Tree."

One of the key sources for these supernatural tales is *Shivhei ha-Ari*, the legends of Rabbi Isaac Luria, known as the Ari, who lived in Safed in the sixteenth century. The circle of the Ari accepted mystical beliefs, including many of a supernatural nature about *dybbuks* and reincarnations. These beliefs are reflected in the tales of the Ari. Among those included are "The Punishment" and "The Finger." From later legends about the circle of the Ari comes "The House of Witches," which derives from Damascus, where the teachings of the Ari found a strong following.

Many supernatural tales, such as "The Speaking Head" and "The Chronicle of Ephraim," are found in the various Hebrew anthologies published in the eighteenth and nineteenth centuries. Most of these tales are of eastern European origin, and several can be found in one of the two primary modern Hebrew anthologies of medieval tales, Mordecai ben Yezekel's *Sefer ha-Maaysiot* (Tel Aviv: 1928) and M. J. Bin Gorion's *Mimekor Yisrael*. (2nd ed., Tel Aviv: 1966).

The supernatural tale, including ghost stories and tales of horror, seems to have been a more dominant genre in Yiddish folklore, and a proportionally large number of tales come from Yiddish sources. Best known of the medieval Yiddish collections is, of course, *The Maaseh Book*, from which two tales have been drawn ("Rabbi Samuel the Pious and the Magicians" and "The Dead Man's Accusation"). Far more obscure, but equally rich in material, is *Maaseh Nissim*, also from the sixteenth century, all tales of which are set in the city of Worms, the home of the scribe who recorded them, Jeptha Yozpa ben Naftali. These tales, like those in *Sefer Hasidim*, portray the helplessness of the virtuous faced with the powers of evil, a dark vision indeed. The tales from *Maaseh Nissim* include "The Queen of Sheba," "The Sorcerer and the Virgin" and "The Charm in the Dress."

One of the primary sources for the supernatural tales of the eighteenth and nineteenth centuries are the tales drawn from Hasidic texts, especially those told of the founder of Hasidism, the Baal Shem Tov and the tales told by his great-grandson, Rabbi Nachman of Bratslav. Tales about the Baal Shem include "The Werewolf," "The Beckoning of the Besht," "The Black Hand," and "A Combat in Magic." The tales of Rabbi Nachman include "The Perfect Saint," "The Tale of a Vow," and "A Tale of Delusion." Also from Hasidic sources is "The Dead Fiancée," one of the best ghost stories found in Jewish folklore.

One rich and relatively obscure source of these tales is the multivolumed anthology of the Jewish folktales of Prague called *Sippurim*. The first of these German-language volumes was published in Prague in 1847 by Wolf Pascheles and contains the earliest written folktales of Rabbi Judah Loew and the Golem. (Other tales about Rabbi Loew are found in the controversial text *Niflaot Maharal* by Rabbi Yudel Rosenberg [Piotrkow: 1909]. Rabbi Rosenberg claimed these stories dated from the sixteenth century, but most scholars insist they derive from the nineteenth century, although they may have been based on earlier oral sources.) Among the tales from *Sippurim* included here are "The Homunculus of Maimonides," "The Cause of the Plague," and "The Underwater Palace," as well as "The Kiss of Death," a variant of the famous twelfth-century tale *"Maaseh Yerushalmi."* (See "The Demon Princess" in Howard Schwartz, *Elijah's Violin & Other Jewish Fairy Tales*, pp. 107–117.)

A number of these tales have been drawn from oral sources. These include "The Wizard's Apprentice," collected by Y. L. Cahan, an early collector of Yiddish folktales, and "The Demon of the Waters," collected by Reuven ben Yakov Naana, an early collector of Jewish folktales in Palestine. Several of these tales have also been drawn from the abundant oral collection of the Israel Folktale Archives (IFA), formed by Professor Dov Noy of Jerusalem. (The vast majority of IFA tales—and all those referred to here—were recorded in Hebrew.) These include "The Beast," (Egypt); "The Demon's Wedding" (Turkey); "The Hair in the Milk" (Turkish Kurdistan); "Rabbi Shabazi and the Cruel Governor" (Yemen); "The Elusive Diamond" (Iraqi Kurdistan); and "The Bridegroom" (Rumania). In general these kinds of supernatural tales—linked to the genre of horror tales—are less common in the IFA than are the kinds of supernatural tales linked to the genre of fairy tales.

Two of the stories included are taken from medieval manuscript sources and are published here for the first time. These are "The Demon in the Tree" and "The Soul of Avyatar." Others, such as "Rabbi Joseph and the Sorcerer," have been published only in scholarly articles. Also previously unpublished are three of the stories from the IFA, "The Beast," "The Bridegroom," and "The Elusive Diamond."

All of these tales evoke a world dominated by the dark forces of the supernatural, and as such are a direct mirror of the popular beliefs and superstitions of the people. For further background information about these folk beliefs, see the Bibliography and, in particular, *Jewish Magic and Superstition* by Joshua Trachtenberg. Refer to the Index to trace a specific legend or legendary figure.

Most of the following tales have been categorized according to the Aarne-Thompson (AT) system, as found in *The Types of the Folktale* by Antti Aarne, translated and enlarged by Stith Thompson. Specific Jewish additions to these types are listed according to the type index of Heda Jason, found in *Fabula* and in *Types of Oral Tales in Israel: Part 2*. Reference to these tale types will be of use to those seeking both Jewish and non-Jewish variants of these tales included in this collection. References to the editor's previous collections of Jewish folktales, *Elijah's Violin & Other Jewish Fairy Tales* and *Miriam's Tambourine: Jewish Folktales from Around the World*, are abbreviated as *EV* and *MT,* respectively.

1. THE QUEEN OF SHEBA (Germany)

From *Maaseh Nissim* (Yiddish), compiled by Jeptha Yozpa ben Naftali (Amsterdam: 1696). A variant of "The Fisherman and His Wife" from *Grimm's Fairy Tales*. AT 555, AT 810.

In the oldest sources the Queen of Sheba is portrayed as a demonic witch and snatcher of children. In both Jewish and Arabic folklore Lilith is identified with the Queen of Sheba. This identification originates in the Targum to Job 1:15, where Lilith is said to have tortured Job in the guise of the Queen of Sheba. It is based on a Jewish and Arabic legend that the Queen of Sheba was actually a genie, half human and half demon. The riddles of the Queen of Sheba were said to be the same ones with which Lilith seduced Adam

(*Livnat ha-Sappir*, edited by Joseph Angelino, Jerusalem: 1913). In one Arab legend King Solomon suspects the Queen of Sheba of being Lilith. In the present tale the demoness plays a variant of the seductive role of Lilith, while calling herself the Queen of Sheba. And to the merchant, whose life she takes possession of, she does indeed embody an erotic fantasy. In later tradition the Queen of Sheba becomes identified with one particular demoness, who behaves, as one of the daughters of Lilith, in a seductive and destructive fashion, but establishes an identity of her own. Note that this is one of the few stories in which the Lilith-like figure demonstrates both mythic roles of the incarnation of lust and of the child-destroying witch: she strangles the children she had with the innkeeper as well as seducing him. The curiosity of the innkeeper's wife suggests the themes of both Pandora and Bluebeard. In this case, however, both man and wife are guilty of breaking the taboo: he by engaging in a secret tryst with a demoness; she by entering the locked room. A longer, more complex variant of this tale is found in "The Cellar," which dates from a century later. This tale, like "The Queen of Sheba," shows some of Lilith's disguises. For another example, see "The Other Side." See also "Helen of Troy" for additional legends about Lilith. For another fine example of a Lilith-type fantasy, see "The Woman in the Forest" (in *Nine Gates to the Hasidic Mysteries* by Jiri Langer, pp. 133–134), which recounts a folktale told by the Belz Hasidim. In this tale, another sexual fantasy, a pious rabbi encounters the hut of a demoness in the middle of a forest, and she seeks to seduce him, almost succeeding before his resistance breaks the illusion. A brief eastern European oral tale about the Queen of Sheba (IFA 7248, collected by Samuel Zanvel Pipe) describes her smoking a pipe and beckoning to children from the water. When the children approach her, curious about how the pipe can stay lit, she drags them into the depths. The magic circle in which the groom protects himself from a hoard of demons plays a similar role in "The Chronicle of Ephraim" p. 147 and protects the Baal Shem Tov from attacking beasts in "The Werewolf" p. 189 and "A Combat in Magic" p. 199.

2. THE BRIDE OF DEMONS (Germany)

From *Sefer Maaseh Nissim* (Hebrew), edited by Pinhas David Braverman (Jerusalem: 1966). AT 508.

One of the most common themes in Jewish folklore involves the angry curse "Go to the Devil!" It is always taken in some literal sense, as here, where the mother's angry words to her daughter are sufficient opening for Lilith to capture her as a bride for one of her demon sons. This superstition is the origin of the popular aphorism, "Don't open your mouth to the Devil." This theme is also used by Rabbi Nachman of Bratslav in his first tale, "The Lost Princess" (*EV*, pp. 210–218), casting light on his use of folk motifs in tales.

This theme is found as well in the tales of the monks, *Gesta Romanorum* #72. Note that "The Bride of Demons" is one of only a handful of tales in which Lilith and Asmodeus, who are reputed to be King and Queen of Demons, appear together. Another is "Helen of Troy." The roles of Asmodeus and the Devil are blurred here. But it often happens in Jewish lore that Samael, Satan, and Asmodeus are used interchangeably to refer to the Devil. There is a Palestinian tradition that unless a woman pronounces the names of God when she puts her wedding dress away in its chest, a demoness will take it out and wear it, attempting to seduce the woman's husband. (See Thompson, *Semitic Magic*, pp. 71–72.)

3. THE HOMUNCULUS OF MAIMONIDES (Eastern Europe)

From *Sippurim: eine Sammlung jüdischer sagen, Märchen und Geschichten für Volker-kunde* (German) (Wien, Austria and Leipzig: 1921). AT 922*D (Andrejev). Version of L. Weisel. First published in Prague, 1847.

The theme echoed here is that of the creation of the Golem by Rabbi Judah Loew, and like that tale this one derives from Prague. But although the Golem is created out of necessity, in order to protect the Jews of the ghetto from the dangers of the blood libel, the homunculus of Maimonides is created purely in order to discover the secrets of creation. (It has been suggested on several occasions that the Golem-cycle of legends may have inspired Mary Shelley's *Frankenstein*, since both concern the creation of a man, the Golem by kabbalistic magic and Frankenstein by science. If there was indeed a folk source that served to inspire Mary Shelley it may have been the present tale about Maimonides, which was first published at the same time as the earliest Golem legends, and which has a theme—and mood—far closer to that of *Frankenstein* than do the tales of the Golem. It would be difficult to demonstrate this conclusively, since *Frankenstein* was published in 1818 and *Sippurim*, the volume in which the present tale and earliest Golem legend appear, was not published until 1847. However, since all indications are that the stories in *Sippurim* are based on authentic folk sources, there is every reason to assume that an oral version of this tale about Maimonides was current at the time Mary Shelley wrote her famous novel— and probably a century or two before then.) The theme that such daring leads to disaster is common in tales with kabbalistic themes such as this. This theme goes all the way back to the famous talmudic tale about the four sages who entered Paradise (B. Hag. 14b)—Ben Azzai looked and died; Ben Zoma looked and lost his mind; Elisha ben Abuyah cut the shoots, that is, became an apostate; and only Rabbi Akiba "ascended and descended in peace." This tale has always been understood to refer to mystical contemplation and the dangers attending it. The moral is clear: if three of four of the greatest sages could not withstand the dangers of the mystical ascent, how could the average person? Therefore restrictions were made—no more than three at a time could discuss the chariot (*merkevah*) of Ezekiel, and no more than two could study the creation. In addition, kabbalistic study was forbidden until a man was married, forty years old, and ordained. This tale indicates that one of the dangers associated with this kind of mystical indulgence is the creation of a false messiah, as Maimonides fears that the man will become, once his gestation is complete, because he will be immortal. This suggests the theme of the hastening of the Messiah by various kabbalistic means, including the use of holy names and other methods. Such attempts have always been portrayed as forbidden and doomed to failure. For a famous example, see "Helen of Troy," p. 42, about the attempt of Rabbi Joseph della Reina to force the coming of the Messiah. The present folktale is of particular interest because of its apparent antagonism toward Maimonides, one of the most revered figures in Judaism. As such it must be considered to be a folk expression of the controversy that raged at several periods—including that from which this tale emerged—over the writings and teachings of Maimonides. For the background of this dispute, see *Maimonidean Criticism and the Maimonidean Controversy, 1180–1240*, by Daniel J. Silver. Folktales are not the usual mode of expression for such interreligious conflict, tracts, books, and fiery speeches being more commonly used. But long before the eighteenth century, Maimonides had become a figure of folk proportions not unlike the greatest sages, such as Rabbi Akiba or the Ari, and was the hero of many folktales. (For an example of a more typical tale about the Rambam, see "The Healing Waters" in *MT*, pp. 209–216.) Therefore it was not enough to resist his teachings in the usual ways, but to undermine his folk image as well. That seems to be the intention of this tale, which also fits into the pattern of many other cautionary anti-Kabbalistic warning tales. The anti-Kabbalistic elements may be part of the reaction against the false messiah Shabbatai Sevi in the same century. The lack of knowledge of the true teachings of both Maimonides and the Kabbalah is evident in the choice of the secret texts from which Maimonides is said to have learned his secrets. One of these, *The Book of Creation*, is the name of an actual kabbalistic text, *Sefer Yetzirah* (Hebrew—literally, "The Book of Formation" or "The Book of Creation") (New York: 1887), which is one of the earliest and most enigmatic kabbalistic works. It does not attempt to impart, however, secrets of the kind required to bring the slain assistant to life. Instead it concentrates on the mysteries of letters and numbers and is far more abstract and oblique. (See Phineas Mordell, *The Origin of Letters & Numerals According to the Sefer Yetzirah*.) Nor does the quotation from *The Book of Creation* quoted in the story appear in the actual text of *Sefer Yetzirah*. The combination of anti-Maimonidean and anti-Kabbalistic elements suggests that this tale emerged from the Jewish center of Poland–Lithuania, where the old quarrel broke out again in the late Middle Ages. At the same time, the present tale is itself a variant of other, positive folktales about the great medical skill and supernatural powers of Maimonides. In one of these tales, found in *Shalshelet ha-Kabbalah*, compiled by Gedalyiah ibn Yachiya (Zolkiew, Russia: 1801), Maimonides is forced to swallow poison in a confrontation with the king's physicians, but provides the antidote to save himself, while the king's physicians all die from the poison provided by Maimonides. In another such tale, an even closer variant to the one at hand, the Caliph has Maimonides beheaded, but before his execution Maimonides instructs his students in how to reattach his head, and he fully recovers, much to the consternation of the Caliph. It is not, after all, a giant step from the powers demonstrated in these tales to the creation of the immortal man in "The Homunculus of Maimonides." Note that the parallel theme to the creation of the Golem by the Maharal differs in the essential issue of the success or failure of the creation—the Golem fulfills its purpose, but the creation of Maimonides does not. As such this tale of the Rambam, no doubt a contemporary of the other, also adds a note of caution to those who found the mystical approach of the Maharal appealing as a way to resolve the problems of their time. It goes without saying that this tale has no historical kernel, nor is it characteristic of Maimonides in any way.

4. THE WIZARD'S APPRENTICE (Eastern Europe)

From *Yiddishe Folksmayses* (Yiddish), edited by Yehuda L. Cahan (Vilna: 1931). Told by Moshe Zimnick, heard from his grandfather in Belz. A Yiddish variant from Bessarabia is found in "Marchen und Schwanke," collected by Leo Wiener, in *Mitteilugen zur judischen Volksunde*, vol. 10, no. 2, (1902), pp. 104–107. An oral variant is IFA 426, collected by Hananya Vaaknin from David Elkhanan of Morocco. Another oral variant is IFA 6849, collected by Dov Noy from Isaac Auzon of Morocco. AT 325.

This is a variant of the famous tale of "The Sorcerer's Apprentice." This is one version popular among eastern European Jews, although the tale is found in many variants, especially the ending, with its series of transformations. This motif is found in many tales, including some Judezmo ballads. See "The Nightingale and the Dove" in *EV*, pp. 122–126. Another variant, with a richer Jewish context, is "The Chronicle of Ephraim," included here. When the boy in "The Wizard's Apprentice" turns himself into a ring that is found by a princess bathing in the river, it brings to mind the biblical account of how the infant Moses was pulled from the Nile by the daughter of Pharoah (Ex. 2:5–6). So too, the fact that the ring turns into a serpent when it falls to the floor echoes the contest of Moses and Aaron with Pharoah's magicians, when Aaron's staff was thrown down and became a serpent (Ex. 7:10). In this way Jewish elements are imprinted on these universal tales.

5. HELEN OF TROY (Palestine)

From *Iggeret Sod ha-Ge'ullah* (Hebrew), by Abraham ben Eliezer ha-Levi (Jerusalem: 1519). A later version is found in *Sippur Rabbi Yosef della Reina* (Hebrew) by Shlomo Navarro. A third version is found in *Eder ha-Yekar* (Hebrew) in *Samuel Abba Horodezky Jubilee Volume* (Tel Aviv: 1947), edited by Zalman Rubashov (Shazar), Yiddish version of Rabbi Leib ben Ozer Rosenkranz, based on the Hebrew version of Rabbi Shlomo Ayllon (Tel Aviv: 1946). AT 424*.

The seeds for this tale were planted in the Talmud. The talmudic tales of the four sages who entered Paradise (B. Hag. 14b) served as a warning against overarching ambition in attempting to discover the secrets of creation. Of the four rabbis who engaged in this kind of mystical contemplation, three were destroyed by it, and only Rabbi Akiba "returned in peace." There is another talmudic tale (B. Baba Mezia 85b) that establishes the pattern for the effort to hasten the coming of the Messiah by forcing the end:

> Elijah used to frequent Rabbi's academy. One day he failed to come. When they asked him why he delayed, he replied: "I had to wait until I awoke Abraham, washed his hands and he prayed; likewise for Isaac and Jacob." They asked: "But why not wake them together?" Elijah replied: "I feared that they might pray together and bring the Messiah before his time." "And is their like to be found in the world?" they asked. Elijah said: "There is Rabbi Hiyya and his sons." Thereupon Rabbi decreed a fast, and Rabbi Hiyya and his sons were called upon to read. As Rabbi Hiyya said *He causeth the wind to blow*, a wind began to blow; when he said *He causeth the rain to descend*, a heavy rain began to fall. When he was about to say *He quickeneth the dead*, the world trembled and in Heaven it was asked "Who hath revealed this secret?" "Elijah," they replied. Elijah was then brought forth and struck with sixty flaming lashes. Then he went forth disguised as a fiery bear and entered among them and scattered them from there.

This tale of Joseph della Reina builds on both of these models, creating the archetypal tale of the holy madman, or the holy man who becomes mad. Another key talmudic tale, that of the capture of Asmodeus, King of Demons, by King Solomon (B. Git. 67b), is also echoed in the account of the attempted capture of Asmodeus and Lilith, who were identified at this time as King and Queen of Demons. So too is the escape of the two demons paralleled by the ending of that same legend, in which Asmodeus throws King Solomon a great distance, after which the king is forced to become a beggar for many years, while Asmodeus, in disguise, rules in his place. (See "The Beggar King" in *EV*, pp. 59–66.) This story might be compared with the later "The Homunculus of Maimonides," p. 31. In both cases the undisputed holy men are tutored by Elijah, echoing the talmudic tale. The historic role of Maimonides is, however, intentionally distorted in the latter tale. See the note to "The Homunculus of Maimonides," p. 243. Traditionally Helen of Troy was linked with Lilith in Jewish folklore, as was the Queen of Sheba. Thus Joseph della

Reina returns to the arms of Lilith—the arms of death—at the end. According to a legend linked to Rabbi Isaac Luria of Safed, Joseph della Reina was reborn as a large black dog that frightened everyone with its barking. The Ari (as Isaac Luria was known) once confronted the dog, and it confessed its identity. The story emphasizes the punishment of Joseph della Reina for his sins. Thus Joseph della Reina becomes identified with that he once tried to subdue—the forces of evil, Lilith and Asmodeus, who likewise took the form of black dogs. For a version of this legend see Mordecai ben Yehezkel, *Sefer ha-Maaysiot* (Tel Aviv: 1918), vol. 6, #67. The Israeli writer Dan Tsalka has written an interesting adaptation of this legend, "The Terrible Tale of Joseph de la Reina." See Ezra Spicehandler and Curtis Arnson, *New Writing in Israel*, pp. 130–177. Other interesting retellings of this legend by the Israeli writers Yehoshua Bar-Yoseph ("The Fettered Messiah") and Asher Barash ("Rabbi Joseph Della Reina") can be found in Howard Schwartz, *Gates to the New City*, pp. 415–418 and pp. 408–414, respectively. It is possible to recognize a reference to the capture of Lilith and Asmodeus in this tale in the final stanza of Rabbi Isaac Luria's Sabbath hymn, "Askina Seudasa," dating from sixteenth-century Safed:

> Defeated and cast out,
> The powers of impurity,
> The menacing demons,
> Are now in chains.

6. THE PUNISHMENT (Palestine)

From *Shivhei ha-Ari* (Hebrew), compiled by Shlomo Meinsterl (Jerusalem: 1905). A variant of this tale is found in *Niflaot Maharal* (Hebrew) by Yudel Rosenberg (Piotrkow, Poland: 1909). AT 1313.

The wisdom of the Ari, Rabbi Isaac Luria, is demonstrated in this tale, along with his mastery of this world and the spirit world as well. He first recounts the man's past, then invokes the spirit of the servant with whom he had sinned. Finally, when the man has confessed and agreed to accept the fatal punishment—hot lead poured into his mouth—the Ari unexpectedly pours in honey. The moral is clear: the man's fear has forced him to repent; the potential for *teshuvah*, repentance, always exists, and if it is authentic, it will be accepted by God. This story reinterprets the law that adultery should be punished by death, applying it in an allegorical manner; that is, the primary intention of the Law was that the sinner should repent, and the man's fear and remorse before the sentence was carried out purified his soul and thus made his repentance complete. The motif of molten metal that must be drunk as a terrible punishment is also found in "The Devil's Fire," included here. In the latter tale, however, those souls being punished in

Gehenna are forced to drink molten gold and are not spared the punishment, as in this tale of the Ari. A variant of this tale concerns Rabbi Judah Loew of Prague. In this tale ("The Great Rabbi Loew and the Count," *Sippurim*, Prague: 1847, version of C. Ludwig Kapper) Rabbi Loew invokes the soul of an evil count's sister, with whom the count had sinned and then murdered, along with their child. The count, confronted with them, confesses and abandons a demand that Rabbi Loew teach him the secrets of Kabbalah. In both cases the soul is brought from the beyond to wrench the truth out of the sinners and, in the case of Rabbi Loew, to protect some ancient mystical secrets as well.

7.   THE FINGER (Palestine)

From *Shivhei ha-Ari* (Hebrew), compiled by Shlomo Meinsterl (Jerusalem: 1905). A variant is found in a sixteenth century Yiddish manuscript in Cambridge (Trinity College) Hebrew mss. 136 #5, "The Story of Worms." AT 365, AT 365B*.

This tale follows the pattern of the marriage with demon tales, except that it is a corpse rather than a demon that the young man inadvertently marries. The tale confirms the folk belief that the dead carry into the grave the unfulfilled longings of their life. In this case the dead woman had not experienced her "hour of joy," a reference to the joy of the bridegroom and bride. The unexpected reanimation of the corpse is an unusual motif, in that in virtually all other cases where one who has died is brought back to life, this is done with the power of the Name, which is usually inscribed on a piece of paper that is inserted into the mouth of the corpse, reviving it. (See "The Sorcerer and the Virgin" and "The Dead Man's Accusation," both included here.) "The Finger" most closely resembles "The Demon in the Tree," p. 104, a previously unpublished tale from an eastern European manuscript also dating from the sixteenth century.

8.   THE HOUSE OF WITCHES (Syria)

From *Sefer Maaseh Nissim* (Hebrew), edited by Pinhas David Braverman (Jerusalem: 1966). A variant of "The Witches of Ashkelon" from the Jerusalem Talmud, tractate Sanhedrin 6.9 and Haggigah 2.2. AT 334.

This oral tale is clearly intended to fit into the canon of tales about Rabbi Isaac Luria, known as the Ari, and his disciple Hayim Vital, such as those found in *Shivhei ha-Ari*. At the same time it is a retelling of the famous tale of "The Witches of Ashkelon," found in the Talmud (see *EV*, pp. 25–28). There the witches were tricked by Rabbi Shimon ben Sheeta, while here that role is played by Hayim Vital. The black dogs that the witches become recall the forms that Lilith and Asmodeus take in "Helen of Troy." This strong echo emphasizes the seminal importance of these tales, those of the Ari and of Joseph della Reina in particular, in the Jewish folklore of the region. *Shivhei ha-Ari* also includes a famous tale about a black dog who is the reincarnation of an evil man, and later lore identifies the dog as Joseph della Reina. (See the note to "Helen of Troy" for the legend of Joseph della Reina.)

9. THE BEAST (Egypt)

From IFA 2675, recorded by Z. M. Haimovitch from Shaul Ephraim. Previously unpublished. AT 934B, AT 934B*.

This is an Elijah tale and also an excellent example of how the folktale treats themes of horror. The theme of parents seeking unusual remedies to cure barrenness is a staple of all folklore, as is the notion that the child who is born out of such a cure may have some unusual destiny. Here that fate is to be devoured by a beast, and of course the prophecy is fulfilled. At the same time, however, the tale is one of sexual initiation, and the devouring understood, no doubt, as a sexual kind. The innocent bridegroom imagines his bride to be shy; when confronted with her bold desire, he is devoured with fear. A similar prophecy of future danger is found in "The Black Hand," included here, where, however, the warning is heeded, and the prophecy of doom avoided. See Haim Schwarzbaum, "The Hero Predestined to Die on His Wedding Day, AT 934B," *Folklore Research Center Studies* 4 (1974).

10. THE RABBI AND THE WITCH (Babylon)

From the Babylonian Talmud, tractate Sanhedrin 67b. AT 430.

This tale perfectly mirrors the ambivalent rabbinic attitude toward magic. Rabbi Jannai discerns that the woman who offers him the drink is a witch and turns the tables on her, causing her to turn into an ass. In this he demonstrates the defensive approach of the rabbis to magic, using it only to protect themselves when they are forced to do so. Later Rabbi Jannai rides the ass triumphantly in the street, where it is recognized by a fellow witch and turned back into a woman. Thus is Rabbi Jannai humiliated in public, where he is seen riding on a woman. This implies that because of his involvement in magic and his flaunting of his victory, he requires humiliation in order to be punished. Thus the story demonstrates both mastery of the supernatural and repugnance toward it at the same time.

11. THE DOOR TO GEHENNA (France)

From mss. Oxford Bodleiana OR 135, published in "Un Recueil de Contes Juifs Inedits" (Hebrew, with French translations) edited by Israel Levi, *Revue* *des Etudes Juives*, vol. 35 (Paris: 1897). (A variant of "Bluebeard.") AT 466**, AT 471A*.

This story reworks the theme of Eve plucking the forbidden fruit and bringing down disaster on herself. Note how little time passes between the sin and punishment, a theme that is found as well in the legends of the Fall. See B. Avot 5:9. Also echoed is the myth of Pandora, where the result of breaking the taboo provokes an immediate punishment, and the fairy tale "Bluebeard," in which the archetypal forbidden door is found. "The Door to Gehenna" thus becomes an emblem for all taboos, hinting at the punishment lurking behind every forbidden door. In the Talmud, Paradise and Gehenna are said to be as close as three finger breadths, implying that it is very easy to sin. Therefore the door to Gehenna confronts us at every turn. The descriptions of the tortures in Gehenna echo traditions found in the Talmud and Midrash. See *Hell in Jewish Literature*, by Samuel J. Fox, which collects these sources. The role of the husband in the tale is enigmatic—it is he, after all, who kept from her the true danger lurking behind the door, and it is the steward who goes on the difficult quest. But the steward can also be seen to represent him in the tale as an alter ego. Another visit to Gehenna is portrayed in "The Devil's Fire," the following tale. These two stories are distant variants, and the motif of the burning ring is found in both.

12. THE DEVIL'S FIRE (Eastern Europe)

From mss. Oxford Bodleiana OR 135, published in "Un Recueil de Contes Juifs Inedits" (Hebrew, with French translations) edited by Israel Levi, *Revue des Etudes Juives*, vol. 33 (Paris: 1896). Also published in *Ozar Midrashim* (Hebrew), edited by J. D. Eisenstein (New York: 1915). A variant is found in *Rosinkess mit Mandlen: Aus der Volksliterature der Ostjuden* (Yiddish), edited by Immanuel Olsvanger (Basel: 1931). Another variant is found in *Sippurim: eine Sammlung jüdischer sagen, Märchen und Geschichten für Volkerkunde* (German) (Prague: 1847). AT 466**, AT 471A*, AT 676.

In the rabbinic view Abraham's sacrifice of the ram in place of Isaac on Mount Moriah establishes for all time the end of human sacrifices, which were regularly practiced by the neighbors of Israel. (See Shalom Spiegel, *The Last Trial* and Hyam Maccoby, *The Sacred Executioner.*) Continuing this practice was, from the rabbinic standpoint, one of the worst possible sins. This story rebuts in a narrative fashion the lingering belief attributed to some pagan peoples that those who were sacrificed were rewarded in some fashion. It has something of the structure of a mystery, where the rabbi has, at first, nothing more to go on than his intuition that the one who returns after being sacrificed is not the one who has lost his or her life. His discovery of a diabolical plot is intended to debunk this belief in the strongest fashion. The role of the Devil in this tale draws upon more Christian elements than do most Jewish folktales concerning Satan or Samael, the more common names used for the Devil. The tortures of Gehenna are the traditional ones found in the aggadic literature. See *Hell in Jewish Literature* by Samuel J. Fox for additional background about Gehenna. The Talmud also mentions three entrances to Gehenna: "One in the wilderness, a second in the sea, and a third in Jerusalem" (B. Erub. 19a).

13. RABBI JOSEPH AND THE SORCERER (Germany)

From the commentary on the Bible by Rabbi Moses, the son of Rabbi Judah HaHasid, Ginzberg Hebrew manuscript 82, folio 78b, published in *Tarbiz XXX* (Tel Aviv: 1961) by Joseph Dan. AT 430.

This tale, discovered by Professor Joseph Dan of Hebrew University, is remarkable because it portrays Rabbi Joseph as a peerless Jewish sorcerer, although there is no other record or known tales of this rabbi. Most interesting of all is the method he uses to transport himself between cities, entering the Ark of the Torah and emerging in the distant city. It is rare to find magic, even in Jewish sources, brought into such close contact with the sacred Ark. The transformation by the evil sorcerer of the young girls into donkeys is far more conventional, and Rabbi Joseph's method of defeating him—causing the open window to close on his head—is also found in a tale about Rabbi Samuel the Pious in *The Maaseh Book* #174. The motif of transformation into donkeys is also found in the talmudic tale of "The Rabbi and the Witch," p. 66. Later legendary Jewish sorcerers, such as Rabbi Adam and Rabbi Judah Loew, exhibit equal confidence in their ability to defeat the powers of evil and also demonstrate such vast powers. The models for all such Jewish sorcerers are, of course, Moses, and, in particular, King Solomon, as he is portrayed not in the Bible, but in later Jewish folklore.

14. THE HAUNTED VIOLIN (Germany)

From *Sefer Hasidim* (Hebrew) attributed to Rabbi Judah the Pious, Parma edition, Hebrew manuscript de Rossi 33, published by Yehuda Wistynezki, #323 (Berlin: 1891). AT 1699*.

Those most likely to fall prey to the forces of evil were those who transgressed, thereby depriving themselves of the powers of good that guard and protect the righteous. By using a board of the coffin to make a violin, the carpenter was not showing proper respect to the departed soul, who thereby sought revenge. That the warning comes to him through dreams reflects the standard belief that spirits communicate in this way. The tale thus reinforces this belief, as well as the need to respect the dead. The Ashkenazi Hasidim, out of whom emerged the *Sefer Hasidim*, lived in a world in which demons and other evil beings surrounded them everywhere. These tales suggest a complete submergence in supernatural belief, almost to the point of obsession.

15. THE SORCERER AND THE VIRGIN (Germany)

From *Maaseh Nissim* (Yiddish), compiled by Jeptha Yozpa ben Naftali of Worms (Amsterdam: 1696). AT 990.

The theme of the dead man who is revived by the use of holy names is found both in *Megillat Ahimaaz* by Ahimaaz ben Pultiel (in *Medieval Jewish Chronicles*, edited by A. Neubauer, vol. II, pp. 111–132. Oxford: 1895) and in the tales about Rabbi Judah the Pious in *The Maaseh Book* #174. The magical requirement that is the basis of this tale from *Maaseh Nissim* is that the one who casts the spell must be the one who breaks it. Here the evil young sorcerer loses his life to a virgin he seeks to possess, after having cast the spell that put ten rabbis and the girl's father to sleep. This is the same type of spell as that cast by the angry witch in "Sleeping Beauty." There it was the prince's kiss that was the only thing that could break the spell. Here it is the sorcerer himself. It therefore becomes necessary to utilize the supernatural in order to bring him to life. Note that the power of the Name, which makes it possible for the young man to be temporarily restored to life, is used only out of desperation, as a last resort. Any other use of the Name is strictly forbidden. Many elements in this tale are found in Isaac Bashevis Singer's story "Taibele and Her Demon." See *The Collected Stories*, pp. 131–139.

16. THE KNIFE (Germany)

From *Sefer Hasidim* (Hebrew), attributed to Rabbi Judah the Pious, Parma edition, Hebrew manuscript de Rossi 33, published by Yehuda Wistynezki, no. 1456 (Berlin: 1891). AT 576, AT 910*M.

This bleak and frightening tale accurately reflects the state of mind of those most possessed by fears of the demonic and supernatural, which is represented more by the tales found in *Sefer Hasidim* than in any other Jewish text. The witch's practice of putting the knife beneath her pillow so that it would take effect in the next world was paralleled in the superstitious practice of parents who slept with a brick beneath their pillow, in order to make their child homesick. It is one more example of the kinds of magical practices carried out in order to force someone to do something against his or her will, or to cause something, usually evil, to happen to another. The moral of the tale seems to be that those who turn to this sorcery to achieve their own ends will soon enough become the victims of the same sorcery. As with most of the tales found in *Sefer Hasidim*, the moral is enforced with terror.

17. THE CHARM IN THE DRESS (Germany)

From *Maaseh Nissim* (Yiddish), compiled by Jeptha Yozpa ben Naftali of Worms (Amsterdam: 1696). The present version is based on a variant found in *Maaseh Tovim* (Hebrew), edited by Shlomo Bechor Chotzin (Bagdad: 1890), which is reprinted in *Sefer ha-Maaysiot* (Hebrew), edited by Mordecai Ben Yehezkel (Tel Aviv: 1929). AT 325**.

In the earliest version of this tale, found in *Maaseh Nissim* in the sixteenth century, the garment is a coat and the charm is a root. Also, the woman is unmarried. In the present version, from nineteenth-century Iraq, the garment has become a dress, the charm a paper, the woman married, and the time of the sin the eve of Yom Kippur. These last two details make the sin much worse, of course. Otherwise the narratives of the tales are very similar, and the later is clearly a direct variant of the earlier.

18. THE SCRIBE (Germany)

From *Be'urim*, 521 (Hebrew) by Rabbi Israel ben Pethahiah Isserlein (Venice: 1519). AT 813C.

Rabbi Isserlein, who died in 1460, offered this grotesque anecdote about the scribe who went back to work as soon as the Sabbath had ended to explain his own decision to refrain from work that night. To do so was to invite the forces of evil, who here accept the invitation, with awful consequences. The story also reflects the expectation that scribes would devote themselves to their writing only at the proper time and place and only under optimum conditions, such as after coming from a *mikveh*. To do otherwise was to pollute their sacred task. In fact, even the requirements for putting aside their work for the day are stringent: a scribe could not end the page he was writing with a phrase that was considered ominous. *Sefer Hasidim* #1464 gives the example of a man who left off studying with the phrase *And satyrs shall dance there* (Isa. 13:21) and woke to find a demon dancing in his chair. This anecdote is the likely source of the current tale, which applies it to a scribe rather than a scholar. Indeed, Rabbi Isserlein was deeply influenced by the teachings of *Sefer Hasidim* and often followed its rulings.

19. THE BLEEDING TREE (Germany)

From *Sefer Hasidim* (Hebrew), Parma edition, Hebrew manuscript de Rossi 33 no. 1462, published by Yehuda Wistynezki (Berlin: 1891). AT 1168B.

The theme of this tale is quite similar to that of "The Knife"—any dealings with the supernatural, intended or not, can bring about disastrous consequences. Here the woodcutter attempts to cut down an enchanted, bleeding tree and receives a terrible punishment. The moral of the tale seems to imply that any attempt to delve into the realm of the supernatural, even to repair any damage already done, is doomed to failure. Here the supernatural world is portrayed as completely evil and unforgiving, which is very much in character with the dark and brooding vision found in *Sefer Hasidim*. The tree itself is described in *Sefer Hasidim* as the place where *liliot*, the daughters of Lilith, gathered. This is probably a negative echo of the Canaanite (and early Jewish) practice of worshiping in a sacred grove, which is a symbol of paganism for the rabbis. For background to this tradition of tree worship, see *The Hebrew Goddess*, by Raphael Patai. The motif of the bleeding tree is also found in "The Door to Gehenna," included here.

20. THE DEMON IN THE TREE (Germany)

From a Yiddish sixteenth-century mss. in Cambridge (Trinity College) Hebrew mss. 136 #5, "The Story of Worms." Previously unpublished.

The theme of the bridegroom dying on the wedding night, slain by the demon Asmodeus, is found in the apocryphal *Book of Tobit*. In the present tale a demoness, who feels that the bridegroom is already wed to her, kills his brides until she is appeased. The primary theme of this tale, that of marriage with a demon, is a close variant of "The Finger," from Palestine in the same century. There the bride is a corpse, and here, and in the other variants of the tale (such as "The Cellar" and "The Other Side," both included here) she is a demoness. That two variants so close in theme would appear in countries so widely separated shows that there was sharing of folktales between eastern Europe and the Holy Land. In "The Finger" the wedding vow is witnessed by two friends; here the demoness is the only witness. Still, pronouncing the wedding vow on a wedding ring is sufficient to make the marriage legally binding.

21. RABBI SAMUEL THE PIOUS AND THE MAGICIANS (Germany)

From *Maaseh Buch* #160 (Yiddish), compiled by Jacob ben Abraham of Mezhirech (Basel: 1601). AT 730A*.

Duals between Jewish and Gentile sorcerers go back to the match between Moses and Pharoah's magicians and between Elijah and the priests of Baal on Mount Carmel (1 Kings 18). Such magical competitions and duels are one of the primary tale types found among Jewish medieval folktales, especially those from eastern Europe. In *The Maaseh Book*, the most influential collection of medieval Yiddish tales, there are a series of tales (numbers 158–183) about Rabbi Samuel the Pious and his son, Rabbi Judah the Pious, founders of the Hasidim, "pious ones," a twelfth-century movement in Germany whose worldview included a belief in demonic forces that was almost overwhelming. (See the stories included here from *Sefer Hasidim*, the central text of this group, attributed to Judah the Pious. These include "The Haunted Violin" and "The Knife.") By the sixteenth century Rabbi Samuel and Rabbi Judah had become legendary figures themselves, and the tales about them in *The Maaseh Book* constitute an independent text. This folk portrayal of Samuel the Pious and Judah the Pious demonstrates that they had become legendary figures by the sixteenth century. (See *Judah the Pious*, by Francine Prose, for a remarkable modern novel built around the legendary traditions concerning him.) The vivid description of the trance the magician goes into when his soul separates from his body to carry out Rabbi Judah's request is undoubtedly based on the observation of some similarly induced trancelike states, which were a part of supernatural lore of the period. Gershom Scholem has suggested that trances were a part of the early Jewish mystical sects who wrote the Hekhalot texts of the first to eighth centuries, such as *Hekhaloth Rabbati*, which describe journeys into Paradise. According to Scholem, certain contemplative exercises were used by the Jewish sects in order to enter a mystical state. So too is the magical circle invoked by the magicians a method of protection often used by Jewish sorcerers, such as Rabbi Adam and the Baal Shem Tov. See "The Black Monk and the Master of the Name" in *MT* pp. 335–348 and "The Werewolf" and "A Combat in Magic" here.

22. THE DEAD MAN'S ACCUSATION (Germany)

From *Maaseh Buch* #171 (Yiddish), compiled by Jacob ben Abraham of Mezhirech (Basel: 1601). Two oral variants of this tale are found in *Mi-dor Ledor* (Hebrew), edited by Zalman Baharav (Tel Aviv: 1968). One is IFA 3635, told by Yichya Nefesh of Yemen, collected by Zalman Baharav. The other is IFA 6451, told by Rabbi Zevulun Shoshana of Morocco, collected by Zalman Baharav. For another variant, see "The Sorcerer and the Virgin," p. 86. AT 730.

Here the power of God's Name performs the ultimate miracle, bringing a dead man to life. Note that the rabbi does so under dire circumstances—with a mob ready to pillage the Jewish quarter. Likewise, Rabbi Judah Loew creates the Golem—a creature made out of clay, also brought to life with the power of the Tetragrammaton—the secret name of God—only to save the Jews of Prague from the blood libel accusation, which inevitably resulted in pogroms. (An example of the misuse of the power of the Name is found in the eleventh-century Hebrew text *Megillat Ahimaaz* by Ahimaaz ben Paltiel, where a parchment with the Name is sewn into the arm of a corpse, who is restored to life until his true nature is discovered by one who notices how he avoids pronouncing God's name while praying and begins to suspect that he is not one of the living, because the dead are forbidden to pronounce God's name.) Rabbi Judah the Pious is one of the great figures of Jewish folk legend. Along with his father, Rabbi Samuel the Pious, he was the founder of the movement known as Hasidism, which flourished in Germany in the twelfth century, and is the reputed author of *Sefer Hasidim*. This is a remarkable and strange text, full of the fear of God and fear of the supernatural. Many of the tales in this collection are derived from it—short, terrifying anecdotes. See, for example, "The Haunted Violin," "The Knife," and "The Charm in the Dress." In these tales the most powerful magic also makes use of the Tetragrammaton, although the kind of folk superstitions well documented in Joshua Trachtenberg's *Jewish Magic and Superstition* flourished as well. Rabbi Samuel and Rabbi Judah the Pious are also the subjects of a long series of folktales, a text in itself, found in *Maaseh Buch*, the most prominent collection of Yiddish folktales. Here the two rabbis are the subjects in the kind of supernatural tales found in such abundance in *Sefer Hasidim*, which is certainly their primary model, although the Yiddish tales are far more polished and complete. One consistent theme that runs through supernatural Jewish lore is the desire of those restored to life after death to depart from life as soon as possible. This theme first appears when the prophet Samuel is brought forth from the dead by the Witch of Endor for King Saul to question. The angry prophet demands to know *"Why hast thou disquieted me, to bring me up?"* (1 Samuel 28:15). Note that the murdered man who is brought to life in this tale of Rabbi Judah the Pious is also anxious to return to the grave. Likewise, the dead man who has been kept alive by having the name sewn into his arm in *Megillat Ahimaaz* (by Ahimaaz ben Paltiel in *Medieval Jewish Chronicles*, edited by A. Neubauer, Vol. II, pp. 111–132. Oxford: 1895) describes living like a shadow, devoid of feeling, and is greatly relieved to return to the dead. There are, however, instances where this is not true, such as in "The Finger" (p. 55) where the corpse of a woman brought to life demands her "hour of joy" after death, since she felt she had been cheated out of it during her life. Also, the newly dead man in Rabbi Nachman's "The Tale of a Vow" (p. 208) is fully unaware that he is dead and therefore shows no desire for the grave. This gradually changes, as he realizes that this world is closed to him and there is no turning back.

23. MOCKING DEVILS (Rumania)

From *Menschen und Ideen* (German), by Manfred Reifer (Tel Aviv: 1952). A Yiddish variant from Slobodka is found in *Mitteilugen zur judischen Volkskunde*, vol. 10, no. 2, 1902, "Märchen und Schwanke," collected by Leo Wiener. Another variant is found in *Ha-kamea ha-Kodosh*, (Hebrew) IFA 874, collected by Rachel Seri, edited by Aliza Shenhar (Haifa: 1968). AT 830A.

Reifer suggests that this is typical of the tales told to each other by wagoners, who congregated at night at the inns in the towns to which they delivered goods. These stories were then retold in other towns, and in this way they fulfilled a function that previously, in medieval times, had been filled by bards. Such stories are similar to the sea stories told among sailors, such as the fantastic tales of Rabbi bar bar Hannah. (See "A Voyage to the Ends of the Earth" in *MT*, pp. 23–34.) There are, in addition, many other tales that involve travel by wagon. Among them is the talmudic tale "The Rabbi and the Witch," and the Hasidic tale "A Combat in Magic," both included here, and the first tale told by Rabbi Nachman of Bratslav, "The Lost Princess," found in *EV* pp. 210–218. In the variant found in *Mitteilugen zur judischen Volkskunde*, a man going to town to shop for the Sabbath had to pass through a forest, and there saw something lying in the road—a huge sheep. He struggled to lift it and with great effort managed to place it on the wagon. Then, as he turned to go, the sheep burst out laughing, clapped its hooves, and fled. The oral variant collected by Rachel Seri is about a man who finds a goat who speaks. When he throws it on the floor, it turns to flame and the man realizes it wasn't a goat but a demon. The demons in these tales seem to intend to frighten rather than harm; one of this type was called a *lantukh*, a sprite or hobgoblin. See "Lantukh, a Jewish Hobgoblin," by Max Weinreich, in *YIVO Annual of Jewish Social Science*. See also "The Lantukh" in *Stories for Children* by I. B. Singer, pp. 231–236.

24. THE DEMONS' WEDDING (Turkey)

From *Edoth* (Hebrew), vol. 2, (1947), pp. 283–284, collected by Menachem Azuz from Yitzhak Azuz of Gallipoli. Another variant is found in the same issue of *Edoth*, p. 285, told by Moshe Hai Nechama of Jerusalem. A third variant, from the Balkans, is found in the Max Grunwald Archives of Hebrew University Folklore Research Center #25. See *Tales, Songs & Folkways of Sephardic Jews*, by Max Grunwald.

The popularity of this tale is demonstrated by the number of variants in which it exists. The tale itself is a compendium of beliefs and superstitions concerning demons. The underlying principle is that demons prefer whatever is forbidden to people, and thus, because no Jewish marriages are permitted between Passover and Shavuot, the demons have made this period the time of their weddings. This belief led to the subsequent assumption that the demons would select a house in which to perform these weddings and drive the owners out until all the demon weddings had taken place. This closely parallels the theme of the haunted house, except that here it is demons rather than ghosts who are doing the haunting, and it is only for a limited period. Although there is no doubt that the demons are driving the people out of their home, they do not harm them unless they resist. Also, they reward them afterward for the use of their home. This portrait of the demons makes them seem far less threatening than, for example, those found in medieval German Jewish folklore. Even the description of the wedding celebration has an element of good humor to it, with the demons whirling and cavorting.

And because the people leave when the demons order them to, and the demons leave the house in good condition, no damage is ultimately done.

25. THE HAIR IN THE MILK (Turkish Kurdistan)

From *Shishim Sippure Am* (Hebrew), edited by Zalman Baharav (Haifa: 1964). IFA 4563, collected by Zalman Baharav from Yakov Chaprak. AT 1168.

This tale is a virtual compendium of customs connected with Lilith's role as a child-destroying witch. Lilith is described as having long black hair in the Talmud (B. Erubin 100b). Finding a hair in food or drink was regarded as a sign of bad luck; here it heralds the arrival of Lilith herself. Lilith has the ability to transform herself into any shape she desires. That is how she is able to be fully present in just a single hair. The midwife, knowing this from tradition, captures her in the jug and thus gains power over her. The importance of a perfect *mezzuzah* at every door to protect against demons is emphasized, as is the need for an amulet against Lilith to be hung above the child's bed. The forced confession of Lilith or other demons is a common theme in many folktales, which is found first in *The Testament of Solomon*. The theme of capturing a witch and seeing only her head echoes the tale found in the Jerusalem Talmud (Sanh. 7:25d) about how Rabbi Hanania pulled a witch's head from flax that he had magically grown on a table. See "Rabbi Joshua and the Witch" in *MT*, pp. 35–38. There is also an echo of the tales of demons caught in a bottle, including a variant about Asmodeus, King of Demons (IFA 107, Yemen, collected by Heda Yazoh from Yeffet Shvili). This is, of course, the primary way that genies are found in *The Arabian Nights*. "The Hair in the Milk" is one of the few tales it is possible to identify as a woman's tale. (Note the wisdom, strength, and confidence of the midwife, who refuses to be intimidated by Lilith—the way men have been for so many centuries.) Although women are as prevalent as men among the tellers whose tales are collected by the Israel Folktale Archives, most tales seem to represent a male perspective. Of course there were tales that were told exclusively among women, which reinforce their strengths and self-image. One such tale is that about the midwife who goes to the land of the demons to deliver a child, a variant of which is found in "The Underwater Palace," included here, and also exists in dozens of variants collected by the IFA. This is another such tale. See "Is There a Jewish Folk Religion," by Dov Noy, in *Studies in Jewish Folklore*, edited by Frank Talmage.

26. THE SOUL OF AVYATAR (Persia)

From Hebrew manuscript Codex Gaster 66, number 11, in John Rylands University Library of Manchester. Previously unpublished. AT 314.

This is a remarkable manuscript, as it documents one of the few Jewish folktales to employ the theme of the *dybbuk* in which a human is transformed into an animal, here a horse. Demonic possession among Jews, well documented in Gedalya Nigal's *Sippure Dibbuk* (Hebrew) (Jerusalem: 1983), almost always takes the form of an evil soul of one dead entering into a living person and taking possession of him or her. There are also some variations on this, such as "The Exorcism of Witches from a Boy's Body," included here. Such human transformation into other life forms, animate and inanimate, is speculated about in Kabbalah and is one of the tenets of *Gilgul*, the Jewish concept of reincarnation. Although such transformations in Jewish folklore are usually brought about by magic, there are also tales where this is the result of reincarnation, as in this case. Another such tale is found in *Shevhei he-Ari*, where a man is reborn as a black dog. (See the note to "Helen of Troy," p. 245.) By way of a modern parallel, see Bernard Malamud's story "Talking Horse," in *Rembrandt's Hat*. Previously Malamud had published another folktale-like story, "The Jewbird," in *Idiots First*, in which a Jew is transformed into a crow. The tortures of the evil soul by the avenging angels are discussed in detail in this tale of Avyatar, and in this it more closely resembles the model of the *dybbuk* tale found in *Shivhei ha-Ari* from Safed in the sixteenth century, or in *The Maaseh Book* from eastern Europe in the same century. Because this tale derives from Persia, it is evident that the theme of the *dybbuk* was a dominant motif in Jewish folklore throughout the world at that time.

27. RABBI SHABAZI AND THE CRUEL GOVERNOR (Yemen)

From *Hadre Teman* (Hebrew), edited by Nissim Binyamin Gamlieli (Tel Aviv: 1978). IFA 12099, collected by Nissim Binyamin Gamlieli from Shlomo Ben Yakov. AT 730A.

Rabbi Shalem Shabazi was a great Yemenite poet who is the subject of many Yemenite legends. Here he shows the confidence and decisiveness of a great sorcerer, enchanting three soldiers who come to take him to the governor, and then causing three stories of the government building to sink into the ground. In the face of such powers the governor quickly retreats from the evil decrees he had intended to sign. This theme of a rabbi-sorcerer who defends the Jewish populace is found in a great many Jewish tales from all sources. These tales date back to the midrashic legends about the child Abraham defeating the evil king Nimrod and are a dominant theme in the late medieval period in the tales about Rabbi Adam, Rabbi Judah Loew, and the Baal Shem Tov. See "The King's Dream" in *EV*, pp. 197–202, and "The Black Monk and the Master of the Name" in *MT*, pp. 335–348. In the latter the magical use of the peg is also found.

28. THE ELUSIVE DIAMOND (Iraqi Kurdistan)

IFA 8821, collected by Moshe Bort from Mordechai Asher. Previously unpublished. AT 810.

This is a warning tale, intended to affirm the custom among Kurdish Jews prohibiting women who have newly given birth from leaving home for a period of forty days. (For additional background on Kurdish-Jewish customs and lore, see Yona Sabar's *The Folk Literature of the Kurdistani Jews: An Anthology*.) This prohibition derives from beliefs about the dangers faced by both newborn infants and their mothers from demons, especially Lilith and her daughters, who seek to harm them in the periods preceding and following birth. The demons desire to punish, in particular, those women who give birth to sons. According to this tradition, these demons seek to harm boys before the eighth day (that of the *bris*, or circumcision) and girls before the twentieth (or, some say, the thirtieth) day. The most dangerous period comes on the last night before the demons must relinquish their power over the infant, which is the origin of the custom of the Watch Night, in which a father would be joined by others who stayed up all night, guarding a newborn boy on the night before the *bris*. (No such night was observed for female infants, because no similar ritual was performed.) It is not hard to understand how this widely perceived danger (based, no doubt, on widespread infant mortality) was also believed to face the mother of the newborn child. Women often died in childbirth, and in any case required a period of recovery following a birth. The choice of the number *forty* seems obvious, with its regular occurrence in the biblical narrative of the length of the flood, the number of years the Israelites wandered in the wilderness, and so on. Such a custom also reinforced the mother's need to devote all of her time and energy to her newborn child. Finally, demons and spirits were believed to congregate near bodies of water (see "The Demon of the Waters" here) and the most dangerous time was believed to be on the eve of the Sabbath, when demons are free from torturing the evil souls in Gehenna and flock around the world seeking to harm humans (see "The Other Side" and "The Scribe"). One of the purposes of all of these stories, of course, is to reaffirm the injunction and warning against going to the wrong place at the wrong time. And much of the power of the demons portrayed in them comes from their ability to create illusions, which their unfortunate victims believe are real. The theme of illusions created by demonic forces is found in Rabbi Nachman's "A Tale of Delusion," p. 211, where a horse appears and disappears, taunting a man obsessed with it. Here the vision of the glowing diamond also induces a virtual obsession, exactly as the unknown demon has intended. In this sense the story accurately describes the irrational state produced by obsession and thus has the kind of psychological accuracy as that found in "The Demon of the Waters." Note that this folktale is a variant of "The Treasure," a tale of I. L. Peretz (*The Case Against the Wind*), in which a man sees a flame before him while walking on the Sabbath, which tries to tempt him to go beyond the distance one is permitted to walk on the Sabbath. The theme of an elusive glowing object and the setting on the Sabbath in both tales suggests that the Peretz story is based on a folktale, probably of eastern European origin, as are many of his tales, and that variants of that tale were told in Jewish communities as far flung as Kurdistan.

29. LILITH'S CAVE (Tunisia)

From *Le Bestiaire du Ghetto: Folklore Tunisian* (French), edited by J. Vehel and Ryvel (Raphael Levy) (Tunis: 1934). AT 1168A.

The haunted house is a universal folk motif, but in most Jewish tales the haunting is done by demons rather than ghosts. See "The Cellar" for a variant tale. The legend of Lilith first finds full expression in *Alpha-Beta de Ben Sira*, by M. Steinschneider (Berlin: 1868), also from North Africa, dating from around the eleventh century. That the mirror should serve to attract demons is not surprising, considering its appeal to vanity, the strange quality of duplication it confers, and the sense of another world. The possession of the girl by a daughter of Lilith is an example of demonic, rather than *dybbuk*, possession. (A *dybbuk* is the soul of one dead who enters the body of one living.) The earliest examples of demonic possession are found in Josephus (*Antiquities* 8:2.5) and the Talmud (B. Meilah 17b). The theme of the power of the curse is a familiar one in Jewish folklore. ("The Bride of Demons" and Rabbi Nachman's "The Lost Princess" [found in *EV* pp. 210–218] also demonstrate its power.) In the present tale the girl's transformation into a bat fits into a long line of human transformations into various animals found in Jewish folklore. (For the closest parallel in this collection, see "The Beast.") The girl's transformation into a bat is a variant on the theme of those who become birds until they are disenchanted. (See "The Princess on the Glass Mountain" in *EV*, pp. 155–161.) Whether the girl in the present tale will ever be restored to her human form is unclear. The story hints that she will remain a bat as long as her father lives, for that is how long the shame will live in his heart. But once he dies, it is implied, she will become human again. On the other hand, he may carry the shame with him into the grave. Why does the father's curse come true? One tradition holds that at times the Gates of Heaven swing open and all words spoken at that time have the seal of truth imprinted on them, and every blessing and every curse comes true. This custom is identified with the whole day of Yom Kippur and with midnight on the holiday of Shavuot, when the sky is said to open. See "A Tale of Three Wishes" in *Stories for Children* by I. B. Singer, pp. 8–14 for a tale of such a midnight wish.

30. THE BRIDEGROOM (Rumania)

IFA 7424. Collected by Marianna Yoster from her grandmother. Previously unpublished. A variant is IFA 1047, collected by Issachar ben Ami from Lola Yamina of Morocco. AT 1476B.

When the possessive father refuses all suitors, his daughter ends up being wed to the Angel of Death. The moral is obvious—if an important decision such as who to wed is delayed too long, the matter will be taken out of our hands. Tales about fathers seeking the perfect bride or groom for their children are legion, and inevitably relate the disaster that occurs because of their insistence on finding perfection. This is the theme in "The Demon Prince," from *The Maaseh Book* (#179), in which a father ends up marrying his daughter to a demon, and in "The Speaking Head," where the boy ends up being kidnapped by a demon. An even closer variant of this tale is the Karaite tale "The Curse" in *Meagadot Hakarim* (Hebrew), edited by Reuven Fahn (Vienna, no date), where it is the daughter, rather than the father, who cannot make up her mind. In the end she loses her chance to wed—a dire necessity among Karaites, who are faced with extinction—provoking a curse from her father that turns her into a Medusa-like figure with snakes for hair, neither dead nor alive. In the Moroccan variant of this tale, the daughter of the sultan is as beautiful as the sun. She gives impossible conditions to all her suitors, who all fail. Then a demon comes who fulfills the conditions and marries her. She discovers the truth and escapes, but he catches up with her and brings her back. In the end he releases her and tells the king he deceived them in order to teach her a lesson, and right after this she marries a prince who wants her.

31. THE DEAD FIANCÉE (Eastern Europe)

From *Kehal Hasidim* (Hebrew), compiled by Aharon Valden (Warsaw: no date). Also found in *'Adat Tzaddikim* (Hebrew), compiled by M. L. Frumkin (Lemberg, Russia: 1877). A variant, concerning the rabbi of Belz instead of the rabbi of Lublin, is found in *Petirat Rabbenu ha-Kadosh mi-Belz* (Hebrew) (Lemberg: 1894). AT 370A, AT 512B. This story has also been attributed to the Maggid of Kosnitz. But in all versions it is the Seer of Lublin who plays the prophetic role.

The ultimate purpose of this tale was to demonstrate the remarkable wisdom of Rabbi Yaakov Yitzkak of Lublin, known as the Seer of Lublin, in perceiving that the man's failure to have children stems from his broken engagement and in sending him to the fair to meet the ghost of his dead fiancée. Attributing such knowledge of the past and future to various Hasidic *rebbes* is in keeping with the pattern established by the Baal Shem Tov. The theme of a broken vow causing barrenness is found in the famous medieval

Jewish folktale of "The Weasel and the Well" (B. Ket. 62b, also *The Maaseh Book* #73). Here a young man saves a maiden who has fallen into a well, and they fall in love and vow to be wed. They call upon a passing weasel to witness their vow. When the young man marries another instead, the weasel comes and kills each of his children, until he discovers the cause of his misfortune and seeks forgiveness from the spurned maiden, who has always refused to marry any other because of her vow to him. In a more general sense, "The Dead Fiancée" is one of many Jewish tales that turns on the issue of a vow. These vows fall into two categories: those that are honored, which inevitably results in great rewards, and those that are ignored, which always provokes misfortune.

32.   THE KISS OF DEATH (Eastern Europe)

From *Sippurim: Prager Sammlung jüdischer Legenden in neuer Auswahl und Bearbeitung* (German) (Wien, Austria and Leipzig: 1921). First published in Prague, 1921. A variant of *Maaseh Yerushalmi* (Hebrew) edited by Yehuda L. Zlotnik (Jerusalem: 1946). An oral variant of this tale is IFA 8129. Collected by Lili David from Rachel ha-Rambam of Persia. AT 424S*, AT 470*.

This tale is a variant of the famous twelfth-century tale "Maaseh Yehrushalmi," ("The Tale of Jerusalemite"), retold as "The Demon Princess" in *EV*, pp. 107–117. Although this version follows that older tale fairly closely, there are some interesting differences. The emphasis on the oath in the former tale is deemphasized here, replaced with a greater focus on the narrative flow. Also, the daughter of Asmodeus here is half-human and half-demon, unlike the princess in the former tale, who is entirely a demoness. Note that the verdict of the rabbinic court is reversed here, ruling against the demon princess. The reference to the peddler's father having visited the land on the other side of the sea is a virtual acknowledgment that the tale is retelling the earlier version and that the tales are linked—as are father and son. But unlike the original, the princess in this tale is isolated and lonely, suggesting another famous tale, "The Princess in the Tower" (*EV*, pp. 47–52), in which the daughter of King Solomon is sent to a remote island to live after a prophecy is made that she will marry a poor man. A giant eagle drops the poor man on the balcony of the tower she lives in, and in that way they are united, much as happens in this tale, except that here the eagle is a griffin. It would seem, then, that two classic Jewish folktales have been combined into one in this tale. The oral variant from Persia concerns a shepherd who meets the daughter of Asmodeus and is forced to marry her. Once a month he is permitted to return to his family to give them money. Curious to know what has happened to him, his wife and mother follow him, discover the truth, and expel him from the house after learning that he has had three children with the demoness. When he returns to the daughter of Asmodeus, she has left with his demon offspring. He cries and sings her songs, but she doesn't come back to him until he is near death. This follows the tradition that Lilith brings a man's demon children to his deathbed, where they too mourn over him. This variant has a strong echo of "The Queen of Sheba," p. 22, where the man receives money from the demoness until his wife discovers their secret; then the demoness vanishes, taking back all that she has given. The notion of a kiss of death is found as early as the Talmud (B. Ber. 8a). See "Concerning the Nature of the Motif 'Death by a Kiss' (Mot. A 185.6.11.)" by Aliza Shenhar in *Fabula* 19.

33. SUMMONING THE PATRIARCHS (Eastern Europe)

From *Sippurim: Prager Sammlung jüdischer Legenden in neuer Auswahl und Bearbeitung* (German) (Wien, Austria and Leipzig: 1921). Version of L. Weisel. First published in Prague, 1847. AT 470*.

Numerous tales concerning Rabbi Judah Loew of Prague are to be found. The most famous of these tales concerns the creation of the Golem, the man made out of clay, with which Rabbi Loew was said to have protected the Jewish community of Prague from a series of blood libels. But there are many other tales recounting the marvels of the Maharal, as Rabbi Loew was known. Many of these concern his use of powers deriving from his knowledge of the Jewish mystical tradition, known as Kabbalah. Only the purest and most eminent sages were considered capable of engaging in kabbalistic studies, and a great many stories are told of those who lost their sanity or even their lives by undertaking such studies without the proper background or preparation. Here the king is saved from destruction only because the pious Rabbi Loew is able to prevent the ceiling from collapsing. The magic of being able to invoke the presence of the patriarchs reflects the midrashic principle that the past is alive and that all generations exist at the same time. The collapsing of the room in which the vision of the patriarchs takes place echoes the famous talmudic legend of Rabbi Eliezer ben Hycranos and other rabbis, who disagreed about a point of the Law:

> Rabbi Eliezer used every possible argument to support his opinion, but it was not accepted by the other sages. Then he said: "Let this carob tree prove that the Law is as I state it is." The carob tree then uprooted itself and moved a distance of one hundred ells. But the sages said: "The carob tree proves nothing." Then Rabbi Eliezer said: "Let the waters of the spring prove that I am right." Then the waters began to flow backward. But again the sages said that this proved nothing. Then Rabbi Eliezer spoke again and said: "Let the walls of the house of study prove that I am right." And the walls were about to collapse when Rabbi Yehoshua said to them: "If scholars are discussing the Law, why should you interfere?" Thus they did not fall, in deference to Rabbi Yehoshua, but neither did they straighten out, out of

respect for Rabbi Eliezer, and they are inclined to this day. Rabbi Eliezer then said: "If the Law is as I say, let heaven prove it." Thereupon a heavenly voice came forth and said: "Why do you quarrel with Rabbi Eliezer, whose opinion should prevail everywhere?" Rabbi Yehoshua then stood up and said: *"The Law is not in heaven"* (Deut. 30:12). "What does that mean?" asked Rabbi Yermiyahu. "It means that since the Torah was given to us on Mount Sinai, we no longer require a heavenly voice to reach a decision, since it is written in the Torah: *"Follow after the majority"* (Ex. 23:2). Later Rabbi Nathan encountered Elijah and asked him, "What did the Holy One, blessed be He, do at that time?" And Elijah replied: "He smiled and said: 'My children have overruled Me, My children have overruled Me!' " (B. Bab. Met. 59b)

Another, probably earlier, version of the summoning of a patriarch is found in *Maaseh Nissim*. This describes how Rabbi Lezer, a master of the Name, who lived in Worms, invoked King David's General Joab. Joab turned out to be of such great size that every step he took caused the house to shake and terrified the young men who observed the invocation, so they begged the rabbi to make him disappear, which he did. So frivolous was this use of the Ineffable Name, that in the version recounted in "Summoning the Patriarchs" it is the emperor who makes the demand, rather than the young Jewish students.

34. THE CAUSE OF THE PLAGUE (Eastern Europe)

From *Sippurim: Prager Sammlung jüdischer Legenden in neuer Auswahl und Bearbeitung* (German) (Wien, Austria and Leipzig: 1921). Version of L. Weisel. First published in Prague, 1847. AT *730A.

In this tale the Maharal uses his spiritual powers to discover the cause of a terrible plague that is affecting the children. Because it is the children who are affected, it is from the spirit of a child that Rabbi Loew learns the cause of the plague. This sets the stage for the magical combat between Rabbi Loew and the sorcerer responsible for the plague, although in this case Rabbi Loew catches him unaware and turns the evil sorcerer's own spell against himself.

35. THE SPEAKING HEAD (Eastern Europe)

From *Noraot Anshe Maaseh* (Hebrew) (Warsaw: no date) and *Pe'er Mi-kedoshim*. (Lemberg, Russia: 1864). A variant is found in *Der Golem: Jüdischer Märchen und Legenden aus dem alten Prag*, edited by Eduard Petiška, a German translation of *Golem a jiné židovské pověsti a pohadky ze staré Prahy* (Czech) (Wiesbaden: 1972). Another variant is found in *Hadre Temen* (Hebrew), edited by Nissim Binyamin Gamlieli (Tel Aviv: 1978). AT 1160.

The theme of the speaking head might, at first, appear to be a variant of that of the Golem, the man of clay brought to life by Rabbi Judah Loew. And indeed this is the legendary tale of the childhood trauma of Rabbi Loew's son-in-law. Joseph Dan, however, identifies this theme with a midrash found in *Midrash Tanhuma* (edited by Solomon Buber, 1885. Reprint, New York: 1946, 2 volumes) dating from around the eighth century, which explains that the reason Rachel stole the *teraphim*, the family idols, from Laben, her father, was because the idols could be made to speak by the use of holy names and would therefore have revealed where she had gone. (See "Teraphim: From Popular Belief to a Folktale" by Joseph Dan in *Scripta Hierosolymitana*.) The visit from the grave of Mordecai's grandfather to Rabbi Loew is typical of the grateful dead motif in Jewish folklore, where a person sees that another receives a proper burial and is later saved in some supernatural fashion by the spirit of the deceased. It is interesting to note that a tale on a similar theme as this one is found in The Arabian Nights (see the Richard F. Burton translation, *The Book of the Thousand Nights and a Night*, vol. I, "The Tale of the Wazir and the Sage Durban," p. 69):

> "Among my books I have one, the rarest of rarities, which I would present to thee as an offering: keep it as a treasure in thy treasury." "And what is this book?" asked the King, and the Sage answered, "Things beyond compt; and the least of secrets is that if, directly after thou hast cut off my head, thou open three leaves and read three lines of the page to thy left hand, my head shall speak and answer every question thou deignest to ask of it." The King wondered with exceeding wonder and shaking with delight at the novelty, said, "O physician, dost thou really tell me that when I cut off thy head it will speak to me?" He replied, "Yes, O King!"

Since some of the tales in the Arabian Nights are as old as the seventh century, and the midrashic source for this tale, *Midrash Tanhuma*, dates from around the eighth century, it is possible that this was a widely known folk motif in the Middle East during that period. Note also the parallel themes found in "The Homunculus of Maimonides," p. 29. The plotline of the first part of "The Speaking Head," concerning the betrothal to a wealthy stranger from a distant land, is a variant of that found in "The Demon Bridegroom," story #179 from *The Maaseh Book*, published in the sixteenth century. Here a father demands an excessive dowry for his daughter, as well as an equally noble lineage. The demon, disguised as a noble, persuades the father to give him the daughter as a wife. After the wedding he insists on taking her back to his kingdom at once. They are accompanied by friends of the family until they reach the gates of his city—the very gates of hell. The unfortunate bride is forced to go with him, while the others return to the father to inform him of her terrible fate. It is interesting to note that this same essential plot is found in the story "Schalken the Painter" by Sheridan Le Fanu, published in 1839, which is widely regarded as one of the earliest, if not the first, supernatural work of fiction. (See *Lost Souls: A Collection of English Ghost Stories* edited by Jack Sullivan, pp. 1–3 and pp. 14–33). As such "The Demon Bridegroom" might be one of the missing links between folklore and fiction. It is widely recognized that anonymous folktales eventually evolved into more self-conscious works of fiction, composed by a single author, but this is the rare case where it is possible to find the folktale—or at least a variant of it—that may well have served as the inspiration for such an early and important fictional tale of the supernatural as "Schalken the Painter."

36. THE CHRONICLE OF EPHRAIM (Eastern Europe)

From *Sippure Kedoshim* (Hebrew) (Leipzig: 1866). AT 938*-*A.

Although it is not immediately apparent, this tale is a variant on the theme of the sorcerer's apprentice, and thus is a variant of "The Wizard's Apprentice," p. 35. This link is disguised by the legendary nature of this tale, which establishes the miraculous birth and childhood of Rabbi Shlomo Ephraim ben Aaron of Lunshitz (Lenczycza) Poland, who succeeded Rabbi Judah Loew as the chief rabbi of Prague. Just as there are legends connected with Rabbi Loew, so is his successor the subject of such legends, which link him to Noah, Joseph, and Moses. The light cast from the newborn child recalls the *midrash* about the birth of Noah (*Drashot al ha-Torah*, by Joshua ibn Shu'aib, Crakow: 1573, reprinted in Jerusalem, 1969). The pit into which he is thrown suggests the pit into which Joseph was cast by his brothers (Gen. 37:24). Also echoed is the *midrash* in which Moses is left in a pit for ten years by the father of Zippora, during which time he is secretly fed by her (*Sefer Zichronot* 46:9). Zippora's father, like the duke in this tale, is astonished when he discovers that his prisoner is still alive. And in both cases this discovery leads to a release from the pit. Thus this story reworks biblical and midrashic elements from several sources and uses them within the framework of the sorcerer's apprentice. This demonstrates the remarkable extent to which Jewish folklore is built on the traditions preceding it. The motif of the magic circle in this story is a popular one, found as well in "The Bride of Demons" and "A Combat in Magic," both included here. A modern retelling of this legend, "In the Evening," not associated with Rabbi Shlomo Ephraim of Luntshitz, is found in *Whither? and Other Stories* by the Hebrew writer Mordecai Ze'ev Feierberg pp. 81–105. See Israel Bettan's *Studies in Jewish Preaching*, chapter 7, for more information on Rabbi Shlomo Ephraim. The mysterious instrument Shlomo Ephraim plays appears to be the legendary *magreifah*, a ten-holed instrument said to exist in the days of the Temple, which could play a thousand notes (Mishnah Tamid 3:8; 5:6). See "The Prince and the Slave" in *MT*, pp. 299–314, where the *magreifah* is also found. For another tale of parents separated from their son for many years see "A Plague of Ravens" in *MT*, pp. 8–14.

37. RABBI LOEW AND THE ANGEL OF DEATH (Czechoslovakia)

From *Die Legenden der Juden*, edited by J. Bergmann (Berlin: 1919) and *Die Wundermanner im Judischen Volk*, edited by J. Gunzig (Berlin: 1921). AT 1199B.

The most famous tale of an encounter with the Angel of Death is that of King David, found in the Talmud. Here David learns that he is fated to die on a Sabbath. Knowing that the Angel of Death is forbidden to snatch a man while he is studying, David spends every Sabbath immersed in study. In frustration the Angel of Death creates a ruse by shaking a tree outside his study, and when David goes out to investigate, the angel snatches his life (B. Shab 30a–b). A common theme found in folklore is that of the snake hidden in a rose, who bites the one who picks it. Such a theme is found in "The Princess and the Rose" in the medieval collection *Sefer Shaashuim*, edited by Israel Davidson (New York: 1914). Another key legend of an encounter with the Angel of Death is found in the pseudepigraphal text *The Testament of Abraham*. Here the Angel of Death disguises himself as a young man of mild appearance, but reveals his true appearance when Abraham demands it. The description of its terrible face is one of the most horrible to be found anywhere. It is such a face that overwhelms the father and mother in "The Bridegroom and the Angel of Death," in *Hibur ha-Maasiyot ve-Midrashot ve ha-Aggadot* (Hebrew) (Venice: 1551), wherein the next of kin of the bridegroom all offer to take his place to spare him being snatched by the Angel of Death—until the moment of truth, when all back away, except for the bride, who so impresses God with her willingness to die that both bride and bridegroom are spared. Two legendary versions of the death of Rabbi Loew have been combined in this tale, that of his snatching the list of victims from the Angel of Death and that of the angel hidden in the rose. The former theme originates in a famous talmudic legend about Rabbi Joshua and the Angel of Death, wherein Rabbi Joshua snatches the angel's sword, preventing him from fulfilling his duties (B. Ket. 77b). A major, as yet unpublished, study of the legends of the Angel of Death was completed by Haim Schwarzbaum shortly before his death.

38. THE OTHER SIDE (Eastern Europe)

From *Tsefunot ve-Aggadot* (Hebrew), Micha Joseph Bin Gorion (Berditchevsky) (Tel Aviv: 1957). AT 424*, AT 470*.

The injunction to refrain from going to the *mikveh* or swimming of any kind on the fourth night or the night of the Sabbath derives from a statement in the Talmud, tractate Pesahim 112B: "One should not go out alone on the fourth night of the week or on the night of the Sabbath. And if he does, his blood is on his own head, because of the danger. What is the danger? An evil spirit." This evil spirit is identified as Agrat bat Mahalath, who controls eighteen myriads (180,000) malicious spirits. Agrat, who is also described as the Queen of Demons, is generally identified as Lilith, in her most dangerous manifestation. This injunction against going out naturally applied even more to swimming, because demons were believed to proliferate in large bodies of water. Of great interest in this tale is the concept of the demonic double. Although it is not stated explicitly, the tale suggests that the man who emerges from the river at the same time as the betrothed man does is his demonic double. The place he leads the betrothed man to is thus the *Yenne Velt*, the Other World, the world of spirits and demons, where he meets his demonic bride. She was destined to be his, just as was his human fiancée, and here the demons intercede to force the man to consummate his marriage with the demon bride. This is a late variant of *Maaseh Yerushalmi*, edited by Y. L. Zlotnik (Jerusalem: 1946), from the twelfth century, and follows the pattern of that tale in the calling of the rabbinic court as well.

39.   THE CELLAR (Eastern Europe)

From *Kav ha-Yashar* (Hebrew), by Tsvi Hirsh Kaidanover (Frankfurt: 1903). Also found in *Ma'assiyot me-Tzaddik Yesode 'Olam* (Hebrew) (Podgaitsy, Russia: 1903) and *Mora-im Gedolim* (Hebrew), compiled by Y. S. Farhi (Warsaw: 1909). The first episode is found in the Bodleian Library, Oxford Hebrew mss. Oppenheim 540 (no. 1567 in Neubauer's *Catalogue of the Hebrew Manuscripts in the Bodleian Library*). It is attributed to Judah the Pious, who died in 1217. Joseph Dan dates it around 1210 and identifies this tale as a variant of that found in *Maaseh Yerushalmi* (Hebrew), edited by Yehuda L. Zlotnik (Jerusalem: 1946). See "The Demon Princess" in *EV*, pp. 107–117, for a version of this tale. AT 424S*, AT 470*.

All men are susceptible to the powerful attraction of female demons. According to the kabbalistic interpretation, even the patriarch Abraham had demonic offspring. The prooftext for this exegesis is found in Genesis 25:6: *To the sons of the concubines that he had taken, Abraham gave gifts. Then, while he was still alive, he sent them to the country of the East, away from his son Isaac.* The concubines in this reading are, of course, demons. (See Gershom Scholem, *On the Kabbalah and Its Symbolism*, pp. 153–157.) "The Cellar" is an elaborate embellishment of the theme of marriage with demons, which provides the history of how the man came to be forced to marry the demon, how their life together was carried on, and the history of the house and the cellar in which the demons lived after his death. Joseph Dan identifies this tale as one of the many variants of the earlier tale "Maaseh Yerushalmi," a late version of which is included here as "The Kiss of Death." What these variants primarily have in common is the theme of marriage with demons. Apart from that, however, there are two basic tale types: one that follows the pattern of "The Demon Princess" in which a traveler ends up in the Kingdom of the Demons and is forced to marry the daughter of the King of Demons in order to save his life, and the pattern of the present tale, in which a man ends up married to a demoness who lives in his own house. Thus the closest variant and likely source is "The Queen of Sheba," from the sixteenth century, p. 22, and "The Queen of Sheba" itself is likely to have been inspired by "The Demon Princess." The source for "The Demon Princess" is probably the brief legend about the man seduced by a demoness on Yom Kippur noted on p. 9 in the Introduction. Thus is the pattern established in which one brief tale gives birth to a more embellished version, which itself inspires a whole host of variants. The power of the demoness over the goldsmith is linked to the enslavement of the Israelites in Egypt when he leaves the *Seder* to join her in the cellar. Thus her power over him is not only a physical enslavement, but a psychological one as well. As in virtually all the variants of this tale, the issue of the rights of the demons versus the humans is resolved by a rabbinic court. In his retelling of this tale, "The House of Demons," Martin Buber reverses the verdict of the original tale, ruling in favor of the demons. See Martin Buber, *Tales of Angels, Spirits and Demons*, pp. 24–34.

40. THE WEREWOLF (Eastern Europe)

From *Shivhei ha-Besht* (Hebrew), by Rabbi Dov Baer ben Samuel, edited by Samuel A. Horodezky (Berlin: 1922). AT 810, AT 1162*.

This is probably the most famous story of the young Baal Shem Tov, demonstrating his faith, wisdom, supernatural abilities, and courage all in one tale. The only other well-known werewolf tale in Jewish lore is "The Rabbi Who Became a Werewolf," from *The Maaseh Book* #228. One unusual aspect of the present tale is that it involves a double transformation: An evil spirit takes possession of a sinful woodcutter, making him into an evil sorcerer. He then transforms himself into the werewolf, who attacks the children led by the Baal Shem Tov because their singing is so pure that Satan fears that it might hasten the coming of the Messiah. This theme is one of the most prominent in Hasidic literature. Basically, there are two ways to hasten the coming of the Messiah: one is to use kabbalistic formulas and holy names to force the Messiah to come (as portrayed in "Helen of Troy"), and the other is to bring the Messiah by a faith so strong that the Messiah would be beckoned and could not resist the call. This tale is in the latter category. Satan's fear that the singing of the children might induce the Messiah to come establishes that the soul of the Baal Shem Tov, even as a young man, was so holy that it was a worthy adversary to Satan and could even shake the heavens.

41. THE BECKONING OF THE BESHT (Eastern Europe)

From *Sippurim Noarim* (Hebrew), edited by Yakov Kudnir (Lemberg, Russia:

1875). One variant is found in *Adat Tzaddikim* (Hebrew), edited by M. L. Frumkin (Lemberg, Russia: 1877). Another variant is found in *Otsar ha-Maasiyot* (Hebrew), edited by Reuven ben Yakov Naana (Jerusalem: 1961). AT 1168A.

The supernatural powers of the Baal Shem Tov are recounted here. In this tale the use of magic seems to suggest hypnosis in the way the Baal Shem puts the evil Bishop in a trance the moment he sees him. Later the Bishop is unable to find his image in the mirror, another effect that could be explained by hypnotism. The explanation given by the Baal Shem is occult: he has snatched away the soul of the Bishop and replaced it with the wandering spirit of a righteous Jew. This explains the sudden transformation of the personality of the Bishop, who soon expresses a desire to convert to Judaism. Both of the possible explanations of this tale—either that the Baal Shem hypnotized the Bishop and created illusions for him, which frightened him into changing his ways, or else that a supernatural exchange of souls actually did take place—are firmly in the rabbinic tradition. The former follows the talmudic dictum that the use of illusion is not forbidden and is therefore acceptable (B. Sanh. 67b), and the latter mirrors the kabbalistic perspective that where there is intense activity between the spirit world and this one, something like an exchange of souls would not be impossible. This indicates how the Hasidic doctrine drew upon both the talmudic and kabbalistic sources and even, as in this tale, wove them together. See "Rabbi Samuel the Pious and the Magicians," p. 107, in which the soul of a foreign priest is conjured from his body and Rabbi Samuel prevents its reentry until the other priests acknowledge his superior power.

42.   THE BLACK HAND (Eastern Europe)

From *Shivhei ha-Besht* (Hebrew), by Rabbi Dov Baer ben Samuel, edited by Samuel A. Horodezky (Berlin: 1922). AT 506*, AT 934B-*A.

Here the Baal Shem Tov demonstrates his ability to foresee the future. He not only knows that a man will have a son, but that on a day far in the future the son will drown if allowed to reach the river. So too does the Baal Shem give the father a sign to remind him that the day has arrived: his son will put two socks on the same foot. Thus when the time of the prophecy arrives, the father is able to save his son by preventing him from reaching the river. There a black hand is said to have been seen that day searching for its victim. This tale defines the Hasidic view of fate as both predestined and mutable. Such a belief was necessary to the assumption that although the time of the coming of the Messiah was preordained, it was also possible to hasten his coming. The supernatural motif in this tale personifies death in an unusual fashion; here some kind of monstrous sea creature functions as the

Angel of Death. Tales about the Angel of Death being turned back are often found in Hasidic sources, but because the Angel of Death is not associated with the sea, another creature has replaced it in the tale. Another tale of a predestined birth, in this case predicted by Elijah the Prophet, is "The Beast," p. 63, wherein, however, the unfortunate fate is not avoided as it is here. The parallel to "The Beast" and similar tales involving Elijah also serves to link the Baal Shem Tov to Elijah, the dominant figure of Jewish folklore, as both are portrayed as having the power to foresee the future.

43. A COMBAT IN MAGIC (Eastern Europe)

From 'Adat Tzaddikim (Hebrew), compiled by M. L. Frumkin (Lemberg, Russia: 1877). An oral variant, which does not involve the Baal Shem Tov, is found in Sheva' Havilot Zahav (Hebrew), collected in Yiddish by Dvora Fus, from her parents, Kalman and Esther Lipkind, translated into Hebrew by Israel Rosenthal, edited and annotated by Otto Schnitzler (Haifa: 1969). IFA 3071. A variant concerning Rabbi Yoel Baal Shem, involving an evil midwife who takes the form of a cat, is found in Ayzik-Meyer Dik, Alte Yidische Zagen Oden Sipurim, (Yiddish) (Vilna: 1876). AT 922, AT **747A (Hansen), AT **748A (Hansen), AT 1168.

This tale type, that of the rabbi-sorcerer engaged in magical combat with an evil wizard, is found in many variants in Jewish lore. The earliest such combat is that of Moses and the magicians of Pharoah. In the medieval period such tales often involve Rabbi Adam, who is drawn into magical combat with various opponents. See "The Magic Mirror of Rabbi Adam," in EV, pp. 187–196. The most famous such story recounts how a Jewish wizard from beyond the River Sambatyon defeated the terrible Black Monk. See "The Black Monk and the Master of the Name," in MT, pp. 335–348. Note that there is a strong element of illusion in the combat, with the flaming animals of the wizard vanishing when they reach the enchanted circle the Baal Shem has drawn. The Baal Shem demonstrates similar illusionary powers in "The Beckoning of the Besht." The first part of the present tale tells of the Watch Night, the night before the circumcision, when a child was believed to be in danger from Lilith, who would try to strangle it. Lilith was believed to come as a black cat, the same form taken by the evil sorcerer. In Sefer Hasidim, #465, a witch is described as turning herself into a cat. There it is said that if such a cat receives a blow from someone, the witch will die unless she manages to get bread and salt from the one who struck her. This, then, can be seen as a Lilith-type tale that has been recast in the context of a magical combat between sorcerers. Such shifting of one tale type to another and the combining of tale types is characteristic of folklore in general and Jewish folklore in particular.

44.   THE PERFECT SAINT (Eastern Europe)

From *Sippure Maasiyot* (Hebrew), by Rabbi Nachman of Bratslav (Ostrog, Russia: 1816). AT 839A*.

Rabbi Nachman of Bratslav tended to see sexual desire as the temptation of the *Yetzer Hara*, the Evil Impulse. At the same time, not even the greatest talmudic sages could overcome lust, as recounted in several parallel tales, such as one in which Rabbi Akiba sees a naked woman in a tree and climbs up after her. When he is halfway there, the woman turns into Satan, who says: "Were it not that it is said in Heaven to respect Rabbi Akiba and his teachings, your life would have come to naught" (B. Kid. 81a). A parallel legend is told about Rabbi Meir, who glimpsed a naked woman on the other side of a river, jumped in, and proceeded across, getting halfway there before she turned into Satan, repeating the same warning given to Rabbi Akiba (B. Kid. 80a). Because Rabbi Nachman's tales usually have a strong personal dimension, this tale seems to indicate an awareness that sexual desire cannot be escaped and may have been intended as a subtle confession that he himself may have engaged in a misguided attempt to do so. See I. L. Peretz, "The Hermit and the Bear," in *Selected Stories* by I. L. Peretz, pp. 34–39, which has a similar theme that may have been inspired by Rabbi Nachman's tale.

45.   THE TALE OF A VOW (Eastern Europe)

From *Sippurim Niflaim*, compiled by Samuel Horowitz (Jerusalem: 1935). A tale of Rabbi Nachman of Bratslav. AT 470.

The fate of the soul after death was of great interest to Rabbi Nachman of Bratslav, who told this tale. In another tale, "The Synagogue in Jerusalem," he describes a living rabbi interceding for the soul of one who has come before the heavenly court. (*Sippure Maasiyot Hadashim* [Hebrew], Warsaw: 1909):

> In Jerusalem there is a synagogue to which are brought all the dead in the world. No sooner does a man's soul depart than he is brought there at once. And there, in that House of Prayer, it is decided where he shall be buried. How does that *Beit Din* decide? According to the clothing that a man wears. If he arrives in a garment that is white and pure and perfect in every way, they give him the most honored place. But if the sash is missing, or one sleeve of the garment is soiled, or worse, missing, each is treated accordingly, based on laws handed down long ago.
>
> And what if a man is naked? In that case all hope is lost, and he will be left outside the boundary of the blessed.
>
> So it was that one day the body of a naked man was carried into the synagogue. The judges looked askance and were about to sentence him to be taken beyond the boundary when a living man arrived, the Tzaddik of his generation. And the Tzaddik took one look at the naked body and took off one of his own garments and covered his nakedness. And when the judges of the *Beit Din* saw this,

they were amazed, and one of them said: "Why do you give him something that belongs to you? Do you want him to be saved by something that does not belong to him?" The Tzaddik replied: "Does not the high minister send his slave ahead of him to prepare for his arrival? This man must go to the same destination to which I will go, and therefore I have the right to dress him in a garment of my own." And in this way the Tzaddik saved the dead man from a terrible fate and redeemed him.

Rabbi Nachman asked to be buried in the town of Uman, where there had been a massacre in the seventeenth century, because he felt that many of the souls of those murdered still hovered there, waiting to be guided to the next world. All of Rabbi Nachman's tales have a strong moral dimension, and this is no exception, as it emphasizes the inviolability of vows. Here two friends vow that the spirit of the one who dies first will visit the other while he is still alive. Because the first to die does not fulfill this vow, his spirit is condemned to wander, and he finds no rest. Only when he finally returns to the grandson of the man to whom he made the vow and reveals all that has happened since his death does his wandering come to an end. The dream-like quality of the story may indicate that it was originally a dream of Rabbi Nachman's. See "Bratslav Dreams" in *Fiction 7*, nos. 1 and 2, 1983, translated by Arthur Green. The failure to fulfill vows is a common theme in Jewish folklore, but the true intention of the tale is to reveal something about the conditions of the spirit after death. This includes a lack of awareness of being dead, at first, and the illusion of continued contact with the world. This portrayal of a wandering soul is completely in keeping with the views presented in the *Zohar*, the primary text of the Kabbalah, and in strongly kabbalistic tales, such as those found in *Shivhei ha-Ari*, about Rabbi Isaac Luria. For a modern story on the same theme as this tale of Rabbi Nachman, see "The Wanderer and the Blind Man," by Yehuda Yaari in *Firstfruits: A Harvest of 25 Years of Israeli Writing*, edited by James A. Michener, pp. 211–239.

46. A TALE OF DELUSION (Eastern Europe)

From *Sippure Maasiyot* (Hebrew) by Rabbi Nachman of Bratslav, edited by Rabbi Nathan Sternhartz of Nimirov (Ostrog, Russia: 1816). AT 810.

This tale clearly seems to have an allergorical intent; it is a portrayal of the ways in which a person will run after a delusion and let it dominate his or her life. Rabbi Nachman said about this tale: "The Other Side constantly deceives a person for no reason. The person is tempted and pursues the temptation. Each time it becomes more important in his eyes, and he desires it all the more. He continues to pursue it until it suddenly vanishes, and everything he desires is taken away from him" (*Sippure Maasiyot*). An oral variant of this tale is found in the Israel Folktale Archives, IFA 7684, collected by David ben Yair from his father, Yakov Yair of Morocco. In this version Satan actually takes the form of the horse, in order to reward a man who has refused to curse him and to punish his enemy, a smith. The smith sells all of his property in order to purchase the horse, losing it in a fashion similar to that in the present tale. In addition, he is blamed when the water of the reservoir becomes polluted and is punished by the king. It is likely that the tale of Rabbi Nachman stands behind this variant, which adds the detail that Satan has taken the form of the horse; Satan merely manipulates the illusion of the horse in Rabbi Nachman's version of the tale.

47. THE BRIDEGROOM WHO VANISHED (Eastern Europe)

From *Hiyo Haya Maseh* (Hebrew), edited by H. B. Ilan-Bernik. (Tel Aviv: 1945).

This is a warning tale about the dangers faced by bridegrooms on the day of the wedding. According to tradition, the groom is supposed to remain isolated and guarded against danger on the day of the wedding. Here the others are preoccupied and do not notice when he wanders outside, where he is met by the spirit of his dead friend (or possibly a demonic figure so disguised in order to lure him away—this latter reading would seem more appropriate). Joining his friend for a few hours, lost in the complexity of their talmudic debate, the time flies and one hundred and thirty years have passed when he finally returns. In providing such a warning, this tale reinforces the restrictive limits on a bridegroom. In fact, one can well imagine that this tale was told to such bridegrooms while waiting for the ceremony to begin, as a way of warning them not to take any risks in that dangerous time. Why is that time particularly dangerous? Because the jealousy of the demons is said to be at its peak at such times. Other tales, such as "The Other Side," p. 173, which reinforces the warning not to go to the river on certain nights of the week, suggest that the jealousy comes in particular from the bride's demonic double, who is about to lose for all time the chance to marry the groom. (See "The Elusive Diamond" for another example of a warning tale that affirms a custom, in this case the Kurdish dictum that women who have given birth must not leave home for forty days.) A secondary reading can also be found in the present tale, a subtle jibe at the excessive withdrawal of certain talmudic students from the world in their attempts to totally immerse themselves in the Torah. This tale closely echoes the famous talmudic tale about Honi (B. Ta'anit 23), who is said to have slept seventy years. (Indeed, this same tale is the likely inspiration of Washington Irving's tale of "Rip Van Winkle." See Irving's *The Sketch Book of Geoffrey Creyon, Gent.*) In the case of Honi, he sees an old man planting a carob tree, which takes seventy years before it bears fruit. Honi make an impudent comment about how the man will not live to see its fruit, and shortly afterward he falls asleep nearby and wakes up seventy years later. Then the first thing he sees is a full-grown carob tree, bearing fruit. He learns from those nearby that the grandson of the man who had planted the tree lives there, and thus discovers that he has slept for seventy years. Such talmudic motifs are often reworked in later Jewish folktales and Hasidic lore. The moral drawn may change, however, as in this case, where Honi is guilty of impudence toward an old man, and the bridegroom has opened himself to danger from demons. It does seem likely that this folktale was of Hasidic origin, for in the nineteenth century such supernatural themes are more often linked to the theme of the primacy of the study of the Torah in Hasidic lore. A variant, set in the time of the Temple, is found in *Stories from the Rabbis* by Abram S. Isaacs, pp. 202–211 (New York: 1928). Here the bridegroom sleeps seventy years (instead of one hundred and thirty) and awakens after the destruction of the Temple.

48. THE EXORCISM OF WITCHES FROM A BOY'S BODY (Eastern Europe)

From *Tsafnat Paaneh* (Hebrew), by Rabbi Eliyahu Gutmacher (Brody: 1875). AT 1168.

This tale, like most of the Jewish accounts of possession, is presented as true. What is unusual is that the possession recounted here is by four witches rather than by a single *dybbuk*. In all other respects, however, the tale follows the established pattern of *dybbuk* tales, including the nature of the exorcism and the escape of the witches through the boy's little finger. The key difference is that here the witches are substituted for the *dybbuk*, and it is unclear if they are dead (i.e., spirits) or alive. The use of Psalm 91 to exorcise the witches is traditional, in that this is considered the anti-demonic psalm, and was recited on many occasions to protect against the threat of demonic forces. The psalm was recited, for example, at funerals, where it was believed to protect the human offspring from the demonic ones. Like "The Door to Gehenna," p. 68, this tale is also a variant on the theme of Pandora.

49. THE DEMON OF THE WATERS (Eastern Europe)

From *Otsar ha-Maasiyot* (Hebrew), edited by Reuven ben Yakov Naana (Jerusalem: 1961). AT 926A, AT 1476B.

This tale was collected orally in Israel from Russian immigrants. The precise details about the names of those involved and the details of place suggest that it is based on an actual incident in which a woman fell into a river from the broken stairway of a *mikveh*, the ritual bath. The shock of this fall likely caused her to lose her mind, leading those around her to conclude that she was no longer the same person and that her place had been taken by a water demon. If these assumptions are correct, then this tale might be regarded as something of a missing link between folklore and psychology, because of the insight it provides into the formation of such a tale and the ways in which mental illness was interpreted in the times before it was understood. Note that the woman's daughter attempts to convince her father that the true cause of the personality transformation was his usurping the mill, which indicates that the fall in the *mikveh* might have been preceded by extreme stress because of this situation and that the combination of the two might well have resulted in the kind of dissolution of personality described in this tale.

50. THE UNDERWATER PALACE (Eastern Europe)

From *Der Golem: Jüdischer Märchen und Legenden aus dem alten Prag* (German), edited by Eduard Petiska, a German translation of *Golem a jiné židovske pověsti a pohádky ze staré Prahy* (Czech) (Wiesbaden: 1972). An oral variant about a drowning man who is saved by the Queen of the Sea is IFA 8831, collected by Ronit Bronstein from Moni Tivoni of Egypt. There are many oral variants of the episode of the midwife, including IFA 8140 from Bukara and IFA 8902 from Morocco. A variant on the theme of a maiden and a demon in a palace beneath the sea is IFA 6057, collected by Zalman Barahav from David Hadad of Libya. In this oral tale, however, the demon is portrayed in completely negative terms. AT 476*-*A, AT 496.

The present tale combines two basic tale types found in Jewish lore. One type is marriage with demons. The other type is a tale in which a *mohel* or midwife is called upon to go to the land of the demons to perform a circumcision or deliver a child. See *Kav ha-Yashar* (Hebrew) by Tsvi Hirsh Kaidanover. (Frankfurt: 1903). The latter type of tale, involving a midwife, is one of the most popular collected from various Middle Eastern sources and exists in dozens of variants in the IFA. The theme of marriage with demons is also found in many variants (see the Introduction, pp. 8–11). To the best of the editor's knowledge, this is the only Jewish tale in which these two tale types have been combined. It is also interesting to observe the tone of this tale, which is upbeat. Most tales of marriage with demons conclude on a disastrous note, but the demonic husband here does not seem threatening and the human wife seems happy, if somewhat lonely, living in the palace beneath the sea. The theme of a palace beneath the sea is a common one in Jewish folklore. See "The Palace Beneath the Sea" in *MT*, pp. 315–334. Leviathan, the King of the Deep, is supposed to live in such a palace. See *The Alphabet of Ben Sira* (Hebrew), edited by M. Steinschneider (Berlin: 1858). All of the midwife tales have an element of a test in them—if the midwife can resist eating anything or accepting any gifts while in the land of the demons, she will be permitted to leave; if she accepts anything, she will be forced to stay. In all of the variants of this tale, the midwife is warned of the fact that accepting anything would force her to remain there. (This test echoes the theme of the Greek myth of Persephone, who is forced to remain in the underworld six months because she ate six pomegranate seeds.) Thus these midwife tales have elements of fear and danger while the midwife remains in the land of the demons, but once she emerges there is an inevitable reward, in which something of little value, such as garlic or coal, is transformed into gold, as happens here. For an important discussion of the midwife theme in this tale, see "Is There a Jewish Folk Religion" by Dov Noy in *Studies in Jewish Folklore*, edited by Frank Talmage.

BIBLIOGRAPHY

The following is a selected bibliography of books and articles in English and in English translation relevant to the theme of the supernatural in Jewish lore. For references from other languages, see the notes to the individual stories, pp. 239–278.

Aarne, Antti, and Stith Thompson, eds. *The Types of the Folktale*. Helsinki: 1961.

Abrahams, Israel. *Jewish Life in the Middle Ages*. New York: 1975.

Agnon, S. Y. *Twenty-one Stories*. New York: 1970.

Ansky, S. *The Dybbuk*. Los Angeles: 1974.

Ausbel, Nathan, ed. *A Treasury of Jewish Folklore*. New York: 1948.

Bamberger, Bernard J. *Fallen Angels*. Philadelphia: 1952.

Barash, Asher, ed. *A Golden Treasury of Jewish Tales*. Tel Aviv: 1965.

Baron, Salo, W. "Medieval Folklore and Jewish Fate." *Jewish Heritage* vol. 6, no. 4 (1964): 13–18.

Bazak, Joseph. *Judaism and Psychical Phenomena*. New York: 1967.

Ben-Ami, Issachar, and Joseph Dan, eds. *Studies in Aggadah and Jewish Folklore*. Jerusalem: 1983.

Ben-Amos, Dan. "Talmudic Tale Tales." In *Folklore Today: A Festschrift for Richard M. Dorson*, edited by L. Degh, H. Glassie, and F. J. Oinas, 25–44. Bloomington, IN: 1976.

Ben-Amos, Dan, and Jerome R. Mintz, trans. and eds. *In Praise of the Baal Shem Tov (Shivhei ha-Besht)*. Bloomington, IN: 1970.

Berger, Abraham. "The Literature of Jewish Folklore." *The Journal of Jewish Bibliography*. 1 (1938–1939): 12–20, 40–49.

Bettan, Israel. *Studies in Jewish Preaching*. New York: 1976.

Bialik, Hayim Nachman. *And It Came to Pass: Legends and Stories About King David and King Solomon*. New York: 1938.

Bilu, Yoram. "Demonic Explanations of Illness Among Moroccan Jews." *Culture, Medicine and Psychiatry* 3 (1979): 363–380.

Bin-Gorion, Micha Joseph (Berditchevsky), ed. *Mimekor Yisrael: Classical Jewish Folktales*. Bloomington, IN: 1976. Three volumes.

Birnbaum, Salomo. *The Life and Sayings of the Baal Shem*. New York: 1933.

Bloch, Chayim. *The Golem: Legends of the Ghetto of Prague*. Vienna: 1925.

Blumenthal, Nachman. "Magical Thinking Among the Jews During the Nazi Occupation." *Yad Vashem Studies on the European Jewish Catastrophe and Resistance* 5 (1963): 221–236.

Bokser, Ben Zion. *The Jewish Mystical Tradition*. New York: 1981.

Braude, William G., and Israel J. Kapstein, trans. *The Midrash on Psalms (Midrash Tehillim)*. New Haven: 1959. Two volumes.

———, trans. *Pesikta de-Rab Kahana*. Philadelphia: 1975.

————, trans. *Pesikta Rabbati: Discourses for Feasts, Fasts and Special Sabbaths.* New Haven: Yale University Press, 1968. Two volumes.

————. *Tanna Debe Eliyyahu: The Lore of the School of Elijah.* Philadelphia: Jewish Publication Society, 1981.

Brichto, H. C. *The Problem of "Curse" in the Hebrew Bible.* Philadelphia: 1963.

Brinner, William M., trans. *An Elegant Composition Concerning Relief After Adversity,* by Nissim ben Jacob ibn Shahin. New Haven: 1977.

Broznick, Norman M. "Some Aspects of German Mysticism as Reflected in the Sefer Hasidim." M.A. Thesis, Columbia University, 1947.

Buber, Martin. *The Legend of Baal Shem Tov.* New York: 1977.

————. *Tales of Angels, Spirits and Demons.* New York: 1958.

————. *Tales of the Hasidim: Early Masters.* New York: 1947.

————. *Tales of the Hasidim: Later Masters.* New York: 1948.

————. *The Tales of Rabbi Nachman.* New York: 1956.

Burton, Richard F., trans. *The Book of a Thousand Nights and a Night* (The Arabian Nights). New York: 1934. Three volumes.

Charles, R. H., ed. *The Apocrypha and Pseudepigrapha of the Old Testament.* Oxford: 1913. Two volumes.

Charlesworth, James H., ed. *The Old Testament Pseudepigrapha.* New York: 1983–1985. Two volumes.

Cohen, A. *Everyman's Talmud.* New York: 1975.

Conybeare, F. C., trans. "The Testament of Solomon." *Jewish Quarterly Review* 11 (1899): 1–45.

Crews, Cynthia. "Judeo-Spanish Folktales in Macedonia." *Folklore* 43 (1932): 193–224.

Dahbany-Miraglia, Dina. "Yemenite Verbal Protective Behavior." *Working Papers in Yiddish and East European Jewish Studies* (YIVO) 13 (1975): 1–12.

Daiches, Samuel. *Babylonian Oil Magic in the Talmud and in the Later Jewish Literature.* London: 1913.

Dame, Enid. *Lilith and Her Demons.* Merrick, New York: 1987.

Dan, Joseph. "An Early Source of the Yiddish Aqdemoth Story." *Hebrew University Studies in Literature* 1 (1973): 39–46.

————, ed. *The Early Kabbalah.* New York: 1987.

————. "Five Versions of the Story of the Jerusalemite." *Proceedings of the American Academy for Jewish Research* 35 (1976):99–111.

————. "Rabbi Judah the Pious and Casarius of Heisterbach—Common Motifs in Their Stories." *Scripta Hierosolymitana* 22 (1971): 18–27.

————, ed. *Readings in Hasidism.* New York: 1979.

————, ed. *Studies in Jewish Mysticism.* New York: 1981.

————. "Teraphim: From Popular Belief to a Folktale." *Scripta Hierosolymitana* 27 (1978): 99–106.

Davidson, Israel, trans. *Sepher Shaashuim: A Book of Medieval Lore,* by Joseph ben Meir Ibn Zabara. New York: 1914.

Davies, Thomas Witton. *Magic, Divination and Demonology Among the Hebrews and Their Neighbors.* New York: 1909.

Einhorn, David. *The Seventh Candle and Other Folk Tales of Eastern Europe.* New York: 1968.

Elbaz, Andre E., ed. *Folktales of the Canadian Sephardim.* Toronto: 1982.

Eliach, Yaffa, ed. *Hasidic Tales of the Holocaust.* New York: 1982.

Elworthy, Frederick Thomas. *The Evil Eye.* London: 1895.

Epstein, I., ed. *The Babylonian Talmud.* London: 1935–1952. Thirty-six volumes.

Epstein, Shifra. "Recent Literature on Jewish Folklore and Ethnography." *Jewish Book Annual* 36 (1978–1979): 106–113.

Feierberg, Mordecai Ze'ev. *Whither? and Other Stories.* Philadelphia: 1978.

Fox, Samuel J. *Hell in Jewish Literature.* Northbrook, IL: 1972.

Frazer, James G. *Folklore of the Old Testament.* London: 1918. Three volumes.

Freedman, H., and Maurice Simon, eds. *Midrash Rabbah.* London: 1939. Ten volumes.

Freidus, Abraham Solomon. *A Bibliography of Lilith.* New York: 1917.

Friedenwald, Harry. "The Evil Eye." *Medical Leaves* (1939): 44–48.

Friedlander, Gerald, trans. *Pirke de Rabbi Eliezer.* New York: 1970.

Gary, Romain. *The Dance of Genghis Cohn.* New York: 1968.

Gaster, Moses, trans. *The Chronicles of Jerahmeel or the Hebrew Bible Historiale (Sefer ha-Zikhronot).* New York: 1971.

———. *The Exempla of the Rabbis.* London: 1924.

———. *Jewish Folklore in the Middle Ages.* London: 1887.

———, trans. *Ma'aseh Book of Jewish Tales and Legends.* Philadelphia: 1934. Two volumes.

———, ed. *Studies and Texts in Folklore, Magic, Medieval Romance, Hebrew Apocrypha and Samaritan Archeology.* London: 1928.

———. *The Sword of Moses: An Ancient Book of Magic.* London: 1896.

Gaster, Theodor, H. "A Canaanite Magical Text." *Orientalia* 11 (1942): 41–79.

———. *The Holy and the Profane: Evolution of Jewish Folkways.* New York: Sloane, 1955.

———. *Myth, Legend, and Custom in the Old Testament.* New York: 1969.

———. *Thespis: Ritual, Myth and Drama in the Ancient Near East.* New York: 1959.

Ginzberg, Louis. *The Legends of the Jews.* Philadelphia: 1909–1935. Seven volumes.

———. *On Jewish Law and Lore.* Philadelphia: 1955.

Goldemberg, Isaac. *The Fragmented Life of Don Jacobo Lerner.* New York: 1978.

Goldsmith, Arnold L. *The Golem Remembered: 1909–1980.* Detroit: 1981.

Goldstein, David. *Jewish Folklore and Legend.* London: Hamlyn, 1980.

Graves, Robert, ed. *Greek Myths.* London: 1955. Two volumes.

Graves, Robert, and Raphael Patai, eds. *Hebrew Myths: The Book of Genesis.* New York: 1966.

Green, Arthur, trans. "Bratslav Dreams" in *Fiction*, nos. 1 and 2, 1983, pp. 185–202.

———. *Tormented Master: A Life of Rabbi Nachman of Bratslav.* University, Alabama: 1981.

Grimm, Jacob and Wilhelm Grimm. *Grimm's Tales for Young and Old: The Complete Stories.* Trans. by Ralph Manheim. Garden City, N.Y.: 1983.

Grunwald, Max. *Tales, Songs & Folkways of Sephardic Jews.* Edited by Dov Noy, Jerusalem: 1982. Folklore Research Center Studies VI.

Hadas, Moses, trans. *Fables of a Jewish Aesop.* (Fables of Rabbi Berechiah Ha-Nakdan.) New York: 1967.

Hadas, Pamela. *The Passion of Lilith.* St. Louis: 1976.

Harris, L. "Dreams in *Sefer Hasidim.*" *Proceedings of the American Academy of Jewish Research* 31 (1963): 51–80.

Heinemann, Joseph, and Dov Noy, eds. *Studies in Aggada and Folk Literature.* Jerusalem: 1971.

Heinemann, Joseph, and Shmuel Werses, eds. *Studies in Hebrew Narrative Art Throughout the Ages.* Jerusalem: 1978.

Higgins, Elford. *Hebrew Idolatry and Superstition: Its Place in Folklore.* London: 1893.

Himmelfarb, Martha. *Tours of Hell: An Apocalyptic Form in Jewish and Christian Literature.* Philadelphia: 1983.

Hirsch, W. *Rabbinic Psychology: Beliefs About the Soul in the Rabbinic Literature of the Talmudic Period.* London: 1947.

The Holy Scriptures According to the Masoretic Text. Philadelphia: 1955. Two volumes.

Irving, Washington. *The Sketch Book of Geoffrey Crayon, Gent.* London: 1819–1820.

Isaacs, Abram S. *Stories from the Rabbis.* New York: 1928.

Ish-Kishor, Shulamit. *The Master of Miracle.* New York: 1971.

Jacobs, Irving. "Elements of Near-Eastern Mythology in Rabbinic Aggadah." *Journal of Jewish Studies* 28 (1977): 1–11.

Jacobs, Louis. *Jewish Mystical Testimonies.* New York: Schocken Books, 1978.

Jason, Heda. "Rabbi Wazana and the Demons: Analysis of a Legend." In *Folklore Today: A Festschrift for Richard M. Dorson,* edited by L. Degh, H. Glassie, and F.J. Oinas, 272-290. Bloomington, IN: 1976.

———. "Types of Jewish-Oriental Oral Tales." *Fabula* 7 (1965): 115–224.

———. *Types of Oral Tales in Israel: Part 2.* Jerusalem: 1975.

Josephus. *Jewish Antiquities.* Trans. by J. Thackeray. London: 1950. Nine volumes.

Jung, Leo. *Fallen Angels in Jewish, Christian and Mohammedan Literature.* Philadelphia: 1926.

Kafka, Franz. *The Complete Stories.* New York: 1971.

Kaplan, Rabbi Aryeh, trans. *Rabbi Nachman's Stories (Sippure Maaysiot)* by Rabbi Nachman of Bratslav. Jerusalem: 1983.

———, trans. *Rabbi Nachman's Wisdom.* New York: 1973.

Kasher, Menahem M., ed. *Encyclopedia of Biblical Interpretation.* New York: 1980. Nine volumes.

Kazis, Israel J., trans. *The Book of the Gests of Alexander of Macedon.* Cambridge: 1962.

Kelly, Henry A. *The Devil, Demonology and Witchcraft.* Garden City, N.Y.: 1968.

Klapholtz, Yisroael, ed. *Stories of Eliyahu Hanavi.* Jerusalem: 1978-1979. Four volumes.

———. *Tales of the Baal Shem Tov.* Jerusalem: 1970-1971. Five volumes.

———. *Tales of the Heavenly Court.* Jerusalem: 1982. Two volumes.

Klar, B. *The Chronicles of Ahimaaz.* New York: 1945.

Klein, Aron, and Jenny Machlowitz Klein, trans. *Tales in Praise of the Ari (Shivhei ha-Ari)* by Shlomo Meinsterl. Philadelpha: 1970.

Kluger, Rivkah Scharf. *Satan in the Old Testament.* Evanston, Ill.: 1967.

Koltuv, Barbara Black. *The Book of Lilith.* York Beach, Maine: 1986.

Kramer, Simon. *God and Man in the Sefer Hasidim.* New York: 1966.

Lachs, Samuel T. "The Alphabet of Ben Sira: A Study in Folk Literature," *Gratz College Annual of Jewish Studies,* 1973, pp. 9–28.

———. "Serpent Folklore in Rabbinic Literature." *Jewish Social Studies* 27 (1967): 168–184.

Langer, Jiri. *Nine Gates the the Chassidic Mysteries.* New York: 1976.

Langton, Edward. *Essentials of Demonology.* London: 1949.

———. *Good and Evil Spirits: A Study of the Jewish and Christian Doctrine, Its Origin and Development.* London: 1942.

———. *Satan: A Portrait.* London: 1945.

Lauterbach, Jacob Z. *Studies in Jewish Law, Custom and Folklore.* New York: 1968. Three volumes.

Leivick, Halper. *The Golem,* in *Great Jewish Plays,* edited by Joseph Landis. New York: 1972.

Levner, J. B. *The Legends of Israel*. London: Clarke, 1946.

Lind, Jakov. *The Stove*. New York: 1983.

Lorand, Sandor. "Dream Interpretation in the Talmud." *The International Journal of Psychoanalysis* 38 (1957): 92–97.

Louis, S. "Palestinian Demonology." *Proceedings of the Society of Biblical Archeology* 9 (1887): 217–228.

Maccoby, Hyam. *The Sacred Executioner: Human Sacrifice and the Legacy of Guilt*. New York: 1982.

Macdonald, George. *Lilith*. London: 1962.

Maitlis, Jacob. *The Ma'aseh in the Yiddish Ethical Literature*. London: 1958.

Malamud, Bernard. *Idiots First*. New York: 1963.

———. *Rembrandt's Hat*. New York: 1973.

———. *The Stories of Bernard Malamud*. New York: 1983.

Mandl, Leopold. "Teraphim." *Am Ur-Quell* 5 (1894): 92–93.

Marcus, Ivan. "The Recensions and Structure of *Sefer Hasidim*." Proceedings of the American Academy of Jewish Research XLV (1978): 131–153.

Meltzer, David. *Hero/Lil*. Los Angeles: 1973.

———, ed. *The Secret Garden: An Anthology in the Kabbalah*. New York: Seabury, 1976.

Meyrink, Gustav. *The Golem*. Translated by Madge Pemberton. New York: 1976.

Michener, James, Ed. *Firstfruits: A Harvest of 25 Years of Israeli Writing*. Philadelphia: 1973.

Mintz, Jerome R., ed. *Legends of the Hasidim: An Introduction to Hasidic Culture and Oral Tradition in the New World*. Chicago: 1968.

Mirsky, Mark, and David Stern, eds. *Fiction: Rabbinic Fantasy*. Vol. 7, Nos. 1 & 2 (1983).

Montgomery, J. A. *Aramaic Incantation Texts from Nippur*. Philadelphia: 1913.

Mordell, Phineas. *The Origin of Letters & Numerals According to the Sefer Yetziruh*. New York: 1975.

Morris, Epstein, ed. and trans. *Tales of Sendebar*. Philadelphia: 1967.

Nadich, Judah, ed. *Jewish Legends of the Second Commonwealth*. Philadelphia: 1983.

Nahmad, H. M. *A Portion in Paradise and Other Jewish Folktales*. New York: 1970.

———. "Superstitions Among Jews." *The Jewish Chronicle*, London, 19 December, 1969.

Neubauer, A. and A. Cowley. *Catalogue of the Hebrew Manuscripts in the Bodleian Library*. Oxford: 1886–1906. Two volumes.

Neugroschel, Joachim, ed. *Yenne Velt: The Great Works of Jewish Fantasy & Occult*. New York: 1976. Two volumes.

Newall, Venetia. "The Jew as a Witch Figure." In *The Witch Figure*, edited by Venetia Newall, 95–124. London: 1973.

Noah, Mordecai Manuel, trans. *The Book of Yashar (Sefer ha-Yashar)*. New York: 1972.

Noy Dov, ed. *Folktales of Israel*. Chicago: 1969.

———. "The Jewish Versions of the 'Animal Languages' Folktale (AT 670): A Typological-Structural Study." *Scripta Hierosolymitana* 22 (1971): 171–208.

———. *Moroccan Jewish Folktales*. New York: 1966.

———. "Motif Index of Talmudic-Midrashic Literature." Ph.D. diss., Indiana University, 1954.

———, Francis Utley, and Raphael Patai, ed. *Studies in Biblical and Jewish Folklore*. Bloomington: 1959.

Oesterreich, Traugott. *Possession: Demoniacal and Other, Among Primitive Races, in Antiquity, Middles Ages and Modern Times*. New York: 1930.

Ozick, Cynthia. *Bloodshed and Three Novellas.* New York: 1976.
———. *Levitation: Five Fictions.* New York: 1982.
———. *The Messiah of Stockholm.* New York: 1987.
———. *The Pagan Rabbi.* New York: 1971.
Patai, Raphael, ed. *Gates to the New City: A Book of Jewish Legends.* Detroit: 1981.
———. *The Hebrew Goddess.* New York: 1967.
———, ed. *The Messiah Texts.* Detroit: 1979.
———. *On Jewish Folklore.* Detroit: 1983.
Peretz, I. L. *The Book of Fire.* New York: 1959.
———. *The Case Against the Wind.* New York: 1975.
———. *In This World and the Next.* New York: 1958.
———. *Selected Stories.* Edited by Irving Home and Eliezer Greenberg. New York: 1974.
Perrault, Charles. *The Glass Slipper: Charles Perrault's Tales of Times Past.* Trans. by John Bierhorst. New York: 1981. First published 1697.
Petuchowski, Jakob J., ed. *Our Masters Taught: Rabbinic Stories and Sayings.* New York: 1982.
Porter, J. R. "Witchcraft and Magic in the Old Testament, and Their Relation to Animals." In *Animals in Folklore,* edited by J. R. Porter and W. M. S. Russel, 70–85. Norwich, England: 1978.
Pritchard, J. B., ed. *Solomon and Sheba.* London: 1974.
Prose, Francine. *Judah the Pious.* New York: 1973.
Rabinowicz, H. *A Guide to Hassidism.* New York: 1960.
Rand, Baruch, and Barbara Rush. *Jews of Kurdistan.* Toledo, Ohio: 1978.
Rappoport, A. S. *The Folklore of the Jews.* London: 1937.
———. *Myth and Legend of Ancient Israel.* London: 1928. Three volumes.
Rogerson, John W. *The Supernatural in the Old Testament.* London: 1976.
Roskies, Diane K. and David G. Roskies. *The Shtetl Book.* New York: 1975.
Roth, Cecil, ed. *The Dark Ages. World History of the Jewish People.* Vol. XI. New Brunswick, New Jersey: 1966.
———. "Folklore of the Ghetto." *Folklore* 59 (1948): 75–83.
Roth, Cecil, and G. Wigoder, eds. *Encyclopedia Judaica.* Jerusalem: 1972. Sixteen volumes.
Rothenberg, Jerome, Harris Lenowitz, and Charles Doria, eds. *A Big Jewish Book.* Garden City, N.Y.: 1978.
Rudwin, Maximilian. *The Devil in Legend and Literature.* La Salle, Ill.: 1973.
Rush, Barbara, and Eliezer Marcus, eds. *Seventy and One Tales.* New York: 1980.
Sabar, Yona, ed. *The Folk Literature of the Kurdistani Jews: An Anthology.* New Haven: Yale University Press, 1982.
Schochet, Jacob Immanuel. *Rabbi Israel Baal Shem Tov.* Toronto: 1961.
Scholem, Gershom G. "The Curious History of the Six-Pointed Star." *Commentary* 8 (1949): 243–251.
———. *Jewish Gnosticism, Merkabah Mysticism, and Talmudic Tradition.* New York: 1960.
———. *Kabbalah.* Jerusalem: 1974.
———. *Major Trends in Jewish Myusticism.* New York: 1964.
———. *The Messianic Idea in Judaism and Other Essays on Jewish Spirituality.* New York: Schocken Books, 1971.
———. *On Jews and Judaism in Crisis.* New York: 1976.
———. *On the Kabbalah and Its Symbolism.* New York: 1965.
———. *Origins of the Kabbalah.* Philadelphia: 1987.
———. *Shabbatai Sevi: The Mystical Messiah.* Princeton, N.J.: 1973.

Schrire, T. *Hebrew Magic Amulets: Their Decipherment and Interpretation*. London: 1966.

Schwartz, Howard. *The Captive Soul of the Messiah: New Tales About Reb Nachman*. New York: 1983.

———, ed. *Elijah's Violin & Other Jewish Fairy Tales*. New York: 1983.

———, ed. *Gates to the New City: A Treasury of Modern Jewish Tales*. New York: 1983.

———, ed. *Miriam's Tambourine: Jewish Folktales from Around the World*. New York: 1986.

———. *Rooms of the Soul*. Chappaqua, New York: 1984.

Schwarz-Bart, Andre. *The Last of the Just*. New York: 1961.

Schwarzbaum, Haim. "The Hero Predestined to Die on His Wedding Day, AT 934B." *Folklore Research Center Studies* 4 (1974): 223–252.

———. *The Mishle Shu'alim (Fox Fables) of Rabbi Berechiah Ha-Nakdan: A Study in Comparative Folklore and Fable Lore*. Kiron, Israel: 1979.

———. *Studies in Jewish and World Folklore*. Berlin: 1968.

Segal, S. M. *Elijah: A Study in Jewish Folklore*. New York: 1935.

Seymour, St. John D. *Tales of King Solomon*. London: 1924.

Shahar, David. *The Palace of Shattered Vessels*. New York: 1976.

Shelley, Mary Wollstonecraft. *Frankenstein*. London: 1818.

Shenhar, Aliza. "Concerning the Nature of the Motif 'Death by a Kiss' (Motif A185.6.11)." *Fabula* 19 (1978): 62–73.

Sherwin, Byron L. "Bar-Mitzvah." *Judaism* 22 (1973): 53–65.

———. "The Exorcist's Role in Jewish Tradition." *Occult*, October 1975.

———. *The Golem Legend: Origins and Implications*. New York: 1985.

———. *Mystical Theology and Social Dissent: The Life and Works of Judah Loew of Prague*. Rutherford, N.J.: 1982.

Shrut, Samuel D. "Coping with the 'Evil Eye' or Early Rabbinical Attempts at Psychotherapy." *The American Imago* 17 (1960): 201–213.

Silver, Daniel J. *Maimonidean Criticism and the Maimonidean Controversy, 1180–1240*. New York: 1965.

Singer, Isaac Bashevis. *The Collected Stories*. New York: 1982.

———. *The Golem*. New York: 1982.

———. *Stories for Children*. New York: 1984.

Singer, Isadore, ed. *The Jewish Encyclopedia*. New York: 1901. Twelve volumes.

Singer, Sholom Alchanan. *Medieval Jewish Mysticism: Book of the Pious (Sefer Hasidim)*. Wheeling, IL: 1971.

Slabotsky, David. *The Mind of Genesis*. Ottawa: 1975.

Soloveitchik, Hayim. "Three Themes in the *Sefer Hasidim*." AJS Review I (1976): 311–357.

Sperling, Harry, and Maurice Simon, eds. *Zohar*. London: 1931–1934. Five volumes.

Spicehandler, Ezra and Curtis Arnson. *New Writing in Israel*. New York: 1976.

Spiegel, Shalom. *The Last Trial*. Philadelphia: 1967.

Steinman, Eliezer. *The Garden of Hasidism*. Jerusalem: 1961.

Steinschneider, M. *Jewish Literature*. New York: 1965.

Stillman, Yedida K. "The Evil Eye in Morocco." *Folklore Research Center Studies* 1 (1970): 81–94.

Stone, Michael E., trans. *The Testament of Abraham: The Greek Recensions*. Missoula, Mont.: 1972.

Sullivan, Jack. *Lost Souls: A Collection of English Ghost Stories*. Athens, Ohio: 1983.

Sussaman, Aaron. *The Flying Ark*. St. Louis: 1980.

Talmage, Frank, ed. *Studies in Jewish Folklore*. Cambridge: 1980.

Thieberger, Frederic. *The Great Rabbi Loew of Prague*. London: 1955.

Thompson, R. Campbell. *Semitic Magic: Its Origins and Development.* 1908. Reprint. New York: 1971.

Thompson, Stith. *Motif-Index of Folk Literature.* Bloomington: 1975. Six volumes.

Trachtenberg, Joshua. *The Devil and the Jews.* New Haven: 1943.

———. "The Folk Element in Judaism." *The Journal of Religion* 22 (1942): 173–186.

———. *Jewish Magic and Superstition.* New York: 1939.

Urbach, Ephraim. *The Sages: Their Concepts and Beliefs.* Jerusalem: 1975. Two volumes.

Vilnay, Zev. *The Sacred Land.* Philadelphia: 1973–1978. Three volumes.

Wakeman, Mary K. *God's Battle with the Monster: A Study in Biblical Imagery.* Leiden, the Netherlands: 1973.

Waxman, Meyer. *A History of Jewish Literature from the Close of the Bible to Our Own Days.* New York: 1960. Six volumes.

Weinreich, B. S. "The Prophet Elijah in Modern Yiddish Folktales." M.A. thesis, Columbia University, 1957.

Weinreich, Max. "*Lantukh*: A Jewish Hobgoblin." *YIVO Annual of Jewish Social Science* 2–3 (1947–1948): 243–251.

Weinreich, Uriel and Beatrice. *Yiddish Language and Folklore: A Selective Bibliography for Research.* The Hague: 1959.

Werblowsky, R. J. Zwi. *Joseph Karo, Lawyer and Mystic.* Philadelphia: 1977.

Westcott, W. Wynn, trans. *Sepher Yetzirah: The Book of Formation.* New York: 1882.

Wiesel, Elie. *The Golem.* New York: 1983.

Winkler, Gershom. *Dybbuk.* New York: 1980.

———. *The Golem of Prague.* New York: 1982.

Yassif, Eli. *Jewish Folklore.* New York: 1986.

Zangwill, Israel. *The Master.* New York: 1897.

Zeitlin, Solomon. "Dreams and Their Interpretation from the Biblical Period to the Tannaitic Time: A Historical Study." *Jewish Quarterly Review* 66 (1975): 1–18.

Zenner, Walter P. "Saints and Piecemeal Supernaturalism Among the Jerusalem Sephardim." *Anthropological Quarterly* 38 (1965): 201–217.

Zimmels, H. J. *Magicians, Theologians and Doctors.* New York: 1952.

Zinberg, Israel. *A History of Jewish Literature.* New York: 1972–1978. Twelve volumes.

GLOSSARY

All of the following terms are in Hebrew unless otherwise noted.

Aggadah rabbinic legends found in the Talmud and Midrash.

Ari acronym for Rabbi Isaac Luria of Safed.

Baal Shem Tov (lit. "Master of the Good Name"). Israel ben Eliezer, founder of Hasidim.

Bar Mitzvah the ceremony at which a thirteen-year-old Jewish boy becomes an adult for ceremonial purposes.

Beit Din a rabbinic court convened to decide issues relating to the Law.

Beit Midrash a House of Study.

Besht acronym for the Baal Shem Tov.

Cheder (lit. "a room"). It has come to refer to the schoolroom where children are taught Jewish studies.

Dybbuk the soul of one who has died that enters the body of one who is living and remains until exorcised.

Gehenna the place where the souls of the wicked are punished and purified; the equivalent of Hell in Jewish legend.

Gemara (lit. "to study" in Aramaic). The commentary surrounding the Mishnah. The Gemara and Mishnah together make up the Talmud.

Gematria a technique used by Jewish mystics to discern secret meanings in the Torah. In this system each Hebrew letter has a numerical value, and the commentator seeks out words or word combinations that have the same totals, which are then regarded as linked.

Gilgul transmigration of souls; reincarnation. A central *Kabbalistic* concept.

Golem (lit. "shapless mass"; see Ps. 139:16). A creature, usually in human form, created by magical means, especially by the use of the Tetragrammaton. The best-known legends are connected with the Golem created by Rabbi Judah Loew of Prague to protect the Jewish community against blood libel accusations.

Haggadah the text used for the Passover *Seder.*

Halachah the code of Jewish religious law.

Harai at mi'kudeshet li	the traditional wedding vow, "You are betrothed to me," which is repeated three times in the presence of two witnesses in order to be valid.
Hasid	(pl. *Hasidim*, lit. a "pious one"). The term is sometimes applied to the talmudic sages, as well as to the followers of Samuel ha-Hasid and his son, Judah ha-Hasid (that is, Judah the Pious). It also identifies the followers of Hasidism, a Jewish sect founded in the eighteenth century by the Baal Shem Tov.
Havdalah	the ceremony performed at the end of the Sabbath, denoting the separation of the Sabbath from the rest of the week.
Heder	the religious school to which young Jewish children were sent.
Huppah	a wedding canopy beneath which the bride and groom stand.
Kabbalah	Jewish mysticism; also, the texts of Jewish mysticism, in particular, the Zohar.
Kaddish	the prayer for the dead, recited by mourners.
Ketubah	a traditional Jewish wedding contract.
Kohen	member of the priestly tribe.
Kol Nidre	the prayer service on the eve of *Yom Kippur*.
Lantukh	(Yiddish) a goblin or imp known for its pranks.
L'hayim	a traditional toast, meaning "to life."
Lilah	(lit. "night").
Liliot	daughters of Lilith.
Maaseh	a tale or story, often a folktale.
Maggid	a preacher who confined his sermons to easily understood homiletics.
Maharal	acronym for Rabbi Judah Loew of Prague.
Matzoh	unleavened bread baked by the Israelites in the wilderness. Ritually used during the period of Passover.
Menorah	Seven-branched candelabrum.
Merkavah	(lit. "chariot"). The merkavah is the divine chariot in the vision of Ezekiel.
Mezzuzah	(lit. "doorpost"). A small case containing a piece of parchment upon which is written the prayer that begins *Shema Yisrael* ("Hear O Israel"). This case is affixed to the right doorpost of a Jew's home in accordance with the biblical injunction.
Midrash	the body of rabbinic legends; also, an individual legend.
Mikveh	the ritual bath in which women immerse themselves after menstruation has ended. It is also used occasionally by men for purposes of ritual purification.

Minyan	a quorum of ten males that is required for any congregational service.
Mishnah	the earliest portion of the Talmud, codified in the second century C.E.
Mitzvah	(pl. *mitzvot*) a divine commandment. There are 613 *mitzvot* in the Torah. The term has also come to mean a good deed.
Mohel	a rabbi who performs a ritual circumcision, known as a *bris*.
Pilpul	(lit. "pepper"). A discussion of a fine point of the Law.
Rebbe	(Yiddish) the term used for hasidic masters.
Responsa	letters sent between rabbis discussing *halachic* decisions.
Seder	the traditional Passover ceremonial meal, during which the Haggadah describing the deliverance from Egypt is recited.
Sefer	book.
Sendak	man given the honor of holding the infant boy during circumcision.
Shavuot	the Feast of Weeks festival, which falls exactly seven weeks after Passover.
Shekhinah	(lit. "to dwell"). The Divine Presence, usually identified as a feminine aspect of the Divinity, which evolved into an independent mythic figure in the Kabbalistic period. Also identified as the Bride of God and the Sabbath Queen.
Shofar	a ram's horn trumpet sounded as part of some Jewish religious observances.
Simhat Torah	the concluding day of the festival of Sukkot on which the cycle of reading from the Torah is concluded and begun again.
Sitra Ahra	(Aramaic) (lit. "the Other Side"). The Kabbalistic term for the domain of evil emanations and demonic powers.
Sukkah	a booth in which Jews were commanded to live for seven days so as to remember the Israelites, who resided in booths during their exodus from Egypt. Its roof must be covered with loose boughs, through which the stars are visible.
Tallis	a four-cornered prayer shawl with fringes at the corners, worn by men during the morning prayer services. It is also worn throughout the day of Yom Kippur.
Talmud	the second most sacred Jewish text, after the Bible. The term *Talmud* is the comprehensive designation for the *Mishnah* and the *Gemara* as a single unit. There are Babylonian and Jerusalem Talmuds, which have different *Gemaras* commenting on the same *Mishnah*. The material in the Talmud consists of both *Halachah* and *Aggadah*, law and legend, and there are in additional discussions on philosophy, medicine, agriculture, astronomy, and hygiene.

Tefillin	phylacteries worn at the morning services (except on the Sabbath) by men and boys thirteen and older.
Terephim	pagan idols, such as those of Laban, stolen by Rachel.
Torah	the Five Books of Moses. In a broader sense the term refers to the whole Bible and the Oral Law. And in the broadest sense it refers to all of Jewish culture and teaching.
Tseshuvah	repentance.
Tzaddik	an unusually righteous and spiritually pure person.
Yarmulke	the skullcap worn by observant Jewish men.
Yenne Velt	(Yiddish, lit. "the Other World"). The world populated by spirits and demons.
Yeshivah	school for Jewish learning, with particular emphasis on the Talmud.
Yetzer Hara	the Evil Inclination.
Yetzer Tov	the Good Inclination.
Yom Kippur	the Day of Judgment, the most solemn day of the Jewish religious year.

INDEX